THE GOVERNANCE GAP

Shashi Budhiraja has held numerous critical leadership positions across the private, public and academic sectors. An alumnus of St. Stephen's College, a Gold Medallist from IIT Roorkee and a Fellow at Harvard's Weatherhead Center for International Affairs, he became the youngest-ever Managing Director of Indian Oil Corporation at the age of 43. Additionally, he served as MD IBP/Balmer Lawrie and British Oxygen (now Linde), Director of MDI Gurgaon, President of the Institute of Management Consultants, Advisor in the UN Secretary-General's office, and governing council member in industry bodies such as the All India Management Association and the Indian Chamber of Commerce. He has also been an Independent Director for IIM Lucknow, Bombay Port Trust, and Neuland Laboratories, among others. A former President of Rotary, he currently chairs the Budhiraja Foundation and instituted the Shashi Budhiraja Chair of Strategic Management at IMI, Delhi. He has also authored *Cases in Strategic Management* and *The Education Revolution*. Now in his 94th year, he shares his views on Governance in India.

Rajeev Budhiraja resides in Dubai and is currently focused on initiatives that promote well-being and behaviour change. He began his career in marketing with Cathay Pacific Airways, after studying Economics and Law at Cambridge University. He then founded and managed four pioneering advertising start-ups for McCann Worldgroup in the Middle East, across the digital, healthcare and data sectors, serving as equity partner and CEO. These included Promoseven 360, MRM and McCann Health. Committed to creating positive social impact, he recently earned an MSc in Behavioural Science from the London School of Economics and, continuing this journey, is currently pursuing a Master's in Positive Psychology at the University of Pennsylvania. Concurrently, he advises Emirates NBD, Dubai's leading bank, on a UAE-wide financial well-being initiative, supports resilience and AI-based coaching initiatives on behalf of the Positive Psychology Center (PPC) at UPenn, sits on the advisory board of Rochester Institute of Technology, Dubai, and guest lectures at various universities.

THE GOVERNANCE GAP

UNLOCKING INDIA'S SUPERPOWER POTENTIAL

SHASHI BUDHIRAJA

Edited by **RAJEEV BUDHIRAJA**

RUPA

Published by
Rupa Publications India Pvt. Ltd 2025
161-B/4, Gulmohar House,
Yusuf Sarai Community Centre,
New Delhi 110049

Sales centres:
Bengaluru Chennai
Hyderabad Kolkata Mumbai

P-ISBN: 978-93-7003-717-5
E-ISBN: 978-93-7003-216-3

First impression 2025

10 9 8 7 6 5 4 3 2 1

The moral right of the author has been asserted.

Printed in India

To
Lalu Budhiraja
my wife, friend and source of strength

CONTENTS

Preface   *ix*

Part I

1. Democracy in Action   3
2. House of Lawmakers   25
3. The Business of Governance   48
4. House of Justice and Justices   69
5. Federalism: An Integral Part of the
   Governance Structure   85
6. Reservations: Not a Magic Bullet to
   Resolve Backwardness   104

Part II

7. Indian Agriculture: Sputtering Along   125
8. A Deeply Unjust Education System   153
9. Public Health: In Need of Revitalization   181
10. Human Capital: The Story of India's Workforce
    Potential   207
11. Criticality of Data in Decision-Making   229
12. India: The Way Forward   249

Acknowledgements   256
Notes   258

PREFACE

In August 1947, when India threw off the colonial yoke to take its place among the free nations of the world, I was 16 years old. The euphoria of freedom was mixed with the pain of Partition and the frenzy of violence. Some months later, when Gandhiji fell to an assassin's bullets at Birla House (now Gandhi Smriti) in central Delhi, where his prayer meetings were held, the entire nation plunged into mourning. I remember walking with a classmate from Kashmere Gate, where our college, St Stephen's, was located, to Birla House as soon as we heard the news.

The generation that witnessed these cataclysmic events was filled with a quiet resolve: to forge a nation that would uphold the highest ideals of governance by building upon its strengths of diversity and addressing the social and economic challenges peculiar to Indian society. This resolve was reflected in the Constitution that the people—We, the People—gave themselves in January 1950. India had chosen to be a parliamentary democracy based on universal adult suffrage, where all power would flow from the people. The institutional pillars of Indian democracy would be infused with the core idea of citizen-centric governance.

Inspired by this juncture, we youngsters were fired by a sense of purpose. Freedom meant taking the opportunity to explore one's potential for the good of the country.

My quest led me to science, from St Stephen's College to the University of Roorkee (later rechristened Indian Institute of Technology [IIT] Roorkee). An active life unfurled as I explored new horizons, but each time circling back, nudged by a sense of purpose. Starting in the private oil industry, I was well settled but drawn in the 1960s to the public sector. The job paid much less, but I was energized by the thought of contributing to the home-grown effort.

Later on, after spending four eventful years earning a dollar salary in the Middle East, and with options internationally, I opted to return to India.

From technical grounding to management expertise and then overseeing management education comprised a professional arc that encompassed many organizations, national and international, but the focus was always on India. There was a palpable interest in seeing which way our nation was headed.

Over the years, this concern has grown. Now I am in my 90s. India too has experienced nearly eight decades of independence. Looking back at our country's progress over these decades, I must confess I have mixed views. There are many who say that one has only to compare India with its neighbours or many other nations that gained independence around the same time to realize how much it has achieved. The question, however, is—where could we have been?

Freedom leading to self-governance was meant to ensure opportunities for all Indians to realize their potential, thus collectively propelling the nation to unlock its strengths and climb the heights of growth and well-being. This was the promise we made to ourselves in the Constitution.

Have Indian citizens experienced the fruits of good governance over the decades? Moreover, has India's long-acknowledged potential been realized?

As I see it, India is a flawed democracy. It has made significant progress but still has some way to go to meet the ideal goals of governance.

Many years ago, in his final address to the Constituent Assembly, Dr B.R. Ambedkar, the chairman of the Drafting

Committee, emphasized, 'however good a Constitution may be, it is sure to turn out bad because those who are called to work it, happen to be a bad lot. However bad a Constitution may be, it may turn out to be good if those who are called to work it, happen to be a good lot.'

He was clear that the working of the Constitution does not depend wholly upon the nature of the Constitution. 'The Constitution can provide only the organs of State such as the Legislature, the Executive and the Judiciary. The factors on which the working of those organs of the State depends are the people and the political parties they will set up as their instruments to carry out their wishes and their politics.'

Therefore, it is only fitting that as ardent Indians we look at the multiple stories that facts tell us about the state of governance in India. That will shine a mirror on the factors holding our nation back from reaching our true potential. We owe it to ourselves.

PART I

∿

This part examines the governance structure of India and gives an insight into the inner workings of its legislature, judiciary, politics and administration from the day the country gained Independence till now.

1

DEMOCRACY IN ACTION

Less than two years after India's constitution came into effect, the newly independent nation's first free general elections took place. In a radical departure from the experience of some of the most powerful democracies in the world, India's elections were based on universal adult suffrage as the fundamental principle underpinning its democracy.

Conducted between 25 October 1951 and 21 February 1952, the first general elections were a truly ambitious exercise in a country with over 80 per cent illiteracy. The total electorate stood at 17,32,12,343, of whom 10,59,50,083 cast their vote in 1,96,084 polling stations across the country.[1] The state- and UT-wise data has been provided in Table 1.1. The successful organization of the polls established India's credentials as the world's largest democracy.

Table 1.1
Voter turnout in the general elections of India in 1951[2]

Sl. no.	State and union territories	Voters	Poll percentage
1	Bilaspur	0	0.00
2	Himachal Pradesh	2,23,189	25.32
3	Vindhya Pradesh	7,05,838	30.06
4	Madhya Bharat	19,53,571	35.08
5	Orissa	36,59,493	35.39

Sl. no.	State and union territories	Voters	Poll percentage
6	Rajasthan	35,26,957	38.40
7	Uttar Pradesh	1,70,74,975	38.41
8	Bhopal	1,69,457	40.35
9	Bihar	99,92,451	40.35
10	West Bengal	76,13,933	40.49
11	Kutch	1,19,580	41.46
12	Hyderabad	48,54,862	44.70
13	Madhya Pradesh	71,92,591	45.98
14	Tripura	1,57,371	47.72
15	Assam	26,47,127	47.96
16	Saurashtra	7,62,705	49.41
17	Manipur	1,52,467	51.07
18	Mysore	28,24,427	51.93
19	Bombay	1,15,28,290	52.38
20	Ajmer	1,78,999	54.33
21	Punjab	49,92,338	55.33
22	Madras	1,99,34,161	56.33
23	Delhi	6,55,900	57.92
24	Patiala and East Punjab States Union	14,75,112	59.56
25	Coorg	63,813	67.46
26	Travancore–Cochin	34,90,476	71.00
	Total	**10,59,50,083**	**44.87**

In his essay 'Democracy's Biggest Gamble: India's First Free Elections in 1952', historian and commentator Ramachandra Guha captures the mammoth task that confronted India's first chief election commissioner Sukumar Sen, a member of the Indian Civil Service (ICS).[3] His brief: to steer along with state election commissioners the battle of the ballot for Parliament (489 seats) as well as for the state assemblies, a total of 4,500 seats.

Guha's description brings alive the sense of commitment with which a seemingly impossible task was approached: '16,500 clerks were needed to type up and collate the electoral rolls. (About 3,80,000 reams of paper were used to print the rolls.) Some 56,000 presiding officers would supervise the voting, aided by another 2,80,000 "lesser staff", and 2,24,000 police would be required to prevent violence and intimidation.

'The electorate was spread out over an area of more than a million square miles [...] Bridges had to be specially constructed across rivers to reach remote hill villages; naval vessels would be required to carry the rolls to the voting booths on small islands in the Indian Ocean.'

Moreover, sensitive to the challenge of organizing an election for an overwhelmingly illiterate electorate, the Election Commission came up with the idea of designing quotidian pictorial symbols through which the voters could opt for the party of their choice—symbols such as two bulls with yoke on, tree, standing lion, human hand, horse and rider, hut, elephant, ears of corn and a sickle, flaming torch, a cultivator winnowing grain, among others. There were separate ballot boxes for each party, making the exercise easy for voters. The indelible ink that marks our fingers to this day to prevent voters from casting their vote again made its appearance for the first time.

In 1955, the Election Commission brought out a report on the first general elections.[4] In volume one, Chief Election Commissioner Sen noted: 'The task was a formidable one and could not have been carried out satisfactorily without the whole-hearted cooperation of everybody concerned. The greatest credit, of course, goes to the millions of voters who gave ample proof of having realized that it was their right as also their duty to participate in the elections by exercising their franchise. They have earned world-wide admiration by the enthusiasm that they displayed during the elections and the orderly and peaceful manner in which they went to the polls. The political parties and the candidates contributed in no small measure to the success of the experiment.'

A DEFINING MOMENT

Few in the developed world had any hopes about India's capacity to keep together, let alone sustain, a democracy. That too a Westminster-style democracy. Granted, the Indian political class was familiar with it. But the circumstances in which India took its first steps towards independent nationhood in 1947 were overwhelming. What the world saw was a country on the brink—torn asunder by the trauma of partition's mass killings and displacement and shocked into numbness by Gandhi's assassination. A country already burdened by poverty, illiteracy and innumerable social and economic fault lines. The way the bulk of the international community saw it, the Westminster model of democracy could only work with an educated and informed electorate.

In fact, the colonial government had introduced the idea of electoral democracy during the elections to provincial assemblies and the Central Legislative Assembly in 1937 and 1946. It was a tightly controlled exercise based on a pernicious idea of separate electorates for members of different religions. Moreover, the electorate was restricted to about 14 per cent of the population, chosen on the basis of educational qualifications, professional standing and property, which excluded the bulk of Indians.[5] For that matter, even countries like Britain and the United States of America had not experimented with universal adult suffrage right from the very beginning.

The members of the Constituent Assembly thought otherwise. When they started debating the letter and spirit of the Constitution, and the architecture of governance it would spell out, they were clear in their minds that the adoption of universal adult suffrage, a long-held goal of the Indian freedom movement, would be the most defining characteristic of the kind of democracy they wanted—the fullest democracy, in Jawaharlal Nehru's words. It would be the one act that would unshackle them from their colonial past. As scholar Ornit Shani puts it in her exemplary book, *How India Became Democratic:* 'It was through the implementation of the universal franchise [...] that electoral democracy came to life in India.'[6]

Shani points out that work on the first draft of the electoral roll began in September 1947 when work on the Constitution was still going on. Ordinary people from all walks of life asserted themselves by vociferously debating their voting rights with bureaucrats. It helped ground the idea of electoral democracy in people's minds by the time the Constitution came into effect in 1950, transforming them from voters into citizens.

The idea that every eligible adult in a highly hierarchical society—whether rich or poor, man or woman, of a low or high caste or belonging to different religions—had an equal vote in the making of a government that would represent its citizens' will was compelling. It was on this foundation that a robust multiparty democracy was established in India.

Most importantly, the first general elections of 1951–52 demonstrated what a committed leadership and bureaucracy along with an enthusiastic electorate could achieve even in a fraught context.

Nearly eighty years on, electoral democracy as the basis of parliamentary democracy, with a few aberrations such as the Emergency imposed by Indira Gandhi in 1975, has become part of the muscle memory of the nation, as it were. In fact, in his immensely readable book, *The Raisina Model*, Meghnad Desai makes an important point[7]: 'Why, despite the differences and the almost continuous trouble in one or other part of India, has the country survived as a single political entity? The answer in one word is democracy. India's experiment with democracy has been unique because it has tamed and "Indianized it". Desai calls it the Raisina model.'[8]

FROM WESTMINSTER TO RAISINA

Indeed, as I look back the pattern becomes evident. The story of the relationship between Indian citizens and democracy has been quite eventful.

Through the 1950s into the early 1960s, the memory of the Congress Party's role in the freedom movement and the struggle to keep the country together following Partition was still fresh in voters' minds. Moreover, the towering presence of Nehru was very much in the forefront, as was his message of nation-building and strengthening society by cultivating a scientific temper. It was an inspiring message for a society that had gone through a terrible convulsion not so long ago. As I pursued science and mechanical engineering, I noticed how many a youngster was influenced by the general ambience of working towards excellence in a chosen field as a way of contributing to the development of the nation.

That is why, in spite of the presence of political parties with different ideological persuasions, the Congress maintained its dominant position in the first three general elections, as can be seen in Table 1.2 and Figure 1.1.

Table 1.2
Electoral results of the Indian National Congress
in the general elections[9]

	Total no. of elected seats	*Seats won by Congress*
1952	489	364
1957	494	371
1962	494	361
1967	520	283

A GENERATIONAL SHIFT

Nehru's death in 1964 signalled the end of an era for Indians. Three years later, in 1967, I left the private sector where I had worked for 14 years to join the Indian Oil Corporation in the public sector that Nehru had prioritized. I wanted to use the expertise I had gained in the private oil sector for the benefit of the country.

The year 1967 was significant for another major reason. The general elections to the Fourth Lok Sabha, the first after Nehru's death, demonstrated signs of a break from the first two decades of independence. Under the leadership of Indira Gandhi, the Congress Party, which had prided itself on being the only national party of consequence until then, received a strong jolt. While it retained the status of the ruling party, its vote and seat shares declined drastically.

In a House of 523 members, Congress secured a little over the majority mark, by bagging 283 seats, losing 78 seats in comparison to its tally in the previous election. C. Rajagopalachari's Swatantra Party, floated in opposition to Congress and the Communist parties, came a distant second with 44 seats. The Bharatiya Jana Sangh, which emerged out of the erstwhile Hindu Mahasabha, emerged third, with 35 seats.

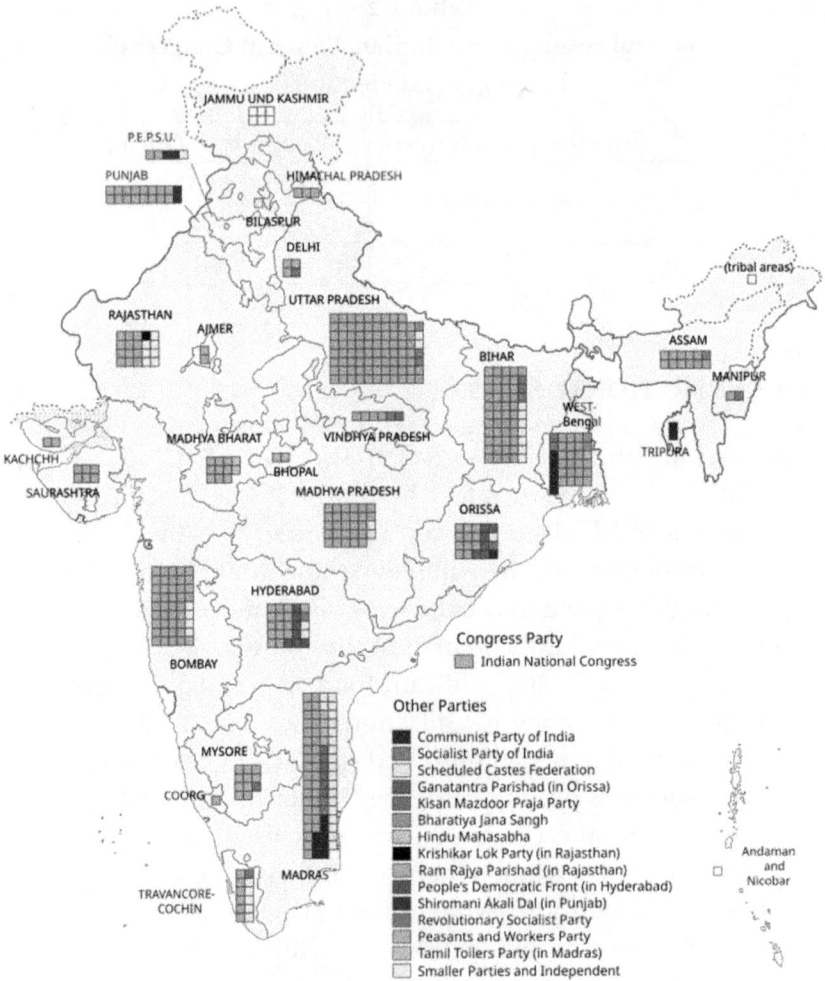

Figure 1.1: Results of the Indian general elections, 1951–1952[10]

The Fourth Lok Sabha was quite different from its earlier avatars. The political field was becoming more crowded. Several regional and smaller parties like the Dravida Munnetra Kazhagam (DMK), Samyukta Socialist Party, Bangla Congress, and Jammu and Kashmir National Conference, among others, made it to Parliament. With the rise of regional parties following the creation of linguistic states, politics had gained the cadence of Indian languages rooted to the ground.

It wasn't only at the Centre that the Congress received a jolt in 1967. The grand old party had been trumped by the DMK in the Tamil Nadu assembly elections, and coalitions had sprung up in Bengal, Punjab, Bihar, Uttar Pradesh and Rajasthan. It was with some amazement that one read those news reports—the party that had seemed invincible had a chink in its armour.

That Indira's Congress and her idea of governance was a far cry from that of Nehru became evident during one of the darkest phases of Indian democracy, namely, the Emergency (June 1975 to March 1977), for which the electorate handed the party a decisive defeat in the Sixth Lok Sabha polls in 1977. Commentator after commentator said the same thing: Indira Gandhi's authoritarian avatar, intent on centralizing power and weakening institutions of governance, with scant regard for citizens' rights, and political dissent had earned her party its first ever defeat at the Centre.

After that two-year interregnum, the Congress did come back to power at the Centre in 1980 with Indira Gandhi at its helm. Her assassination in 1984 paved the way for Rajiv Gandhi to become prime minister in the Lok Sabha elections later that year, with the Congress getting the largest number of seats ever. Yet, five years later, the same electorate that had voted sympathetically for Rajiv Gandhi in 1984 seemed to have little patience for him. The Bofors scandal proved to be his undoing. The electorate preferred his bête noire, his former colleague V.P. Singh.

THE 1990S: DIFFERENT STROKES

After four decades of Congress dominance, punctuated by a two-year interregnum (1977–79), a new political inflection emerged in the 1989 general elections. The Congress failed to get a majority in the Lok Sabha. V.P. Singh of the Janata Dal, who led the National Front government supported by the Bharatiya Janata Party (BJP) and the Communist Party of India (Marxist) (CPM) from outside, became the prime minister. The age of coalitions had dawned, and the age of the Congress as the single dominant force in national politics was a thing of the past.

With the coming of the National Front government, there was an unmistakable change in the political atmosphere. V.P. Singh's announcement in Parliament on 7 August 1990, regarding the implementation of the Mandal Commission report advocating reservations for Other Backward Classes (OBCs) based on social deprivation rather than economic deprivation, opened the floodgates for political parties that demanded social justice through politics. Hitherto under-represented and unrepresented social groups began to think of exercising political power themselves.

Interestingly, the report prepared by B.P. Mandal was ready by 1980, but the Congress Party, in power at that time, had preferred to keep it in cold storage, sensing the far-reaching consequences it could have. Indeed, Mandal unleashed a political storm across the nation.

Desai sums up this shift in Indian politics succinctly[11]: 'In the place of the polite decorum of British parliamentary practice came the rough and tumble of the Indian streets and pavements, a kind of rural boisterousness. The *demos* had finally arrived, shoving aside the *bhadraloks* and *ashrafs*, the Oxbridge graduates and the established dynasties.'

Around the same time, two other trajectories emerged— one on the political front and one on the political economy front. Parallel to the idea of Mandalization was the BJP's campaign of Mandir, namely, the Ram Janmabhoomi movement, through which it said it wanted to consolidate the Hindu identity, which would eventually weave its way to power at the Centre almost a decade and a half later.

The third trajectory unshackled the chains of the licence raj and quota system and introduced citizens to a new narrative—of liberalization and the embracing of globalization. In 1991, faced with an inherited grim balance of payments crisis, economist and finance minister in Narasimha Rao's minority government, Dr Manmohan Singh announced a series of measures intended to do much more than just solve the immediate crisis. The measures brought to the fore a very different way of approaching the basic issues of economic policy and growth, and governance. Indians were introduced to new catchwords— opening up, liberalization, reforms.

The idea was to foster a more competitive economic environment. Towards that aim, the new policy decontrolled industry and trade. Private enterprise could now produce any amount in response to the demands of free market, in contrast to the ceiling on production in the past.

The popular slogan to describe the times, 'Mandal, Mandir and Market', encompassed the churn in Indian democracy. For citizens the challenge was to try and make their political representatives understand that paying heed to their burgeoning aspirations was the stuff of governance.

GROWTH, WELFARE AND ACCOUNTABILITY

Experts say that the first decade of the 21st century, including the tenure of Atal Bihari Vajpayee's National Democratic Alliance (NDA) government, the Congress-led United Progressive Alliance (UPA) I and the beginning years of UPA II, was good for economic growth. Yet, the government led by the hugely popular Vajpayee suffered a shocking defeat at the hands of the electorate in 2004. Their 'India Shining' campaign did not work.

Again, during UPA I, with Manmohan Singh as prime minister, the focus was on growth as well as on welfare schemes like the Mahatma Gandhi National Rural Employment Guarantee Act (MGNREGA). Alongside, the government enacted legislations like the Right to Information Act to hold public institutions accountable. Moreover, India managed to insulate itself against the Wall Street-induced global recession in 2008–09. The electorate voted the UPA back to power in 2009.

But the same voters gave the Congress-led alliance a drubbing in 2014 for what was described as policy paralysis and corruption scandals.

2014: A NEW ERA OF ELECTORAL POLITICS

In 2014, the Narendra Modi-led BJP became the first single political party in about two and a half decades to come to power with a majority at the Centre, confining the Congress to a shrunken presence.

With the ascendancy of the BJP in 2014, many political experts believe that India has entered a new era of electoral politics.[12] The way they saw it, the BJP, after its decisive victory in the 2019 elections, had taken the place that the Congress once occupied in national politics, that is,

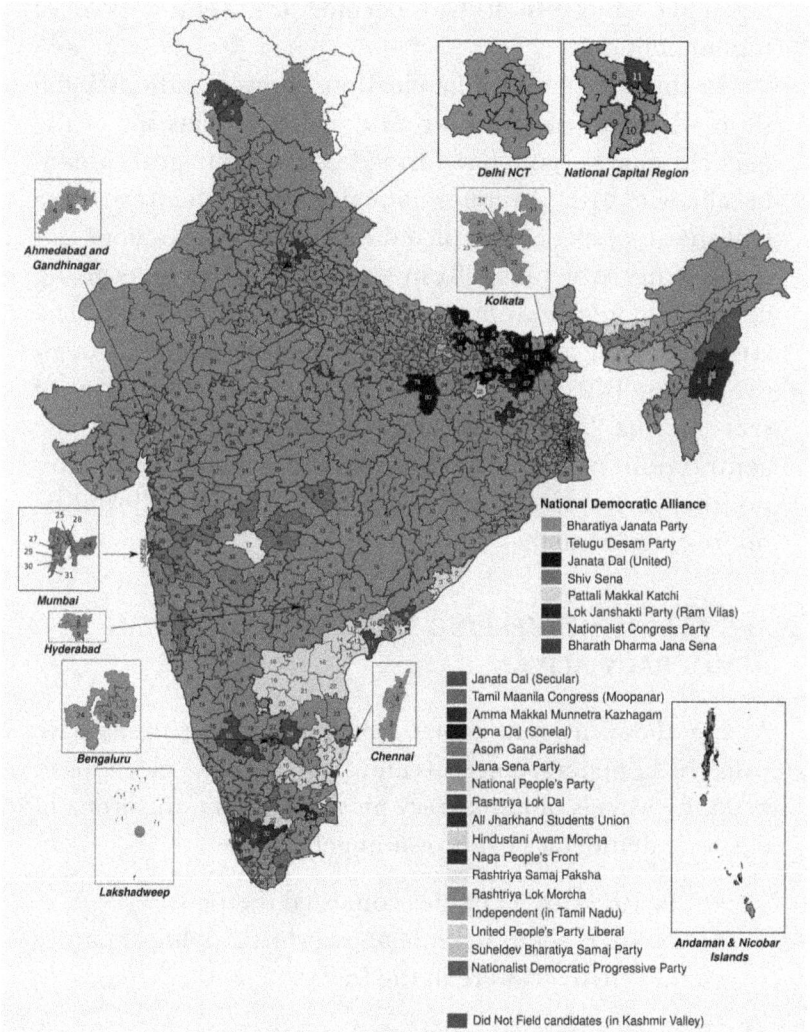

Figure 1.2: 2024 NDA alliance Lok Sabha seat-sharing of all parties[13]

replacing Congress, it had become the central pole of
Indian politics.

In the 2024 Lok Sabha elections, however, the BJP fell
short of a majority, winning 240 seats—32 seats shy of the
majority mark—and has formed a coalition government
in alliance with several regional parties; the respective
seat-sharing has been depicted in Figure 1.2. So, does this
mark a decisive break from the trend of people giving
decisive mandates to one party as in the recent past? The
answer to that question must be a nuanced one. Though
the ruling BJP has not been able to win a majority of
seats in the 2024 Lok Sabha elections, it remains the
central pole in Indian politics. Whether it can retain this
position in the next general elections due in 2029 will be
interesting to watch.

ARE ELECTIONS KEEPING THE SPIRIT OF INDIAN DEMOCRACY ALIVE?

As the above account shows, thus far Indian citizens have
voted in 17 general elections and state assembly elections to
keep the wheels of democracy moving. In fact, the arena of
electoral democracy has grown hugely:

- In 1951–52, 53 parties contested the polls.[14]
- In 2019, there were 2,354 registered political parties
  of which 500 were in the fray.[15]

The electorate, too, has expanded in a big way:

- In 1951–52, the electorate comprised 173 million
  voters.
- In 2019, the electorate numbered 900 million, with
  150 million first-time voters (comprising 85 per cent
  of the electorate in 1951–52).[16]

India has held on to elections as a core feature that is vital to the idea and practice of multiparty democracy for nearly eight decades in spite of ups and downs. The doubts expressed in 1952 by powerful Western nations regarding India's ability to hold elections at regular intervals have been laid to rest during this time. Not only that, in 2011, the then US Secretary of State Hillary Clinton during her visit to India, described the Election Commission of India as the 'global gold standard' in election management.

Does that mean that all is well with our democracy? The simple answer is no.

What is the measure of a true democracy? One can say it is the extent to which citizens are able to elect a representative parliament that believes the laws it frames should have the concerns of citizens at their core. A parliament that holds the government to account in the quest for good governance. Therein lies the rub.

A VASTLY CHANGED SCENARIO: THE POLITICS OF SELF-INTEREST

Certain trends that have marked the political scenario have led to a growing distance between the people and the representatives they end up voting for. It reflects in every aspect of governance.

One of the most visible changes concerns the new generation of politicians who see politics as a career for self-advancement by accessing power and not as a means to serve people. Self-interest is not the mantra of individual politicians alone; it has become the raison d'être of political parties as well.

Nowhere is this more evident than during the election process, which has been overtaken by the power of money and muscle. Winning is the goal and money is the winnability factor in a field of intense political jostling by parties to ensure their influence on a sprawling electorate.

NEXUS OF CRIME AND POLITICS: THE BAHUBALI FACTOR

Often, political parties give tickets to candidates known to be involved in criminal activities, who can provide both muscle and money. Not only can they finance their own campaigns, they can also contribute to the party's coffers during election time, courtesy the stream of unaccounted money generated by their dealings. That helps a party finance other candidates.

Milan Vaishnav, the author of *When Crime Pays*, writes, 'Criminals get elected not in spite of their criminal background but because of it.'[17] After analysing the data of three general elections—in 2004, 2009 and 2014—he concludes that the poorest 20 per cent candidates had 1 per cent chance of winning the polls while the richest 20 per cent had over 23 per cent chance of getting elected. The candidate's hold over the local levers of politics, business and economy is an asset. Candidates with a criminal background thus present an opportunity for political parties wanting to win at any cost.

As per an analysis done by the civil society organization, Association for Democratic Reforms (ADR), among the 543 newly elected Lok Sabha members in 2024, 251 have criminal cases registered against them while 27 of them have been convicted.[18] Table 1.3 presents the data from the last few elections.

Table 1.3
Members of Parliament with criminal cases[19]

	No. of members	*Percentage*
2024	251	46
2019	233	43
2014	185	34
2009	162	30
2004	125	23

MONEY QUEERS THE POLL PITCH FOR THE LESS WEALTHY

For an effective parliamentary democracy, elections need to be free and fair. However, as Gopalkrishna Gandhi puts it in his preface to former Chief Election Commissioner S.Y. Quraishi's book, *An Undocumented Wonder*, 'The biggest attempt at manipulation of the electoral system has come from money and the attempted use of what is best described in a straightforward manner—undisguised bullying.'[20]

A telling example of how money power affects the very idea of a level playing field is provided by ADR. After analysing the 2019 Lok Sabha results, the organization released a report with a valuable finding: almost 30.1 per cent candidates with assets totalling ₹5 crore and above won, whereas the winning percentage among candidates with total assets below ₹10 lakh was just 0.3 per cent.

As Quraishi explains, the cost of rallies and meetings as well as advertisements and posters falls in the category of legal poll expenditure. There is an Election Commission cap for it: between ₹50 lakh and ₹70 lakh for a Lok Sabha candidate, and between ₹20 lakh and ₹28 lakh for a state assembly candidate. This amount is revised during each election.

The actual expenditure is several times that, and
that's where the illegal poll expenditure comes in, from
cash inducements to spirited dinners, and a range of
alluring consumer items as gifts, to name a few. There is
a constant attempt to find ingenious ways of ferrying cash
for these activities—in car boots, concrete mixers and even
ambulances.

Following previous years' trends, it was estimated that
the 2024 election would cost approximately ₹1,00,000 crore.
Table 1.4 shows the election expenditure incurred over the
years.

Table 1.4
Cost of holding elections in India[21]

	Cost (crore)
2024	1,00,000
2019	50,000
2014	3,870
2009	846.67
2004	1,113.88
1999	947.68
1998	666.22
1996	597.34
1991–92	359.10
1989	154.22
1984–85	81.51
1980	54.77
1977	23.04
1971	11.61
1967	10.80
1962	7.32
1957	5.90
1951–52	10.45

ELECTION FINANCING: A THORNY ISSUE

The fact that legal forms of donation to election funds of political parties comprise but a fraction of their total expenditure has long been acknowledged. The ocean of anonymous cash donations, in shades other than white, on which election campaigns sail forth, has been a source of worry for those concerned about the free and fair part of elections. The long-standing stipulation that only donations of ₹20,000 and above needed to be reported has been bypassed regularly by several political parties claiming that all their donations were in far lower sums.

The opacity of donations, especially from corporate sources, has always triggered doubts about a quid pro quo. Who would the elected representative be representing: the electorate that voted or the funder who fuelled the campaign?

In the Union Budget of 2017–18, the scheme of electoral bonds was introduced with the stated objective of bringing about transparency in election funding. Donations to political parties would be permitted through the sale of electoral bonds by the State Bank of India (SBI). Only cheque and digital payments would be allowed. Moreover, the identity of the donor would not be revealed. The argument was that it would curb funding through anonymous cash donations to parties.

In his memoir, *We Also Make Policy*, a former secretary of economic affairs (2017–19) and former finance secretary, Subhash Chandra Garg, writes about a conversation with the then finance minister Arun Jaitley[22]: 'The system he had devised was, he recognized, not the best and most transparent, but was better than any other prevalent system. Companies would be able to make donations from their accounts without the need to search for cash. There would be transparent accounting in companies. The only compromise made […] was that companies or their sponsors would not be required to disclose which party they had made contributions to…'

The scheme was implemented for the first time during the 2019 elections. The maximum sale during the 30 phases in which the electoral bonds were issued was in 2019— between 1 April and 20 April, bonds totalling ₹2,256.37 crore were sold.[23] In the month of January 2024 alone, of the ₹570 crore worth of bonds sold, 94 per cent were in the denomination of ₹1 crore.[24]

On 15 February 2024, a five-judge bench of the Supreme Court gave a unanimous verdict on the many cases before it challenging the electoral bonds scheme as being non-transparent. The apex court struck down the scheme on the grounds that it was unconstitutional; it violated the voter's right to information, which was part of the fundamental right to free speech and expression granted by Article 19(1)(a) of the Constitution.

In an article written a day after the verdict, Quraishi explained that the electoral bonds scheme had been accompanied by some changes[25]:

- Until then, companies could donate up to 7.5 per cent of their profits to a political party. This was changed, 'allowing a company to donate 100 per cent of its profits to a political party'.
- The then Foreign Contribution (Regulation) Act (FCRA) was modified to shield 'any foreign financing of elections from scrutiny'.
- Amendments were made to the Reserve Bank of India (RBI) Act as well. The central bank had voiced a concern that the scheme 'would allow "unauthorized and non-sovereign entities to issue

bearer bonds", in turn undermining the "core principle of central banking legislation"'.

CITIZENS' RIGHT TO KNOW

In fact, by upholding voters' right to know as the basis of its verdict, the Supreme Court was reiterating the same principle it had upheld in 2003. In response to a public interest litigation (PIL) filed by ADR in 1999, the Delhi High Court had ruled that candidates contesting parliamentary and assembly elections would henceforth be required to file a sworn affidavit along with their nomination papers, declaring any pending criminal cases against them.

The then government at the Centre appealed the order in the Supreme Court, and was joined by other political parties as well. Their view was that the Delhi High Court had ruled on a matter that was the preserve of the legislature.

The Supreme Court upheld the high court order in 2002. Its view was that[26]: 'if the field meant for legislature and executive is left unoccupied detrimental to public interest, this Court would have ample jurisdiction under Article 32 read with Articles 141 and 142 of the Constitution to issue necessary directions to the Executive to subserve public interest.'

The government promulgated an ordinance amending the Representation of the People [RP] Act (1951) so that the apex court ruling was made ineffective. Finally, in response to three PILs challenging the amendment of the RP Act as being unconstitutional, the apex court, in 2003, held that the amendment did not pass the 'test of constitutionality'—it went against the citizens' fundamental right to freedom of speech and expression, namely, Article 19(1)(a) of the Constitution.

The Supreme Court gave a ruling in September 2018 on a PIL filed by the Public Interest Foundation. While stating that candidates, and their political parties, would be required to publicize the criminal charges pending against them through media advertisements, the apex court ruled against a request to debar such individuals from contesting parliamentary or assembly elections. The court noted[27]:

> A time has come that the Parliament must make law to ensure that persons facing serious criminal cases do not enter into the political stream. It is one thing to take cover under the presumption of innocence of the accused but it is equally imperative that persons who enter public life and participate in law making should be above any kind of serious criminal allegation.
>
> The nation eagerly awaits for such legislation, for the society has a legitimate expectation to be governed by proper constitutional governance. The voters cry for systematic sustenance of constitutionalism. The country feels agonized when money and muscle power become the supreme power. Substantial efforts have to be undertaken to cleanse the polluted stream of politics by prohibiting people with criminal antecedents so that they do not even conceive of the idea of entering into politics. They should be kept at bay.

◆

Years ago, a newly independent nation managed to pull off a successful election when no one gave it much of a chance. In every election the citizens have exercised their franchise, seeing it as their right and duty to elect representatives to Parliament who will voice their needs, concerns, and aspirations and enable good governance. In this context, it is important to look at the institution of Parliament and assess whether it has stayed true to their faith.

2

HOUSE OF LAWMAKERS

People's representatives trooping into the House with placards in hand, shouting slogans before the Speaker, launching projectiles of copies of the bills they are opposed to, engaging in slanging matches across the aisle and on occasion even in a physical scuffle, aiming footwear at the Speaker—India's Parliament has seen it all in the last few decades. More importantly, the people who elect them to power can also witness them, courtesy the live telecast of Parliament session proceedings on television.

There was a time when Parliament was associated with decorum, informed debates and good-humoured banter. Now the terms that come to mind are pandemonium, disruption, poor debates or none at all, casual attendance, 'horse-trading' and criminal records.

So much so that former Lok Sabha Speaker (2004–09), Somnath Chatterjee, was provoked to comment, 'The behaviour and conduct of some legislators have become the subject of justified criticism and in some cases even of ridicule. Unfortunately, there is developing more and more an attitude of confrontation than cooperation in our political life, which finds its reflection in the House.'[1]

In another instance, he responded sharply to the sloganeering Members of Parliament (MPs) who had made their way to the well of the House: 'I think Parliament should be adjourned sine die. Useless allowances should not be given to you. I think that is the best thing to do. You don't deserve one paisa out of public money.'[2]

This kind of conduct is not unique to Parliament, it is common to legislatures across the country.

Legislatures are considered the soul of our democracy. As the supreme lawmaking bodies, their fundamental function is to enact laws that mirror the aspirations of the people, show a concern for their growth and the nation's development. Legislatures have another mandate as well: holding the executive accountable through various mechanisms available to them in order to ensure that the government fulfils the promises made to the electorate. By acquitting themselves thus, Parliament and state assemblies stay accountable to the citizens, whose will they represent.

Subhash C. Kashyap, former secretary general of the Seventh, Eighth and Ninth Lok Sabhas, lamented in his book *Blueprint of Political Reforms*[3]: 'The number of days on which the Houses of Parliament sit each year to transact business has come down in recent years. Even when they do meet, often little gets done. In the face of disturbances and shouting, the Houses have to be adjourned frequently.'

Seeing the issue in perspective, he added, 'Parliament was conceived as the Legislature or the lawmaking body but of late lawmaking has ceased to be even the most important of its functions either qualitatively or quantitatively. From about 48 per cent, it has come down to occupy less than 14 per cent of its time.'

This holds true for state assemblies as well. Debates have suffered both in quality and quantity, impacting not only the quality of legislation but also the number of laws passed in many cases. Frequent disruptions leading to adjournments delay every pending business, which has a concrete impact on people's lives. The legislatures' mandate of exercising control over the government of the day through various mechanisms has also weakened.

These developments are worrying. Considering that Indian legislatures have come to mirror our society's diversity in large part, much more than during the early decades of independence, this is the perfect moment for them to exercise their mandate, work towards a blueprint for development aimed at reducing disparities. That can happen only when there is a debate on the issues central to the workings of our society with the ultimate aim of building consensus.

Somehow, stridency, acrimony and a disinclination to hear the other person out only leads to one-upmanship or 'political theatre' as commentators call it. Consequently, issues become hardened fault lines on the ground in the absence of informed and sincere deliberations, hampering good governance at every step. As the former President R. Venkatraman commented about our political representatives, they are 'no longer competitors in the endeavour to serve the nation but are bitter enemies drawn in battle array'.[4]

HOUSE OF DISRUPTIONS

According to PRS Legislative Research—which makes the Indian legislative process better informed, more transparent and participatory—the time spent by MPs and Members of Legislative Assembly (MLAs) in Parliament and state assembly sittings has been on the decline.

- The sitting days in the Lok Sabha have declined from an annual average of 121 days during 1952–70 to 68 days since 2000.[5]
- The First Lok Sabha, with Prime Minister Jawaharlal Nehru as the leader of the House, had an average of 135 sittings every year.[6]

- The Seventeenth Lok Sabha (2019–24), which concluded on Saturday, 10 February 2024, had an average of only 55 sittings in a year (the fewest sittings were in 2020 during Covid-19).
- Between June 2019 and February 2024, the Seventeenth Lok Sabha held 274 sittings, the fewest among all full-term Lok Sabhas. A look at Figure 2.1 shows a pattern:

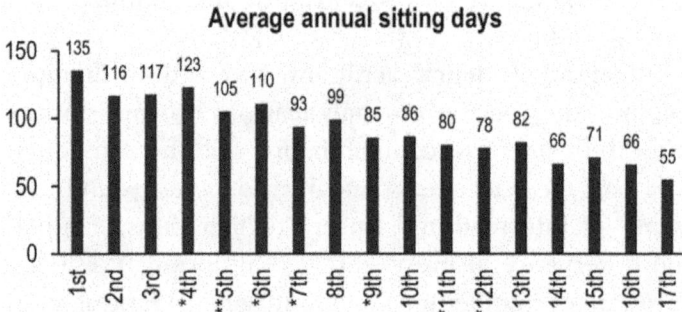

Note: * indicates a term less than five years; ** indicates a six year term.

Figure 2.1: Average annual sitting days across Lok Sabhas[7]

- The 'Annual Review of State Laws 2022' by PRS Legislative Research, which was released in May 2023, indicates that state assemblies demonstrate a similar pattern[8]: on an average, sitting days have been on a declining streak from 2016 to 2022, going even lower in 2020 due to the Covid-19 pandemic. In these years, the average sitting days in 24 state assemblies was 25. Kerala topped the list, followed by Odisha and Karnataka. The states of Haryana, Punjab and Tripura did not average more than 20 days annually since 2016, as can be seen in Figure 2.2.
- In 2022, 28 state assemblies met for 21 days on average. Karnataka led the list, followed by West Bengal and Kerala.

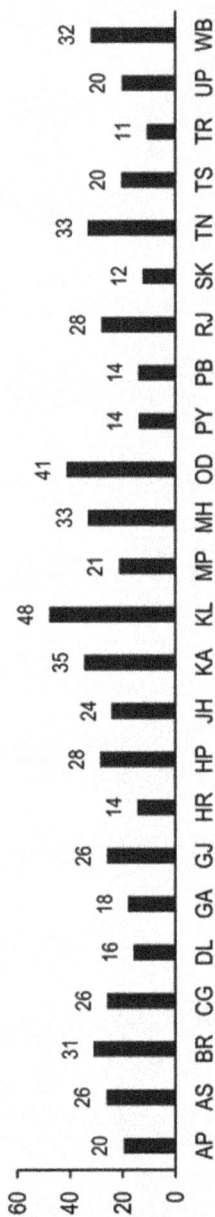

Figure 2.2: Average number of sitting days of state assemblies (2016–2022)[9]

Note: The data for Sikkim and Puducherry is the average number of sitting days for 2017-2022; the chart above does not include Arunachal Pradesh, Meghalaya, Manipur, Mizoram, Nagaland, and Uttarakhand.

Sources: Assembly websites of various states; RTI; PRS.

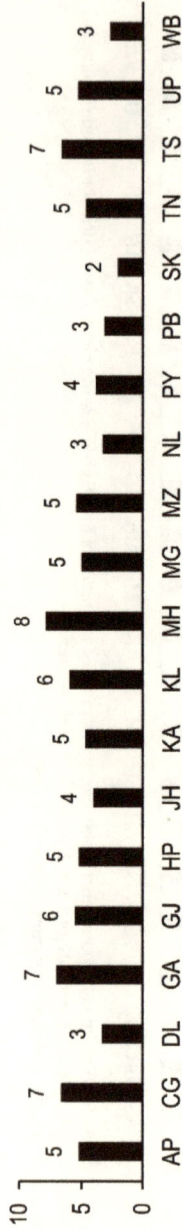

Figure 2.3: Average duration of a sitting in 2022 (hours)[10]

Sources: Assembly websites of various states; RTI; PRS.

- In 2022, the average duration of a sitting in 20 states came to five hours. On average, a sitting in Maharashtra lasted eight hours, while in Sikkim it lasted for two hours. Further data has been shared in Figure 2.3.

FEWER BILLS, LESS TIME FOR DISCUSSION

Of all the Lok Sabhas that have had a five-year term, the maximum number of bills, 355, were passed during the Eighth Lok Sabha (1984–89), and the least, 192, during the Fifteenth Lok Sabha (2009–14).[11]

Every government talks about the productivity achieved during a particular session in terms of the legislative business accomplished in a particular session. The fact, however, is that the number of hours spent on discussing and debating bills have been steadily decreasing.

As mentioned earlier in this chapter, over two decades ago, Kashyap was bemoaning the fact that the time devoted to lawmaking had come down, from about 48 per cent to less than 14 per cent, in Parliament. That trend has continued. The figures released by PRS India bear this out[12]:

- The 2018–19 budget was passed by a voice vote, without discussion, amid continuing protests from the Opposition.
- In the Seventeenth Lok Sabha (2019–24), the government cleared over 18 bills during one of the monsoon sessions. Each bill was discussed for about 34 minutes on an average. The House comprises over 500 MPs.
- The Farm Laws Repeal Bill (2021) was passed in eight minutes—getting three minutes in the Lok Sabha and five minutes in the Rajya Sabha.

About 203 MPs (37.24 per cent) are self-professed agriculturalists.[13]

- The Essential Defence Services Bill (2021) that enables 'the government to prohibit strikes, lockouts and lay-offs in units engaged in essential defence services' saw 12 minutes of debate in the Lok Sabha.

- The Insolvency and Bankruptcy Code (Amendment) Bill (2021) witnessed just five minutes of debate.

- The 2023–24 Union Budget was passed amid sloganeering without any discussion in a matter of 12 minutes. Former Finance Minister Chidambaram commented, 'The "worst message" from a parliamentary democracy is approval to a Budget without discussion. ₹45,03,097 crore will be raised and spent for the "people" in 2023–24 without the people's representatives offering their views on the Budget.'[14]

PRS data in its 'Annual Review of State Laws 2022' shows a similar pattern across state legislatures[15]:

- In 2022, 322 bills (56 per cent of the total number of bills passed across all states on important subjects such as labour, land and social justice) were passed on the day they were introduced or the following day, showing an increase from 44 per cent bills passed in this duration in 2021.

- In 2022, nine states, including Bihar, Gujarat, Punjab and West Bengal, passed all bills within a day of introduction. The states of Kerala, Karnataka, Rajasthan and Meghalaya devoted over five days to pass the majority of their bills.

The world over, as the complexity of issues increases, there's a greater emphasis on legislative debates and discussions, which has a direct impact on the quality of legislation and policies. Treasury benches, by law, and as part of convention, find they have to go through hours of discussion before they arrive at the stage of passing a bill and enacting a law. In September 2013 in the US, Republican senator Ted Cruz was allowed to speak for 21 hours and 19 minutes in the Senate during a discussion on Obamacare. The ruling Democrats listened to him attentively while he grilled them on a number of aspects of the bill that was to come, and he passionately argued against the bill.

In India, except for the early decades of independence, governments that have been comfortably placed in terms of their numbers in the legislature, and they have been of all hues, have not cared much for developing this aspect of legislative business.

The voice vote has been used by many a majority government to push through legislation on the force of their numbers. The votes are not counted or recorded, the decibel level of 'aye' as opposed to 'no' is all the proof that is needed by the Speaker for a bill to be passed. The presumption being that as there are more MPs on the treasury benches, they would vote according to the party line once a whip is issued. This method has come in for criticism when serious bills are passed without deliberation, and votes are not counted or recorded.

In this context, it is important to mention the case of the passage of the Aadhaar Bill (2016) and the controversy around it. In the Indian context, money bills are a specific category of bills introduced in Parliament that exclusively deal with matters related to taxation, government expenditure, government borrowing or the Consolidated Fund of India. Article 110 of the Indian Constitution defines the criteria for classifying a bill as a money bill, stating that 'a Bill shall be deemed to be a Money Bill if it contains *only* provisions dealing with all or any of the following matters, namely... [emphasis added]'

More importantly, money bills can only be introduced in the Lok Sabha; they do not require the assent of the Rajya Sabha, except for recommendations that the President of India may make. This gives the Lok Sabha primacy in matters of taxation and public expenditure. A government with a comfortable majority in the Lok Sabha is able to get the job done without fuss.

If there is a doubt in any quarter that a bill sought to be passed as a money bill does not meet its strict parameters, and reflects other compulsions, legal challenges may arise as to whether it meets the strictly defined criteria specified in Article 110 of the Constitution. In the Seventeenth Lok Sabha, one such challenge did arise.

The Aadhaar Bill was introduced in the Lok Sabha as a money bill in 2016. Of the 59 sections in the bill, there was only one, Section 7, which referred to the Consolidated Fund of India. In *K.S. Puttaswamy* v. *Union of India* (2018), the Supreme Court upheld the constitutionality of the Aadhaar (Targeted Delivery of Financial and Other Subsidies, Benefits and Services) Act, 2016, by a 4:1 majority. It held that no illegality had been committed by passing the Aadhaar Bill as a money bill in Parliament. The lone dissenter was Justice D.Y. Chandrachud.

At the heart of the case was one concern in regard to Article 110: how does one read the Aadhaar (Targeted Delivery of Financial and Other Subsidies, Benefits and Services) Act, 2016, the bulk of which is related to 'incidental matters' but which also contains some provisions of a money bill. Does it pass muster with regard to the conditionalities of Article 110?

The majority opinion penned by Justice A.K. Sikri was that the main objective of the legislation was to extend benefits in the nature of aid, grant or subsidy to the marginalized sections of society with the support of the Consolidated Fund of India, which was expressed in Section 7. Holding Section 7 to be the main provision in the Aadhaar Act, and the other provisions being 'incidental', the apex court ruled that the Act fell within the ambit of Article 110(1)(e) of the Constitution (expenditure charged to the Consolidated Fund) and was valid as a money bill. Concurring, Justice Bhushan affirmed that the matter was subject to future judicial review.

Justice Chandrachud, in his dissenting opinion, pointed to the word in Article 110(1)—'only'—followed by a list of matters connected to taxation and expenditure from the Consolidated Fund of India. In his view, the argument that the Aadhaar Act should qualify being passed as a money bill because it involved extending grants from the Consolidated Fund did not pass the test. He held that such a contention would allow just about anything to be passed as a money bill, which would amount to rewriting the Constitution. His dissenting note also underscored that superseding the Rajya Sabha's authority to look at non-money bills was in conflict with the constitutional scheme and the legitimacy of democratic institutions.

MAKING THE GOVERNMENT ACCOUNTABLE

It is in such contexts that the second role of Parliament, namely, ensuring the accountability of the government of the day, becomes relevant.

Among the means Parliament has had at its disposal are Question Hour, Zero Hour and the various committees that do the heavy lifting when it comes to detailed examination of bills to facilitate informed discussions or scrutinizing budgetary allocations and policies.

Question Hour is the liveliest hour in Parliament.[16] Experienced MPs have taken the government of the day to task by asking incisive questions designed to elicit information and trigger suitable action by ministries. There have been many instances of MPs successfully using this parliamentary device to bring irregularities to public knowledge.

Zero Hour, the hour before lunch, and an Indian parliamentary innovation, evolved organically in the first decade of Parliament during which MPs could raise important constituency and national issues without giving advance notice to the Speaker. It is an opportunity for MPs cutting across party lines to voice issues, and also to advance private members' bills on issues they consider important. When the number and duration of legislature sittings come down, these mechanisms, too, are affected.

A significant aspect of the architecture of accountability is the committee system, comprising members drawn from the ruling party and the opposition as well as from both Houses, which grew in a big way from the 1990s. Seeing the limited duration of legislative sessions, the detailed examination of bills by the standing committees for various departments helps build the expertise of legislators, as a range of stakeholders are invited to provide their point of view. It provides a way of arriving at a consensus.

The Public Accounts Committee (PAC) and the Estimates Committee are heavy-duty financial committees. The former, chaired by a leading member of the Opposition, is constituted every year, and its mandate is to ascertain how the budget allocated by Parliament has been spent by the government. The PAC scrutinizes cases involving financial irregularities on the basis of the

Comptroller and Auditor General's (CAG) reports. While it expresses no opinion on points of general policy, it is well within its brief to point out whether there has been any irregularity in carrying out that policy.

One of the most prominent issues for which the PAC came into the public eye was regarding the 2G spectrum allocation in 2010, during the second tenure of the UPA coalition government. Vinod Rai, who was the CAG at that time, writes about the exemplary vigilance of the PAC, which sought to hold the government to account in the 2G spectrum matter, showing a 'non-partisan approach'.

The PAC began to examine the 2G spectrum allocation procedure even before the CAG audit report had been tabled in Parliament. Rai writes that unlike usual occasions when Opposition MPs ask the rigorous questions, this time it was an MP from the ruling party who wanted the finance secretary to calculate and tell them the possible magnitude of loss that could stem from the way the 2G licences had been allocated. However, writes Rai, ultimately, the PAC was not able to submit the report during the session as the whole affair degenerated along party lines. He also adds that fewer meetings and 'inadequate application' reduces the impact of this mechanism.

The Joint Parliamentary Committee (JPC), too, has occupied a prominent place in public memory from 1987 onwards when it was first constituted to examine the Bofors scandal. Usually looking at matters of national significance, other prominent matters on which a JPC was constituted were the Ketan Parekh stock market scam (2001); issue of pesticide residues in and safety standards for soft drinks (2003); the 2G spectrum allocation case; the Land Acquisition Bill (2015); and the Personal Data Protection Bill (2019). During the Sixteenth and Seventeenth Lok Sabhas, demands for a JPC on the issue of the Rafale deal were not agreed to.

JPC recommendations have persuasive value but the committee cannot force the government to take any action on the basis of its report. The discretion to launch an investigation rests entirely with the government. Of course, the government is required to report on the follow-up action taken on the basis of the recommendations of the JPC and other committees. The committees then submit Action Taken Reports in Parliament on the basis of the government's reply. These reports can be discussed in Parliament and the government can be questioned on the basis of the same.

These mechanisms reflect the mature understanding that in holding the executive accountable, Parliament is conscious of its own accountability to the people. But when there are disruptions or a decline in the quantity and quality of discussions and infrequent meetings by members of significant committees as well as an attitude of taking extreme positions of partisanship, what suffers is governance.

WHERE IS THE OPPOSITION?

In fact, the Opposition plays a crucial role in holding the executive accountable in a parliamentary democracy. A force to reckon with, as the very term suggests. It scrutinizes the government's policies and actions by playing a proactive role in parliamentary discussions, during Question Hour and in committees—highlighting discrepancies, failures and potential shortcomings in government initiatives.

By providing alternative viewpoints and ensuring that minority opinions are not overlooked, the Opposition can enrich the democratic process. And in a situation where the ruling party is in a comfortable majority, by questioning government decisions and proposals, the Opposition can play a constructive role.

In recent times, there have been some constructive interventions by Opposition parties. Their concerns about the impact of the goods and services tax (GST) on small businesses and the complex tax structure come to mind. The points made by the Opposition parties and civil society groups regarding the proposed Land Acquisition Bill (2015), namely, that it would dilute safeguards for landowners and environmental protection, had an impact. The bill was withdrawn and a revised version was introduced. Similarly, when the views of farmers' bodies regarding the three farm laws (2020) were voiced on the floor of the House by Opposition parties, the laws were rolled back in 2021.

As the decades of India's democratic journey have passed, Opposition parties have been blamed for disruption of Parliament and assembly sessions that seriously impacts the business of legislatures. On their part, many an Opposition has accused governments of stifling their voice because they have a comfortable majority.

WHAT IS THE WAY OUT?

During the very first session of Parliament after the first general elections, Prime Minister Nehru had a message for the Opposition: 'We welcome the coming to this House of the Members of the Opposition. Whoever they may be, and however much we might differ from them in many matters, we welcome them because, undoubtedly, they represent a certain section of Indian opinion and it is good in a House of this kind to have a vigorous Opposition so that whether it is Government or the majority party, they do not become complacent.'

Former Prime Minister Atal Bihari Vajpayee, who led the BJP-led NDA government from 1999 to 2004, was a towering figure of the Opposition for most of his political career and is remembered for the standards he set. Speaking at the International Parliamentary Conference to mark the Golden Jubilee of the Parliament of India, held in 2003, he said: 'In a democracy, there are bound to be differences among political parties, and [...] vigorous debate among divergent viewpoints in Parliament. Differences and their well-researched, articulate expression both inside and outside Parliament is the very stuff of democracy. It is what lends vibrancy to democracy. But the vitality of democracy also demands discipline, constructive approach and a readiness to contribute to consensus-building on pressing issues before the nation—and adherence to rules.'

In our times across the world, realpolitik holds sway. Arithmetic matters more than anything else. The situation becomes more complicated in instances where the Opposition parties, too, are in disarray because there are too many parties with few numbers in the legislature and no one party is playing the role of fulcrum due to its small numbers. The task of maintaining checks and balances becomes more difficult.

Moreover, in the context of India, many political observers feel that with the changing social composition of legislatures and, particularly, with the live telecast of legislative sessions, protests and disruptions have become a way of grandstanding. They represent the new vocabulary of opposition.

In the view of Ronojoy Sen, Senior Research Fellow at the Institute of South Asian Studies and the South Asian Studies Programme, National University of Singapore: 'The frequency of protests inside the House and the behaviour of MPs possibly represent a clash between the elite and mass cultures, which undermined British parliamentary rituals. They also represent the intrusion of the politics and political theatre of the street into the precincts of the Parliament, which have often adversely affected its deliberative and legislative functions.'[17]

CRIMINALIZATION OF POLITICS

All these factors affecting the functioning of our legislatures are dwarfed by one major phenomenon—the steady rise in the number of MPs and MLAs with declared criminal backgrounds, as mentioned in the previous chapter. This nexus of crime and politics tars parties across the spectrum, with few exceptions. Having deep pockets, much of it money that is unaccounted for, such candidates are sought after because of their winnability factor, namely money power, in a highly competitive scenario of politics. According to 2023 data published by ADR:

- As many as 40 per cent of sitting MPs (from both Lok Sabha and Rajya Sabha) have declared criminal cases against themselves (as of September 2023). In absolute numbers, this translates to 306 out of 763 MPs. The figure has been worked out based on self-sworn affidavits of 763 sitting MPs out of 776 MPs.
- As many as 25 per cent of MPs (194 out of 763 MPs) have serious criminal cases, including kidnapping, murder, attempt to murder, crimes against women, etc., against them.
- The percentage of Lok Sabha MPs with criminal charges rose drastically from 30 per cent in the 2009 elections to 34 per cent in the 2014 elections to 43 per cent in the 2019 elections.[18] In a grim reminder of the steep and slippery slope on which Indian democracy is standing, that figure has risen to 46 per cent after the 2024 Lok Sabha elections,

according to an ADR analysis.[19] It pointed out that as many as 251 out of 543 Lok Sabha MPs have criminal cases against them. Of these 27 have actually been convicted of crimes. This is the highest number of tainted MPs ever to be elected to the Lok Sabha. There has been a 55 per cent rise in MPs with criminal cases against them since 2009.

The situation in state assemblies is no better, according to the 2023 analysis by ADR and the National Election Watch, which examined both criminal records and assets of the MLAs.[20] The survey examined the affidavits submitted by individuals in the run-up to their most recent election— about 4,001 MLAs out of 4,033 in a total of 28 state assemblies and two UTs. The findings were significant:

- About 44 per cent MLAs had declared that there were criminal cases against them.
- About 28 per cent were facing serious criminal charges such as murder and kidnapping.
- Significantly, MLAs who had criminal cases had on an average higher assets (₹16.36 crore) than MLAs with no criminal cases (₹11.45 crore).
- Karnataka—with all 223 MLAs having average assets of ₹64.39 crore—was first on the list of MLAs with highest assets. Andhra Pradesh with 174 MLAs came second with average assets of ₹28.24 crore, and Maharashtra came third with 284 MLAs having average assets of ₹23.51 crore.
- States with the lowest average assets were Tripura (₹1.54 crore for 59 MLAs), West Bengal (₹2.8 crore for 293 MLAs) and Kerala (₹3.15 crore for 135 MLAs).

SELF-PRESERVATION VERSUS DISQUALIFICATION: A CASE STUDY

According to the Representation of the People Act, 1951, Section 8(3), any MP or MLA convicted of an offence and sentenced to imprisonment for not less than two years faces disqualification from the date of conviction. Section 8(4) of the Act provided protection to the MP or MLA by allowing members to continue provided they appealed within three months.

In 2005, Kerala lawyer Lily Thomas challenged Section 8(4) of the Act. In a landmark judgement in July 2013, the Supreme Court of India, in *Lily Thomas* v. *Union of India,* ruled that any MP or MLA convicted of a crime and sentenced to a minimum of two years would automatically lose membership of the House with immediate effect. It struck down Section 8(4) of the Representation of the People Act as being 'unconstitutional'. In no uncertain terms the apex court held[21]:

> Looking at the affirmative terms of Articles 102(1)(e) and 191(1)(e) of the Constitution, we hold that Parliament has been vested with the powers to make law laying down the same disqualifications for person to be chosen as a member of Parliament or a State Legislature and for a sitting member of a House of Parliament or a House of a State Legislature. We also hold that the provisions of Article 101(3)(a) and 190(3)(a) of the Constitution expressly prohibit Parliament to defer the date from which the disqualification will come into effect in case of a sitting member of Parliament or a State Legislature. Parliament, therefore, has exceeded its powers conferred by the Constitution in enacting sub-section (4) of Section 8 of the Act and accordingly

sub-section (4) of Section 8 of the Act is ultra vires
the Constitution.

The government filed a review petition in the apex court
to allow convicted legislators three months' time to appeal
against their conviction. It was a rare occasion when the
government and Opposition parties put up a joint front in
backing the review petition.

The review petition expressed the argument that
questions of constitutional importance needed to be heard
by a bench of minimum five judges, as per Article 145(3),
and not by a two-judge bench that pronounced the 2013
judgement.

The government said the matter of conviction and
disqualification of MLAs or MPs was a settled principle
in law, given that a five-judge Supreme Court bench had
upheld the three-month duration for appeal in the *K.
Prabhakaran* v. *J. Jayarajan* case in 2005. A two-judge bench
could not override it.

The government's review petition further argued
that the court's ruling in the 2005 case was correct in the
sense that it would prevent an 'anomalous situation'
wherein the conviction of a particular legislator is struck
down by a higher court, but the member has already
been disqualified. And, the government said, there is no
provision thus far to refill the vacant seat, of a Lok Sabha
constituency or an assembly constituency, by a disqualified
member. This would mean letting the seat remain vacant
and depriving particular constituents of their right to have
an elected representative in their respective assemblies or in
the Parliament.

Despite the government and political class's attempts
to show that the order passed by the Supreme Court was
wrong in principle and on legal terms, the apex court

refused to review its order, saying: 'Legislature has created all the problems and they don't want to admit their mistakes. Parliament is to make laws and we are here to interpret them. But when we start interpreting the laws, legislature blames us for encroaching into legislative domain. The law was very clumsily drafted. You have yourself invited all the problems.'

The court also said, 'We found there was a lacuna in the law and we passed orders. Otherwise, a voter would say the law prohibits him from casting his vote when he is inside a jail but allows another person in jail to contest. What kind of a law is this? There was an error in the legislation and you should have changed it.'

The ruling meant that a convicted legislator would lose their membership immediately without any judicial remedy at their disposal, and two, they would be barred from contesting elections for six years subsequent to the date of their conviction.

The Union government announced that it would bring in an ordinance and later a bill to supplant the court's ruling. Then followed the shocking incident of Rahul Gandhi, the then vice president of the Indian National Congress, calling a press conference where he tore up the ordinance devised by his own government. The ordinance was then withdrawn but the act of the political class seeking to go the ordinance way angered public opinion substantially. It created a sense of outrage among the people, a sentiment that, along with the corruption allegations against the government, became one of the reasons for its unequivocal defeat in the 2014 elections

Since the landmark judgement of 2013, only 12 MPs and MLAs have been disqualified following conviction in criminal cases, among them Lalu Yadav, Azam Khan, J. Jayalalithaa, Lakshadweep MP Mohammed Faizal from the Nationalist Congress Party (NCP) and, ironically, Rahul

Gandhi of the Congress Party too (he was given a two-year sentence by a Gujarat court in a defamation case).

However, the rising trend of criminalization of politics in India has not really been stemmed. In the end, it is the legislature as an institution that is devalued, as people look at it with cynical eyes.

As Sen points out in his paper, 'Criminality and corruption, which are increasingly associated with India's political class, pose a severe challenge to the legitimacy and accountability of the Parliament. As far back as 1951, an MP in the Provisional Parliament, H.G. Mudgal, was accused of taking money to ask questions and move amendments in the Parliament. Many years later, the 2008 scandal raised similar crucial questions about the conduct and accountability of MPs.'[22]

Sen's reference was to the stunning image of some MPs brandishing wads of currency in Parliament in 2008, saying they had been offered the money to abstain from voting on the no-confidence motion against the proposed Indo-US nuclear deal that the then government at the Centre was advocating.

Similarly, the almost routine images of legislators being herded by anxious political parties and taken to some destination where they would presumably be safe from the overtures of another party wanting them to defect, in order to stay in power or assume power, are sources of distress for the electorate. One of the recent cases is when 16 of Bihar's 19 Congress MLAs were flown to Hyderabad due to fear in the party about an attempt to split it before the trust vote scheduled for 12 February 2024 in Patna. Ironically, the anti-defection law, which was supposed to increase the stability of governments and prevent legislators from the lures of benefits offered, has ended up doing the very opposite.

When seen in the context of a general decline in the number of sitting hours of legislators, the decline in the quantity and quality of legislative business accomplished, and lesser scrutiny of the executive, the picture that emerges is sombre. There needs to be a rethink, a recalibration on the part of all political parties to ensure that the spirit of their mandate, exemplified by the legislature, stays intact.

In order to do that, there has to be an awareness of how crucial timely steps of governance are, particularly in today's integrated world of immense financial and economic complexity, social change and fast-changing technologies. Governments across the world are finding it a challenging task to govern in the interests of their citizens and nations. We are at a crucial juncture where we need to utilize our pool of resources and skills in a mature fashion to deal with these challenges of governance.

◆

In this context, the role of the legislature becomes all the more important. For it is the vital link between the people, whose will it voices, and the government of the day that it is supposed to keep a strict eye on.

The crucial question in the last almost eight decades and going further is the same: if not the legislature, who will monitor the all-powerful executive?

3

THE BUSINESS OF GOVERNANCE

In theory we know that in a parliamentary democracy, policymaking and governance are the preserve of the executive. Also, that the political executive comprises a Council of Ministers drawn from the legislature, with the prime minister as first among equals. The Council are defined by the two Cs—collegial functioning and collective responsibility. And they are accountable to the legislature for their actions. However, the reality is different.

What we have witnessed in the nearly eighty years of democracy in India is more accurately described as a prime ministerial form of government. After all, the Indian prime minister has a free hand to choose his or her Council of Ministers, comprising the all-important Cabinet, ministers of state and deputy ministers. How a prime minister, or chief minister for that matter, chooses to exercise that power is a different matter. Whether it's a 'my way or the highway' attitude or consensual approach depends on two things—the circumstances in which prime ministers and chief ministers find themselves, such as whether they are heading comfortable majority governments or coalitions, and their temperaments. More importantly, it affects the nature of the functioning relationship between a prime minister and the Cabinet in terms of decision-making.

In his book *The Indian Cabinet: A Study in Governance,* V.A. Pai Panandikar gives an interesting overview of the relationship of different prime ministers with their Cabinets.[1]

During Nehru's time, when Vallabhbhai Patel was alive and the Cabinet had heavyweights, the Cabinet function was 'more or less like a collegial executive'. Nehru and Patel enjoyed a strong partnership, where their distinctive strengths were pooled together in the service of the country they both deeply loved. After Patel's demise 'the spirit of accommodation which kept the Cabinet as a substantial policy coalition' began to wane. However, Nehru was 'cautious at every step not to damage the institution of the Indian cabinet.'

Lal Bahadur Shastri, who became the prime minister after Nehru's death, was a total contrast. By nature and due to circumstances (he was aware of the strong personalities in his party) he chose the path of consensus in his Cabinet. Indira Gandhi, who succeeded Shastri and was aware of her standing in a party of heavyweights, decided to 'short-circuit established procedures' of the Cabinet system by setting up a 'kitchen cabinet' of friends and associates, and doing away with the idea of hierarchy in the Cabinet. Post-1971 and when she returned to power in 1980, it was the time of 'imperial prime-ministership' and irrelevance of the Cabinet.

Before Indira Gandhi's last stint as prime minister came the post-Emergency Janata Party rule (1977–79). Morarji Desai's coalition Cabinet took on a collegial character. However, as it was full of established leaders of the erstwhile Opposition, there was a constant barrage of political challenges, which led to the downfall of the government.

When Rajiv Gandhi stormed to power in 1984 with the largest ever majority, it created conditions for 'the rise of imperial prime ministership in its fullest form'. He ruled with the help of an 'unofficial coterie and some

50   THE GOVERNANCE GAP

of his political camp followers'. When his bête noire V.P.
Singh formed what was only the second non-Congress
government at the Centre in 1989, a coalition government
with the outside support of the CPM and BJP, he could not
but choose 'collegial and democratic functioning of the
Cabinet', writes Panandikar.

It was a short-lived Cabinet, though, for the
government collapsed under the weight of its own political
contradictions.

These trends have informed the trajectory of the
political executive since. It is apparent that there has been
a general move towards centralization of power in political
decision-making, and a movement away from the Cabinet,
at the Centre and in states. Tied to this is the ascendance
of the prime minister's or chief minister's office and a
corresponding decline in the importance of the Cabinet
Secretariat.

In the parliamentary democracy model, the role of
the Cabinet Secretariat is built around the functioning of
the Cabinet. It is the link between the topmost political
executive and ministers as also between the Cabinet
and various ministries. The Cabinet Secretary heads the
bureaucracy.

The Cabinet Secretariat has largely gone the way of the
Cabinet in the Indian scheme of things.

In his book *Portraits of Power*, former Indian
Administrative Service (IAS) officer N.K. Singh traces the
important role that the Prime Minister's Office (PMO)
has come to assume over the years.[2] Under Nehru, the
Cabinet Secretariat stayed the course. Although India's
first prime minister had his own personal staff (referred to
then as PM's Personal Staff or PMS), they never replaced
or overruled the advice of the Cabinet Secretariat to prime
ministers or the Council of Ministers.

Nehru's private secretary M.O. Mathai corroborates this in his book *Reminiscences of the Nehru Age*: 'The staff of the Prime Minister's Secretariat are not responsible for advising on policy or for executing the Prime Minister's decisions on policy. They are only gatherers and conveyors and, in short, mechanics men.'[3]

It was only after Nehru, under Lal Bahadur's tenure as prime minister, that this arrangement was altered. By means of an amendment to the Government of India (Allocation of Business) Rules, 1961, in June 1964, the PMS was given a distinct status. It was now required 'to provide secretarial assistance to the PM'. Lakshmi Kant Jha, a secretary in the Government of India, was appointed as secretary to the PM in July 1964.

Shastri's intention was not to move towards a centralization of power, nor did he want the Cabinet Secretariat to be diminished. He wanted help on economic issues and foreign affairs on which he did not have a sound hold.

Singh recalls his father, reputed ICS officer T.P. Singh, congratulating Jha on his appointment and 'for this remarkable coup, which has now permanently destroyed the traditional ethos of the Civil Services establishment'.

Jha replied: 'How can you say that? I have a profound respect for the cabinet secretary.' The reply he got was succinct: 'Let's not get into semantics. Time will tell.'

The conversation underlines the fact that the 'structural change permanently eroded the primacy of the cabinet secretary', writes Singh.

He further adds that Jha's successor, P.N. Haksar, who was Indira Gandhi's right-hand man, ensured that the 'emasculation of the Cabinet Office was nearly complete. The PMS mirrored a parallel government'.

Under Haksar, Indira Gandhi's PMO became a small

coterie of loyal officers. As a result, says Singh, 'multiple layers of decision-making disintegrated the chain of responsibility and accountability and led to the usual jostling for power and influence.'

Over the years, under successive prime ministers, the PMO acquired more power, diminishing the Cabinet Secretariat and even the Council of Ministers. Journalist and political commentator Neerja Chowdhury records the trajectory in her fascinating book *How Prime Ministers Decide*.[4] According to Chowdhury, prime ministers enjoyed complete autonomy without any check on their power. As a result, governance suffered, making it a non-transparent process, fully centralized and a top–down affair.

The stronger the prime minister, the more opaque the prime minister's office is. The occasions on which there was a semblance of accountability and transparency was under coalition governments. 'When the Prime Minister of India is neither politically strong nor, in terms of personal charisma, a key-turner, then a kind of fog comes to surround that office. It turns hazy, remote and strangely unimportant. Decisions taken by such a Prime Minister, even of key moments, then look like coins minted by unstable occupants of the throne of Delhi—not in proven metals but aspirant alloys,' writes former civil servant Gopalkrishna Gandhi.[5]

Reflecting on the progressive centralization and concentration of power, former RBI governor Raghuram Rajan, in the course of delivering a talk in the US in November 2018, said, 'India can't work from the Centre. India works when you have many people taking up the burden.'[6] This is an aspect that overshadows every aspect of government and, by extension, governance.

Since 2014, the PMO under Narendra Modi has enjoyed almost unbridled authority over every arm of the government. Critics have alleged that the PMO has centralized powers and, thus, reduced the authority of even senior Cabinet ministers and the Cabinet Secretariat. News reports and anecdotal evidence would seem to suggest that there is more than a grain of truth in this allegation. Several important decisions, such as demonetization, the fight against the Covid-19 virus and the Balakot airstrikes, among others, were reportedly driven by the PMO rather than the administrative ministries. These indicate that the current PMO, born under Lal Bahadur Shastri's prime ministership as the Prime Minister's Secretariat, is perhaps the most powerful in the history of this institution. This has strengthened the position of the prime minister—from being the first among equals under the Westminster system of government, the office of the prime minister has evolved into a more presidential office in a manner that the framers of our Constitution may not have envisaged.

WHEN POLITICS TAKES PRECEDENCE OVER GOVERNANCE

Take the formation of the Council of Ministers and the Cabinet. Almost with every government there has been a rise in the number of ministers. The first Cabinet of India's prime minister Nehru comprised 17 ministers. Today, the number hovers around 70–75.

One question comes to mind here. If at the Centre and states there has been a trend of concentration of power in the hands of the topmost political executive, what purpose do these large number of ministries serve?

Secondly, while the collegial aspect of the Cabinet and Council of Ministers has declined in the face of concentration of power in the hands of the topmost political executive, are there clear indications of jumbo

Cabinets leading to improved governance? Over time, there has been a significant betterment in terms of delivery of public services, but can that be attributed to the burgeoning sizes of the Cabinet and Council of Ministers?

The preference for an oversized Council of Ministers may stem more from political than administrative considerations.

Every time a new government is formed, considerations like caste, region, religion, language and gender, among others, are factored into the formation of the Council. It is an act of political signalling aimed at keeping the important groupings among the party's support base happy, reflecting the same election campaign arithmetic that propels the ruling party to power. In this exercise of political manoeuvring, competence and aptitude are not the most important parameters.

The trend of jumbo ministries intensified in the post-Mandal phase, which inaugurated the era of coalitions (1989–2014). The support from coalition partners to single largest parties is conditional. Depending on how critical they are to government formation, coalition partners want to extract their pound of flesh with a requisite number of berths in the ministry. The competition for the top ministries in the government—finance, home, defence, external affairs, agriculture, industry, among others—is intense. Whilst the single largest party usually wants to keep the plum ministries for itself, the demands of coalition partners have to be accommodated at times in the interest of sheer survival—be it the Cabinet, council of ministers, ministers with independent charge or junior ministers. Conventionally, the marking of ministries as important or unimportant is based on the budgets they are allocated. A larger outlay signifies an important ministry for which there is often a scramble. For the single largest party, ensuring that its core philosophy towards governance is retained while accommodating requests from coalition partners is a tough psychological and political challenge.

Usually, the constitution of the ministries is done in instalments. The first swearing-in is relatively modest. It leaves a large number of aspirants hoping, and has proved to be an effective strategy in running coalition governments. Whether a coalition or single-party majority government, it provides manoeuvrability for a government to expand its ministries in order to induct legislators from states where elections are scheduled, or reshuffle ministries to soothe ruffled groups. Often there is little time or opportunity for ministers to develop an in-depth understanding about the ministry they may be put in charge of.

One of the many reasons forwarded to explain the necessity of the phenomenon of jumbo ministries is that Indian governments have felt the need to have more ministries to further the goals of development and welfare across a vastly diverse country with a highly stratified society. That way attention could be given to every domain that has a bearing on the lives of the citizens. It is just that the way governments go about it makes their main motivations evident.

Basically, every political party that comes to power has its own set of priorities on account of which it may do several things—divide one ministry into two separate ones, do away with some, sometimes club different ministries, or create new ministries. The Modi government, for instance, created a new ministry of cooperation.

The larger point is that jumbo Cabinets have become a fact of life even for governments with the motto of minimum government and maximum governance. In fact, criticism of jumbo Cabinets was what triggered the Constitution (Ninety-First Amendment) Act, 2003, which limited the size of the Council of Ministers to 15 per cent of the numbers of the Lok Sabha in the Central and state governments. Even that allows for a fairly large number, say, an 80-member ministry in a House of 540-odd legislators.

THE ART OF CREATING A JUMBO CABINET

Over time, India has had separate ministers for power, renewable energy, petroleum and natural gas, and coal, when all of them can be clubbed into a single ministry of energy, like many countries have. Rather than having one ministry of transport, in India, we have a ministry each for road transport and highways, aviation and railways. Similarly, there are different ministries catering to rural development and urban poverty alleviation, which can be, in a coherent manner, combined with the existing panchayati raj and urban affairs ministries.

Then there are cases when all governments exercise their preference for keeping a ministry like information and broadcasting going when it has been described as anachronistic in many quarters since the 2000s. Earlier, both All India Radio and Doordarshan came under it, but they were brought under the public service broadcasting authority, Prasar Bharati, set up in the late 1990s. As for private television channels, something like the US Federal Communications Commission, which has been effectively regulating television companies for more than half a century, could have been envisaged. These options have not been exercised.

One thing is for sure—a large number of ministries at the Central and state levels give a sense of increased activity, but as the celebrated American basketball coach John R. Wooden said, 'never mistake activity for achievement'.

This diffused approach may help governments manage their political objectives, but the question is if it is better for governance.

The problems are evident, such as lack of coordination and a longer time for files to be cleared. Given that there are at least four levels for a file to pass through in one particular ministry, one can only imagine the number of layers a file has to travel through for final approval if it involves four ministries.

Moreover, for any ministry, law and finance become service ministries for clearance in terms of finances and legal issues. So, more layers get added at every level for a file to be moved and cleared. It could also lead to duplication of effort and overlapping of responsibilities, allowing one ministry to pass the buck to other ministries and departments.

Often it has been said that the policy of economic liberalization increased the quantum of work, necessitating more ministries. However, across the world, countries whose thrust is on minimum government interference, hence fewer ministries, and who allow maximum participation of people by leveraging information and communication technologies (ICT) seem to be better off. These issues have led to India's poor performance in international reports where countries are ranked on the basis of governance indices.

The trend, in many parts of the world, is to bring in technocrats to head key ministries such as finance, law, foreign affairs so that they are able to steer policy and set a direction for key sectors. These areas have become vastly complicated in a fast-changing world that is globally integrated at various levels. Hence the need for domain experts. India has not shown a great deal of keenness to go down that way.

However, India does have some prominent examples, such as Manmohan Singh. An economist who was inducted as the finance minister in Narasimha Rao's government at a critical juncture for India, he was responsible for a series of policies associated with the opening up to global trade and liberalization of India's economy. Later, he served two terms as prime minister as well.

A present-day example that comes to mind is that of S. Jaishankar, India's minister for external affairs. A career diplomat who served as India's ambassador to the US and China, among others, he went on to become India's foreign secretary during 2015–18. In 2019, he assumed charge as India's external affairs minister in the Narendra Modi-led BJP government at the Centre, and continues to do so in the Modi-led coalition government that came to power in June 2024. But such examples are not too common in a scenario where hard political concerns overshadow other considerations.

YES MINISTER: THE ROLE OF THE BUREAUCRACY

If technocrat ministers are desirable, what about the Indian bureaucracy that helps the political executive in policy formulation and is responsible for its implementation? Is the 'steel frame' of India, as Patel characterized the IAS, equipped to handle the increasingly complicated nature of work that governments have to deal with in an increasingly complex world? The kind of negotiations that are required in multilateral fora on issues ranging from economy and finance to climate change and foreign policy necessitate an agile bureaucracy that is able to hold its own in covering all bases while advising the political executive. A bureaucracy that is also aware of the need to grasp the big picture and the granular details on the ground so that it can implement policies and programmes without leaving the most vulnerable out.

In 1964, India's first prime minister, Nehru, remarked, 'I could not change the administration, it is still a colonial administration.' In 2021, on the floor of Parliament, Prime Minister Modi accused bureaucrats of holding India's growth 'hostage' due to their inefficiency. 'Babus will do everything? Because they became IAS (officers), they'll run fertilizer factories [...] Because they are IAS, they will run chemical factories [...] even fly planes [...] What is this big power we have created?'[7]

While there has been a lot of criticism against the IAS, some experts, such as former Cabinet Secretary B.K. Chaturvedi, have cautioned against dismissing it altogether. He writes, 'Carrying out the business of governance will require a strong and professionally competent civil service. Considering India's diversity, fissiparous tendencies in some regions and the need for a strong Centre, there is definitely a need for competent service. This calls for further professionalizing the IAS, putting focus on specialized training, both in India and abroad, and reinforcing a beleaguered "steel frame". Running it down will weaken us as a nation.'[8]

Former bureaucrat N.C. Saxena, who retired as secretary, Planning Commission of India, in 2002 and also served in the mid-1990s as director, National Academy of Administration, Mussoorie, which trains civil servants, does not hold himself back in his book *What Ails the IAS and Why It Fails to Deliver.* He writes, 'A high degree of professionalism ought to be the dominant characteristic of a modern bureaucracy. The fatal failing of the Indian bureaucracy has been its low level of professional competence. The IAS officer spends more than half of his tenure on policy desks where domain knowledge is a vital prerequisite. However, in the present environment, there is no incentive for a young civil servant to acquire knowledge or to improve their skills. As years pass by, there is thus an exponential growth in both his ignorance and arrogance.'[9]

A GENERALIZED SERVICE IS A DRAWBACK

One of the major criticisms levelled at the IAS is that it is too generalized. That goes against the grain in a world that increasingly demands specialized inputs to address issues in different fields. This is because the IAS is modelled on the colonial-era ICS that helped the British Indian government administer vast territories in India. ICS officers then helmed every department, from revenue to diplomacy and defence, which today, the IAS do. The criticism against them is that their perspective has not changed much from that of their colonial predecessors. It is widely believed that the 'steel frame' of India is becoming more of a straitjacket. Governance systems the world over are constantly evolving in terms of technology and administrative frameworks. But the perception amongst IAS officers is that not only are they resistant to change, they fail to correctly gauge the needs of their departments.

This is particularly relevant with regard to the social sector. Saxena mentions that many an IAS officer suffers from a lack of concern for the poorer sections of society, which is exacerbated by a lack of domain expertise. According to him, programmes like MGNREGA and the public distribution system (PDS) could have benefited with a better design.

Across the world, democracies are going in for minimum government interference, focusing on better delivery of public services. In India, however, the attitude of the bureaucrat is a throwback to the licence raj mindset.

There have been attempts to tackle the issue of generalization over the years, but they have not met with much success due to the lack of political will on the part of successive governments. For instance, the Constitution Review Commission in 2002 suggested the 'need to specialize some of the generalists and generalize some of the specialists'. But in the last two decades, the recommendations made by the Commission have not been translated into action.

EXPERIENCE OVER PERFORMANCE, DECLINING CALIBRE

In today's age of competition, which values merit, the world is moving towards a performance-based reward system. Many say that the continued emphasis on seniority within the IAS poses a problem. The Services Rules, drafted in the colonial era and slightly tweaked in the post-independence era, continue to guide service hierarchy, promotions and transfer of officers across the various levels of administration. Many officers, by aligning themselves to the political establishment, find ways to hasten their upward mobility and become more powerful. In the process, governance suffers.

The demonstration of power in this way has today become a major influence for many who seek to join the IAS primarily for that reason. Coaching centres have mushroomed across Tier 2 and Tier 3 cities in India. Like in most coaching centres, swotting is the way to learn. This, say many former bureaucrats, has led to a further decline in the calibre of new recruits. Power is the magnet. Other qualities such as professional ethics and rigour or the ability to understand societal currents on the ground are not too common. Democratization is a positive trend, but the quest for power at the expense of understanding and sensitivity among new recruits is troubling.

In 2007, the Second Administrative Reforms Commission recommended several measures to make the

IAS more transparent, accountable and citizen-centric. These included reducing the size of the bureaucracy, introducing performance-based assessments, and increasing the involvement of citizens in decision-making.

One of the best examples of civil service reform comes from Singapore, which has one of the most efficient and effective bureaucracies in the world. The Singapore Civil Service has been reformed to be more meritocratic, responsive and accountable. The selection process for the civil service is highly competitive, and there is a strong focus on training and capacity building. Additionally, there are strict performance-based assessments, and civil servants are rewarded for their performance.

Another example comes from the United Kingdom, where the civil service has been reformed to be more agile, efficient and customer-focused. The reforms are focused on reducing the size of the bureaucracy, introducing performance-based assessments and improving the quality of service delivery.

In India, the National Civil Services Day was first celebrated on 21 April 2006 and has been observed every year hence as it was on that day in 1947 that Patel addressed the first batch of civil servants. The idea of celebrating the achievements of civil servants so that they re-dedicate themselves to good governance is a positive gesture. But it needs to be accompanied by reforms so that the bureaucracy can perform the role it is supposed to perform. Introducing measures to improve transparency and accountability is essential. Training programmes should be redesigned to focus on skills relevant to the modern workplace, such as technology and communication.

LATERAL ENTRY: A SOLUTION?

Over the years, several serving and retired IAS officers have advocated the need to allow lateral entry into the IAS. NITI Aayog, in its recent document, *Strategy for New India @75*, has suggested that 'domain experts' be brought into bureaucracy. The argument being that when positions in the government are filled with technically competent personnel, who have worked and established themselves in their particular field of work for a considerable length of time, they would be more adept at their work.

Over the years, there have been some cases: Montek Singh Ahluwalia was a domain expert who, encouraged by Manmohan Singh, joined the Finance Ministry in the 1970s, with stints in different capacities in various Congress-led governments between 1991 and 2014; he has been the longest-serving technocrat at the highest level. Other significant names that come to mind include Bimal Jalan, Lovraj Kumar, Vijay Kelkar, Rakesh Mohan, C. Rangarajan, Raghuram Rajan and Arvind Subramanian, whose contributions in senior positions contributed to governance as well.

However, making it a regular practice requires clear criteria for selection, necessitating changes in the recruitment process. Creating conditions that would minimize opportunities for conflict between the lateral entrants and IAS bureaucrats is important.

Lateral entrants should be subject to the same performance evaluation and disciplinary procedures as civil servants, and their appointments should be subject to public scrutiny and review. This will go a long way towards improving the efficiency of the administration as well as its image.

BABU CULTURE OF THE BUREAUCRACY AS A WHOLE IS THE PROBLEM

It is not just the IAS; the mindset of the bureaucracy as a whole at the national, state and local levels is largely such that the average Indian feels alienated from the administration. The word babu encapsulates the personality of people working in the bureaucracy—they may be called government servants, but actually behave more like colonial or feudal masters in their dealings with citizens, using every trick in the system to exploit them.

It is instructive to note that the descriptions of Indian bureaucracy have not changed over the decades. It continues to be described as being riddled with red tape, corruption and lack of accountability, which makes the goals of good governance recede further.

No wonder India's bureaucracy has fared none too well in global surveys and ranking systems.

- In 2012, a survey of bureaucracies across Asia by the Hong Kong-based Political and Economic Risk Consultancy put Indian bureaucracy below that of Vietnam, the Philippines, China, Thailand, South Korea and Indonesia, ranking it the worst in the region. Singapore topped the rankings. Describing India's bureaucracy as 'suffocating', the report said bureaucrats make governance in India a 'slow and painful process'. Also, '[t]hey are a power centre in their own right at both the national and state levels, and are extremely resistant to reform that affects them or the way they go about their duties.'
- In 2020, *The Hindu* wrote that the findings of Transparency International's survey, 'Global Corruption Barometer—Asia', placed India on top of the list when it came to the 'overall bribery rate'

(39 per cent). The survey also showed India having the highest rate of citizens falling back on personal connections to access public services like education and healthcare (46 per cent), followed by Indonesia (36 per cent) and China (32 per cent).[10]

• In the World Justice Project's 'Rule of Law Index 2020', India was ranked 69th out of 128 countries,[11] indicating that the country's legal framework and enforcement mechanisms need vast improvement. The report noted that Indian bureaucracy faces significant challenges in functioning with impartiality, accountability and effectiveness, for it is rife with corruption, bribery and political influence.

MULTIPLE CHALLENGES AND OBSTINACY TO CHANGE

For things to fall in place, the serious challenges facing the bureaucracy need to be addressed, for they affect governance deeply. These problems are reflected at the national, state and local levels.

One of the major problems of the Indian bureaucracy is corruption, depending on the stature of officials and the money involved in their departments. Not only does this affect the delivery of government services to people but also makes a dent in the state exchequer.

Experts who have studied the phenomenon of corruption across the world say that corruption in India thrives because of an entrenched culture of rent-seeking, cronyism and a politician–bureaucrat–businessman nexus. There is a modicum of truth in claims that many a bureaucrat acts as a go-between in striking deals that often bring together the political class and business establishments. It is no wonder then that bribery exists even at the lower levels of bureaucracy as citizens discover during a routine task such as getting a passport or a death certificate issued, or getting copies of documents from a government department.

Given the severity of the problem, many people now consider bribery as a necessary evil for getting their work done. This situation has eroded the public's trust in the bureaucracy.

Another challenge faced by the Indian bureaucracy is political interference with a view to influencing the decisions of officials in matters like awarding government contracts. The Damocles sword of a transfer or suspension is duly produced to twist regulations. Politicians exert pressure on their administrative machinery and its officials to carry out government work in accordance with their self-interest rather than with that of the law of the land. What gets affected is the quality of implementation of government programmes, and beneficiaries are short-changed.

The Indian political establishment, in its dealings with the bureaucracy, has long used the carrot-and-stick approach. If bureaucrats fall in line they are looked after and can even expect cushy sinecures post-retirement. Those who refuse to oblige have experienced the reality of 'punishment postings' or much worse, such as a stint in prison on account of false charges. A leading example of an officer being subject to punishment postings by a Congress and BJP government is the Haryana cadre IAS officer Ashok Khemka, who has been transferred 56 times in three decades.

In the general absence of upright officers who are not afraid of the political masters, the combination of red tape and corruption plays havoc with the system. It not only delays the delivery of government services and the processing of citizens' grievances but causes losses to the exchequer while creating a parallel conduit of black money. It is the citizens who lose out eventually as schemes are implemented haphazardly. Sometimes the delivery of government programmes is deliberately delayed to extract a price from the affected party.

The politician–bureaucrat nexus creates a system of lack of accountability on the part of both. They ensure that they work in tandem for each other's benefit in a way that they escape the law.

Years of experience in the government sector equips these bureaucrats to understand the inner workings of the system, which is used to evade prosecution and arrests. Instead of developing a culture of accountability, a culture of scheming and evasion prevails.

ATTEMPTS TO REFORM THE SYSTEM

Two Administrative Reforms Commissions (ARCs) set up so far have come up with a number of recommendations to improve the efficacy of the bureaucracy and administration in the country.

The First ARC was set up in 1966. During its tenure till the mid-1970s it submitted 20 reports on key areas. It recommended the simplification of procedures, reduction of red tape, and introduction of performance-based incentives for civil servants.

The Second ARC was set up in 2005. During its tenure till 2009, the ARC's focus was on improving the accountability and responsiveness of the bureaucracy. Its recommendations led to the setting up of the Central Vigilance Commission, with an intent to track and prevent corruption. Many of its reports argued in favour of strengthening local self-government institutions, and the establishment of ombudsmen to address citizens' grievances. One of the reports brought out by the Second ARC eventually led to the enactment of the significant Right to Information Act.

Both ARCs, through multiple reports and hundreds of recommendations, suggested pathways for good governance. However, these reports have been largely left to gather dust, with successive governments turning a blind eye to many of the recommendations.

◆

This brings us back to the point from which we started in this chapter—the excessive domination of the political executive, and the tendency of letting political compulsions dictate governance.

Over the decades, the citizens of India have witnessed the declining capacity of legislatures to hold the political executive accountable. In this quest, they have invariably looked to the third pillar of democracy, namely the judiciary, to reiterate their rights and their valid expectation of good governance.

4

HOUSE OF JUSTICE AND JUSTICES

The very mention of the judiciary brings to mind two sets of images. One set bears an unmistakable air of solemnity and occasion—stately corridors, the scales of justice, the imposing judge's gavel, and last but not the least, the serious visages of Supreme Court judges as they gravely pronounce their verdicts on seminal issues.

The other set of images is of crowded lower courts bursting at the seams with a crush of humanity, harried faces of individuals from all walks of life, and a constant buzz of voices. In these courts, life in its interactions with the law is at its rawest.

These two sets of images are very much part of one picture. Like the root and crown of a tree, they represent the two ends of one integrated judicial hierarchy, from the lower courts across the country to the state high courts, with the Supreme Court at the apex of the structure.

It is this judicial structure, associated with the administration of justice, on which citizens pin their hopes in a parliamentary democracy. S.C. Kashyap puts it very simply in his book: 'In a representative democracy, administration of justice assumes special significance in view of the rights of individuals which need protection against executive or legislative interference. This protection is given by making the judiciary independent of the other two organs [...] and supreme in its own sphere. The Constitution attaches great value to the independence of the judiciary

which is essential to rule of law and constitutionalism and for
the effective functioning of the judicial administration.'[1]

GUARDIAN OF THE RULE OF LAW

In layperson's terms, rule of law means two things: rule by
law, which acknowledges the supremacy of the law of the
land, protecting the citizens from arbitrary actions of the
ruler, and it also means that everyone is subject to the same
law as is laid down. The judiciary is the guardian of the rule
of law.

A January 2024 Supreme Court judgement by a two-
judge bench enunciated this principle clearly: 'Importantly,
rule of law means no one, howsoever high or low, is above
the law; it is the basic rule of governance and democratic
polity.' The judgement pointed out that the principle is
linked to adjudication by courts of law and that justice
'should remain loyal to the rule of law'.

The court referred to the late Justice V.R. Krishna Iyer
who stated that 'the finest hour of the rule of law is when
law disciplines life and matches promise with performance.'

COURTS: PENDING CASES, SHORTFALL IN JUDGES

Unfortunately, the more common experience of most
Indians who have had to approach a court of law in distress
is otherwise. The stories of traumatic encounters with courts
and the legal fraternity are legion. So much so that ordinary
citizens think several times before entering the labyrinthine
maze of law as courts across the country fail to do justice to
administering justice.

The most common grievance against courts, whether
laterally or up the hierarchy, is to do with the way cases
drag on for years, often from one generation to the next.

The wait for the next *tareekh*, or date of hearing, is what characterizes people's experiences.

A look at the National Judicial Data Grid (NJDG) gives an idea of the magnitude of the problem[2]:

- As of 24 February 2024, there were 4,44,18,082 cases pending in courts across the country, including the Supreme Court, high courts and district courts. Of these, 1,09,22,035 were civil cases and 3,34,96,047 criminal cases.
- Over 10,000 cases had been pending for more than 30 years; 37,99,164 cases had dragged on for 10 to 20 years; 85,59,716 cases had gone on for five to 10 years; and 70,48,567 cases had been pending for three to five years.
- Of the grand total, 61,97,105 cases had been pending across all high courts. The pending cases in the Supreme Court stood at 65,086 in 2020, 70,239 in 2021, 69,768 in 2022 and 64,854 in 2023.
- The Supreme Court's case disposal rate, that is, the number of cases cleared as compared to the number of cases filed in a given period, saw a drop from 67 per cent in 2018 to 25 per cent till the end of July 2022. The disposal rate in high courts saw a drop from 39 per cent in 2018 to a mere 9 per cent till the end of July 2022.[3]

Timely disposal of cases gives a clear signal to citizens that justice does exist and that it is not an esoteric concept. The impact of delays is significant not just in financial terms. The anxiety experienced is immense. Gradually, individuals lose faith in the ability of the legal system to provide recourse, which can only mean timely recourse. The guilty feel emboldened. There are implications on a national level as well: for instance, the World Bank placed India among the worst performers with regard to enforcing contracts in its Ease of Doing Business ranking of 190 countries in 2018. While India climbed up the ranks overall, from the 100th to the 77th position, it moved from a rank of 164 to 163 when it came to enforcing contracts.[4]

Whenever the number of pending cases is mentioned, the question of number of judges in the judiciary comes up. *State of the Judiciary,* a report prepared by the Centre for Research and Planning of the Supreme Court in November 2023, sees it as an issue of citizens having access to justice. Recalling an earlier Supreme Court judgement, the report states, 'In *All India Judges Association* v. *Union of India,* the Supreme Court held that, "An independent and efficient judicial system is one of the basic structures of our Constitution. If sufficient number of Judges are not appointed, justice would not be available to the people, thereby undermining the basic structure..."' The report states that:

- As on 12 September 2023, there were 5.05 crore cases in a population of a little under 140 crore (1.4 billion) Indian citizens. These were being handled by 20,580 judges across the Supreme Court, high courts and the district judiciary.
- Against the sanctioned strength of 1,114 high court judges, as on 1 October 2023, there was a vacancy of 347 judges; the state-wise details are provided in Figure 4.1. The deficit: 31 per cent. The vacancies of high court judges was the highest in the Allahabad High Court: against the sanctioned strength of 160, the working strength was 93, showing a shortfall of about 41 per cent.
- Against the sanctioned strength of 25,081 judges in district courts, as on 1 April 2023, the working strength was 19,781; the state-wise details are

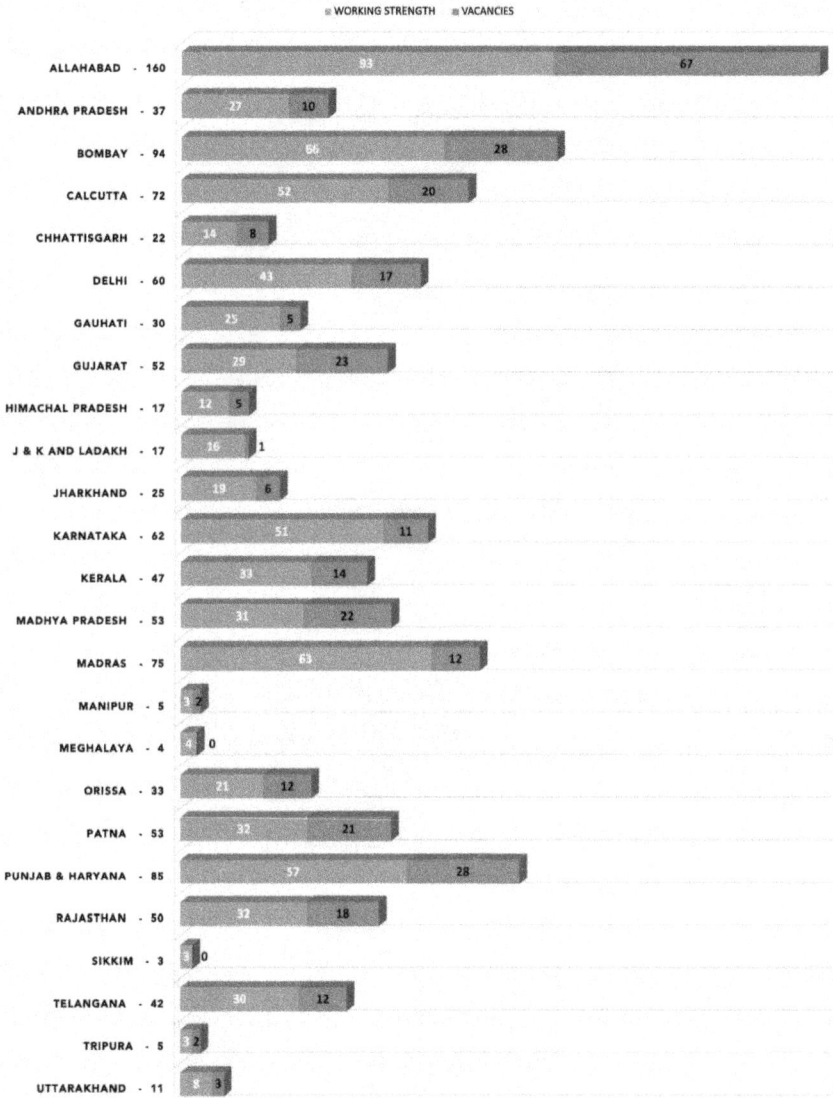

VACANCY OF JUDGES IN HIGH COURTS

WORKING STRENGTH   VACANCIES

High Court	Working Strength	Vacancies
ALLAHABAD - 160	93	67
ANDHRA PRADESH - 37	27	10
BOMBAY - 94	66	28
CALCUTTA - 72	52	20
CHHATTISGARH - 22	14	8
DELHI - 60	43	17
GAUHATI - 30	25	5
GUJARAT - 52	29	23
HIMACHAL PRADESH - 17	12	5
J & K AND LADAKH - 17	16	1
JHARKHAND - 25	19	6
KARNATAKA - 62	51	11
KERALA - 47	33	14
MADHYA PRADESH - 53	31	22
MADRAS - 75	63	12
MANIPUR - 5	3	2
MEGHALAYA - 4	4	0
ORISSA - 33	21	12
PATNA - 53	32	21
PUNJAB & HARYANA - 85	57	28
RAJASTHAN - 50	32	18
SIKKIM - 3	3	0
TELANGANA - 42	30	12
TRIPURA - 5	3	2
UTTARAKHAND - 11	8	3

Figure 4.1: Sanctioned strength, working strength and vacancy of judges in high courts, as on 1 October 2023[5]

VACANCY OF JUDGES IN DISTRICT COURTS

■ WORKING STRENGTH   ■ VACANCIES

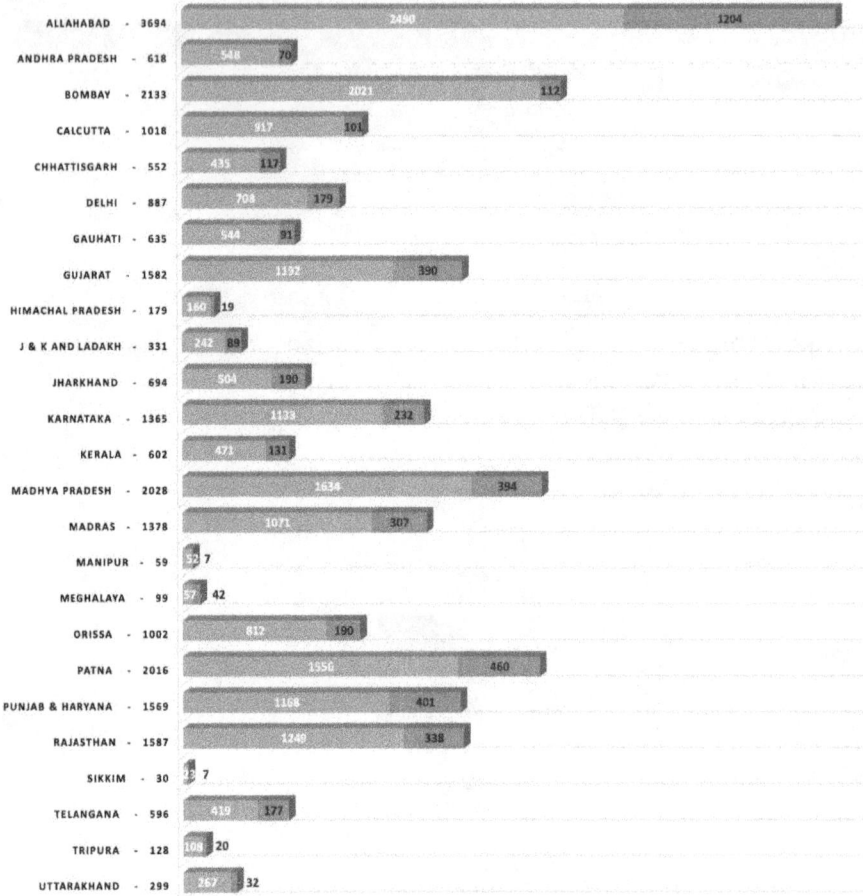

Court	Sanctioned	Working Strength	Vacancies
ALLAHABAD	3694	2490	1204
ANDHRA PRADESH	618	548	70
BOMBAY	2133	2021	112
CALCUTTA	1018	917	101
CHHATTISGARH	552	435	117
DELHI	887	708	179
GAUHATI	635	544	91
GUJARAT	1582	1192	390
HIMACHAL PRADESH	179	160	19
J & K AND LADAKH	331	242	89
JHARKHAND	694	504	190
KARNATAKA	1365	1133	232
KERALA	602	471	131
MADHYA PRADESH	2028	1634	394
MADRAS	1378	1071	307
MANIPUR	59	52	7
MEGHALAYA	99	57	42
ORISSA	1002	812	190
PATNA	2016	1556	460
PUNJAB & HARYANA	1569	1168	401
RAJASTHAN	1587	1249	338
SIKKIM	30	23	7
TELANGANA	596	419	177
TRIPURA	128	108	20
UTTARAKHAND	299	267	32

Figure 4.2: Sanctioned strength, working strength and vacancy of judges in district courts under the jurisdiction of respective high courts, as on 1 April 2023[6]

provided in Figure 4.2. The deficit: 21 per cent. The shortfall of judges in district courts under the jurisdiction of the Allahabad High Court was among the highest: against the sanctioned strength of 3,694, it had a working strength of 2,490 judges, and thus a deficit of 32.5 per cent.

PUBLIC INTEREST LITIGATION: A NEW HOPE

If the number of pending cases and the deficit of judges makes ordinary citizens wonder about the true meaning of justice, there is one dimension of the legal system that has given them hope. It was with a view to making a connection between law, public interest and the real-life concerns of governance that the likes of former Supreme Court justices V.R. Krishna Iyer and P.N. Bhagwati, in the late 1970s and early 1980s, pioneered what came to be known as PIL.

Civic-minded citizens or organizations could file a PIL in a high court or Supreme Court on an issue of public interest if that issue had not been given the due attention it deserved by those responsible for governance. PILs could also be filed by public-spirited citizens to highlight the plight of disadvantaged groups for whom accessing legal recourse was difficult. It goes without saying that the court had to be convinced that the PIL was not a private interest masquerading as public interest.

Inspired by American jurisprudence, the arrival of PILs on the Indian stage demonstrated something significant: in a society where the general public feels overwhelmed and ignored by the legal system, judges were giving them the power to make their voices heard. They were saying that issues ranging from social and economic oppression and environmental challenges to denial of human rights, which impacted people's lives, were of importance in the corridors of justice. In the words of Justice Krishna Iyer, 'The law of all laws is that the "rule of law" must sustain the "rule of life" by climbing down from its high pedestal, to ascertain ground realities for meeting the needs and aspirations of the people in an ever-changing society.'[7]

The evolution of the PIL movement has had an interesting trajectory. The principle was first explored by Justice Krishna Iyer in *Mumbai Kamgar Sabha* v. *M/s Abdulbhai Faizullabhai and Others* (1976) in his landmark judgement. A petition was filed by the Mumbai Kamgar Sabha against Abdulbhai Faizullabhai on the grounds that they had stopped paying yearly bonus to their workers. While the employer questioned their right to initiate action on an issue involving them and their staff, Justice Krishna Iyer's view was that in light of the fact that those affected came from a weaker section of society, the union could file a petition on their behalf. The principle of locus standi, meaning only a person involved in a disputed issue can approach the court, was given a wider interpretation for the first time.

The case of *Hussainara Khatoon* v. *the State of Bihar* (1979) is considered the first PIL case in India. Lawyer Kapila Hingorani filed a petition under Article 32 before a Supreme Court bench led by Justice Bhagwati, drawing the court's attention towards the undertrials in Bihar who were languishing in prison. The time they had spent in jail before trial was far more than the maximum sentence for the offences they had been charged with. The court recognized the right to a speedy trial through its interpretation of Article 21, which states that no person shall be bereft of his life and personal liberty except according to the procedure established by law. On account of the judgement, about 40,000 undertrials in Bihar were released. The court had recognized that lawyer Hingorani, who did not have a personal locus standi, had filed the case in public interest.

Justice Bhagwati would even treat a letter from an individual pointing to a public cause as a writ petition.

The PIL movement took off in a significant way when the Supreme Court Constitution Bench decision in 1982 (*S.P. Gupta* v. *Govt. of India*) recognized that an individual or a group with a bona fide public interest could file a case in a high court, under Article 226, or the Supreme Court, under Article 32 for violation of fundamental rights, to draw attention to those whose constitutional or legal rights were being infringed but they could not access the courts themselves on account of their disadvantaged situation.

Over the years there has been a steady stream of landmark judgements:

- The PILs filed by lawyer and environmental activist M.C. Mehta transformed the way environmental laws would henceforth be looked at, as a connection was made to the right to life of citizens (Article 21). Whether it was the oleum gas leak case (1986) or a PIL drawing the court's attention to industries polluting rivers by releasing their effluents directly into them, they changed the perspective of society.
- In the pathbreaking PIL of *Vishaka* v. *The State of Rajasthan* (1992), filed by women's group Sakshi, the Supreme Court judgement paved the way for comprehensive guidelines to deal with sexual harassment of women at the workplace, seeing it as a violation of the fundamental right to life, liberty, equality and right to pursue any occupation.
- In 1998, acting on a PIL filed earlier by M.C. Mehta drawing attention to rising air pollution caused by vehicles using diesel and leaded petrol, the Supreme Court ordered that Delhi's bus fleet be shifted to compressed natural gas (CNG) fuel by 2001.

- In 2002, the Supreme Court upheld a verdict given by the Delhi High Court in response to a PIL filed by ADR in 1999, drawing attention to the number of individuals charged with serious criminal cases who were contesting elections. The Delhi High Court held that any individual contesting parliamentary and assembly elections would have to file a sworn affidavit along with their nomination papers, declaring any pending criminal cases against them.
- In 2013, in response to a PIL filed by Kerala lawyer Lily Thomas, the Supreme Court ruled that any MP or MLA convicted of a crime would lose their membership immediately without any judicial remedy at their disposal. Further, they would be barred from contesting elections for six years subsequent to the date of their conviction.
- In recent years, several PILs have demonstrated the nature of concerns arising out of current societal preoccupations—opening up the Sabarimala and Haji Ali shrines to women, and decriminalizing same-sex relationship between consenting adults, among others.

Clearly, the idea of PIL, a way of empowering the public through an act of judicial activism, embraces an entire gamut of issues concerning the lives of citizens, seeing them in relation to the violation of their constitutional and legal rights. Moreover, they spotlight inactivity on the part of the powers that be in myriad ways, thus showing vital gaps in governance. For that reason, there is a real need to see that this potent instrument is not ill-used for purposes other than public interest in a democracy like ours. Cases driven by self-interest masquerading as public interest not only end up crowding the caseload of already burdened judges, they also strike at the very root of the idea of PIL. Over the years, due to the practice of PIL, citizens have often viewed the judiciary in a new light: as an ally against an executive they perceive to be overbearing or a legislature they consider unmindful.

RELATIONSHIP OF THE JUDICIARY WITH THE LEGISLATURE AND EXECUTIVE

Whether it is a review of a piece of legislation to see if the rights of citizens are being impacted or the Constitution itself, a review of executive action or a dispute between Centre and state, ultimately it is a question of how the three organs of state are functioning. Are they able to provide the checks and balances required to strengthen democracy and deliver effective governance to the citizens?

Take the relationship between the legislature and the judiciary. Parliament is the lawmaker and has the power to amend the Constitution: the process governing the latter is subject to a higher level of difficulty than the enactment of a law on a routine subject. The judiciary is the interpreter of laws and the Constitution. The Constitution ensures that both institutions have an independent space to function. For instance, court proceedings cannot be initiated against MPs for their utterances in Parliament. Similarly, Parliament cannot just debate the conduct of a judge in the higher judiciary except when there is a move to remove a judge in light of proven misconduct.

One of the most contentious aspects of the relationship between these two arms of the state concerns the judiciary's power of judicial review. The Supreme Court and the high courts, through this power, can strike down laws enacted by Parliament. They can do so on the grounds that a certain law violates the fundamental rights or goes against the essential features of the Constitution or covers a subject that is actually under the purview of state legislatures.

Not surprisingly, the power of judicial review has led to eventful duels between the judiciary and Parliament over the years, particularly on the issue of constitutional amendments:

- In the celebrated case of *Kesavananda Bharati* v. *State of Kerala* (1973), a 13-judge Constitution Bench of the Supreme Court held by a 7:6 majority that Parliament had the power to amend the Constitution as long as it did not alter the basic structure of the Constitution. In giving this ruling the Supreme Court bench used its power of interpretation to establish the essential features of the Constitution that were not amenable to amendment by Parliament. Among them were 'supremacy of the Constitution', 'separation of powers', 'judicial review' and 'judicial independence'.[8] It is a delicate balance here with a view to avoiding instances such as a dispensation with a brute majority going all out to amend the Constitution so that it might enjoy uninterrupted power rather than the usual five-year routine of going to the electorate.

- The *Minerva Mills* v. *Union of India* (1980) case challenged the validity of the 42nd Amendment Act, 1976, which was enacted during the Emergency. The Supreme Court held that the amendments of Article 31C, which gave the Directive Principles of State Policy more importance than the fundamental rights, and Article 368 to curtail the judicial review of constitutional amendments were unconstitutional and violative of the basic structure of the Constitution.

- In 2000, the Information Technology Act was enacted. Under Section 66A any individual sending through a computer or device information that was offensive, false or meant to trick the person receiving it was liable for three years imprisonment and a fine. The Supreme Court struck down Section 66A on the grounds that it violated Article 19(1)(a) of the Constitution, which guaranteed freedom of speech and expression.[9]

- In a landmark judgement in 2015, a five-member Supreme Court Constitution Bench, by a 4:1 majority, struck down as unconstitutional the Constitution (Ninety-ninth Amendment) Act, 2014 and the National Judicial Appointments Commission [NJAC] Act, 2014. The acts had sought to replace the collegium system with the NJAC, which envisaged a larger executive involvement in the appointment of judges to the higher judiciary. In his individual judgement, Justice Jagdish Singh Khehar, the presiding judge, wrote, 'It is difficult to hold that the wisdom of appointment of judges can be shared with the political-executive. [...] The expectation from the judiciary, to safeguard the rights of the citizens of this country, can only be ensured by keeping it absolutely insulated and independent from the other organs of governance.'[10] Ruling that the judiciary's precedence in the appointment of judges was integral to the Constitution's basic structure, the judgement held that the collegium system, through which judges were appointed to the Supreme Court and high courts, would continue, with the Chief Justice of India (CJI) having the final word. It is instructive to note that the acts that were struck down had been 'passed unanimously by the Lok Sabha on 13.08.2014 and Rajya Sabha on 14.08.2014', according to a Press Information Bureau (PIB) release.[11] As face-offs go, this was a big one.

THE JUDICIARY AND THE EXECUTIVE: A TUMULTUOUS RELATIONSHIP

Examining issues such as the constitutionality of executive decisions and actions is part of the judiciary's role. Where the former is concerned, the landmark 1994 Supreme Court Constitutional Bench judgement in the case of *S.R. Bommai* v. *Union of India* comes to mind. The Janata Dal government in Karnataka headed by Bommai was dismissed through the use of Article 356 and President's Rule was imposed on the grounds that due to defections he had lost the majority in the House. In those days, Article 356 was used quite often by the Centre to dismiss state governments that were being ruled by Opposition parties. Denied a floor test in the House, Bommai first challenged the dismissal in the high court and later went to the Supreme Court. Several other state governments had also been brought under President's Rule around that time.

In 1994, a nine-judge Constitution Bench ruled that the power to impose President's Rule was not absolute. Moreover, the decision could be subjected to judicial review. The judgement emphasized the need for a floor test in the assembly before any action is taken to dismiss the state government. The ruling has been viewed as a significant intervention in maintaining the spirit of Centre–state relations.

The other issue that has bedevilled the relationship between the executive and the judiciary is to do with the appointment of judges. The intense public confrontation between the Modi government and the judiciary in

2014–15 was the most recent example of an issue that has been simmering for long.

Presently, the process is clear. The President appoints judges to the Supreme Court and high courts after consultation with the CJI and judges of the apex court and high courts. The judges are chosen through the collegium system: the CJI and four seniormost apex court judges for the Supreme Court, and CJI and two seniormost Supreme Court judges for high court appointments. The President can send back a name but is bound to accept it if the collegium stays with it.

The interpretation of the term 'consultation' has been the main bone of contention. In a 1981 ruling (First Judges Case), the Supreme Court held that with regard to the appointment of judges, the CJI did not have primacy over the other two constitutional functionaries. Consultation with the CJI did not mean that the latter's concurrence was needed. The executive gained the upper hand over the judiciary. This was during the prime ministerial tenure of Indira Gandhi.

Then, in a 1993 ruling (Second Judges Case), the Supreme Court overturned the 1981 judgement. It marked the beginning of the collegium system comprising the CJI and two seniormost judges of the Supreme Court. The collegium's word was final. The system took its current shape in a 1998 ruling (Third Judges Case).

In 2015, the judiciary won the round against the political executive by standing its ground in no uncertain terms. However, there are many well-wishers of Indian democracy who fully support the judiciary's move to retain its independent functioning but are troubled by the lack of transparency in the collegium process of judicial appointments.

◆

A system that is more transparent but also safe from political interference should be the end goal, for the role played by the judiciary is crucial in a parliamentary democracy like India. It holds the beacon of justice for all, but it is important to keep in mind the adage about justice being seen to be done. That is the need of the hour, from the district judiciary, which is the first point of contact with citizens on the ground, to the higher judiciary, which negotiates a vast universe, from the rights and concerns of citizens to the principle of federalism in Centre–state relations.

5

FEDERALISM: AN INTEGRAL PART OF THE GOVERNANCE STRUCTURE

Is India's polity federal or unitary in structure? The answer will depend on who you ask—much like the ancient Indian parable of the blind men and the elephant, which made its way into John Godfrey Saxe's 19th century poem about the six men of Indostan who went to see an elephant and described the animal from their own viewpoints as they were unable to see it in its entirety. The poet writes: 'Though each was partly in the right, and all were in the wrong!' Similarly, the architecture of governance laid down in the Constitution cannot be classified as either unitary or federal. Rather it has elements that have features of both.

Dr Ambedkar, chairman of the Drafting Committee explained, 'The Indian Constitution is a federal Constitution in as much as it established what may be called a dual polity which will consist of the Union at the Centre and the states at the periphery, each endowed with sovereign powers to be exercised in the field assigned to them respectively by the Constitution.'[1]

However, he emphasized that 'The Drafting Committee wanted to make it clear that though India was to be a federation, the federation was not the result of an agreement by the states to join in a federation and that the federation not being the result of an agreement, no state has the right to secede from it. The federation is a Union because it is indestructible. Though the country and the people may be divided into different states for convenience of administration, the country is one integral whole, its people a single people...'[2]

On the federal aspects of the architecture of governance that the Constitution lays down, the relations between the Union and the states are described in Part XI, the salient features of which are:

- Articles 245–255 enunciate the distribution of legislative powers between the Union and the states. The three legislative lists in the Seventh Schedule provide for the Union List on which the Union government has exclusive jurisdiction, the State List over which state governments have exclusive jurisdiction, and the Concurrent List on which both the Union and state governments have concurrent powers.
- Articles 256–263 deal with the distribution of executive powers between the Union and state governments.
- Articles 264–293 lay down the distribution of financial powers between the Union and state governments. According to the Constitution, a Finance Commission is appointed for a term of five years to look at the distribution of tax revenue and grants between the two.

However, many an expert has pointed out that the Indian polity is not 'strictly' federal either. Former secretary general of the Lok Sabha, S.C. Kashyap, highlights the important points:

- The Union government wields residuary powers.
- Parliament has the power, under Article 249, 'to

legislate with respect to a matter in the State List in the national interest'.

- Articles 352–354, deal with the proclamation of Emergency. During such periods the 'Constitution can be converted to an entirely unitary one [...] as during proclamation of Emergency, the executive and legislative powers of the Union extend to matters even in the State List.'
- Articles 356 and 357 provide for the Union government to bring a state under President's Rule on the grounds of a failure of its constitutional machinery.
- Articles 2, 3 and 4 give Parliament the power to create new states or alter boundaries of states simply by means of a law enacted by a simple majority.

In his book, R. Mohan refers to economist Pranab Bardhan's succinct description of this aspect of 'centralized federalism': 'In India, the Centre has the power to take over regional state governments on a temporary basis, to redefine and reformulate the states themselves, to establish "concurrent" jurisdictions with them and to wield far-reaching "residual" and emergency powers. The most elastic sources of revenue generally accrue to the central government, so the states are perpetually dependent on it for finance...'[3]

The reason for this Indian mix of federal and unitary aspects of governance is to be found in the circumstances in which the Constitution was written. Partition was the decisive factor that drove the members of the Constituent Assembly to think of a federal structure that would answer the needs of the vast diversity of communities in India, and a strong Union government that could keep the integrity of the nation intact, carry forth the task of development,

address entrenched inequalities, and present a strong face
to the international community. At the same time, a hope
was expressed that even provisions such as those governing
the imposition of President's Rule in a state would not be
misused.

The federal aspects enable governance that meets the
needs of India's diversity. But the fact is that governance is
always looked at through the prism of politics by political
parties. Over the almost eight decades, the politics of the
day has largely shaped the relationship between the Union
government at the Centre and the states. At various points
the use, rather misuse, of Article 356 and encroachment
upon subjects in the State List by the Union government of
the day has weakened the federal structure.

TRAJECTORY OF INDIA'S POLITY IN ALMOST EIGHT DECADES

During the first decade and a half after Independence,
the Congress held sway over the political firmament, both
at the Centre and in the states. Any issues pertaining to
Centre–state relations were addressed in-house as it were.
Even then, the spectre of Article 356 raised its head in July
1959 when the Union government led by Jawaharlal Nehru
unilaterally used the provision to dismiss the Communist
Party of India government led by E.M.S. Namboodiripad in
Kerala, and impose President's Rule.

Earlier, in 1957, E.M.S. Namboodiripad had come to
power with a slender majority in the then newly formed
state of Kerala, becoming the first ever democratically
elected communist government in the world. Several
reforms introduced by the state government, including an
Education Bill, was opposed by the Catholic Church and
the powerful Nair community. These two communities,

along with the Indian Union Muslim League, launched a series of agitations, reportedly with the tacit support of the Congress. As the law and order situation deteriorated, the governor sent a report to the Centre recommending President's Rule. After a little hesitation, the Nehru government dismissed the state government despite the latter enjoying a majority in the state assembly.[4]

The first portents of largescale political change came in the 1967 elections. The Congress emerged victorious at the Centre, but with fewer seats and vote share than before. With the emergence of regional parties following the linguistic reorganization of states, the DMK defeated Congress in Tamil Nadu while anti-Congress coalition governments were formed in West Bengal, Punjab, Bihar, Uttar Pradesh and Rajasthan. Most of them did not last their full term, but they signalled the emergence of new political formations and a contested polity that led, over the next few decades, to a mushrooming of regional political parties that shifted the balance of power away from the Congress.

Even as this fundamental change was taking place in Indian politics, the Congress was becoming increasingly centralized in the figure of Indira Gandhi post-1969 and especially after their victory in 1971. Indira Gandhi, who had established a direct connect with voters with slogans like 'Garibi Hatao', launched Central schemes for poverty eradication. Hitherto powerful state leaders lost their importance. The Centre became all-important. The peak of Indira Gandhi's authoritarian power was reached in 1975 with the proclamation of Emergency.

The Janata Party, a coalition of anti-Congress groupings, which created conditions for the upsurge of strong regional caste-based parties in the post-Mandal coalition era, trounced Congress in the 1977 elections. After coming to power, it dismissed nine state governments ruled by the Congress on the grounds that the party had not performed well in those states in the Lok Sabha elections, which became a pretext for the Indira Gandhi government to reply in the same coin after it came to power in 1980. This was the high noon of rampant misuse of Article 356.

Interestingly, as R. Mohan points out, in 1977, Jyoti Basu, the then West Bengal chief minister, sent a memorandum to the Janata government, an ally, demanding a restructuring of Centre–state relations. Basu wrote that the 'obsessive preoccupation' of those in power at the Centre to keep power in their hands was affecting the country's unity and severely affecting states' autonomy. Economic growth was not possible through orders given from the Centre. Strong political leaders in Karnataka, Andhra Pradesh and Tamil Nadu further questioned the Centre's heavy-handedness. Karnataka and Andhra Pradesh were then Congress strongholds.

N.T. Rama Rao's newly formed Telugu Desam Party (TDP) stormed to power in Andhra Pradesh in 1983 on the plank of Andhra pride as the people of the state had earlier witnessed the Congress leadership in Delhi change four chief ministers rapidly. This generated a groundswell of public opinion against the high-handedness of the Congress government at the Centre and propelled leaders like Rama Rao to power.

Meanwhile, states like Punjab and Assam were facing armed insurgencies. The energies of the state were spent fighting terrorism and separatism. With two important border states in turmoil, the status of Centre–state relations assumed centre stage.

This set the stage for the Sarkaria Commission, which was set up by the Union government in 1983 to 'examine and review the working of the existing arrangements between the Union and states with regard to powers, functions and responsibilities in all spheres and recommend such changes or other measures as may be appropriate.'[5] The Commission submitted its report in 1988, making over 200 recommendations, but it would be accurate to say that the report did not receive the attention it should have.

The 1980s came to an end with a flagrant misuse of Article 356 in Karnataka. In 1989, the Janata Dal government of S.R. Bommai was dismissed under Article 356. The case for dismissing his government was that following the withdrawal of support of 19 MLAs, the state government had lost its majority. The fact was that 12 of the deserting MLAs had returned before the order for dismissal of the government was issued; thus, keeping Bommai's majority intact was not considered. A nine-judge Supreme Court bench delivered a historic ruling in 1994 that put significant limits on the discretionary power of ill-disposed Union governments blatantly dismissing a state government for political reasons. The essence of the judgement was that Article 356 shall be used sparingly by the Centre, otherwise it will likely destroy the constitutional structure between the Centre and the states. Even Dr Ambedkar envisaged it to remain a 'dead letter' in the Constitution, hoping it would be used only as a measure of last resort.

GOVERNORS AS AGENTS OF THE CENTRE

Of the various aspects of the federal structure as laid down in the Constitution, one feature that has continued to be a thorny issue in Centre–state relations is the office of the governor. Like the President who is the constitutional head of the country, the governor is the constitutional head of a state, meant to uphold constitutional and democratic values.

However, in the decades following Independence, imposing President's Rule under Article 356, ignoring all constitutional propriety, was the most contested aspect of the governor's discretionary power. Critics spoke of Union governments ruling by proxy over states by unseating their governments.

Since 1950, President's Rule has been imposed 134 times and the state-wise data has been shared in Figure 5.1.[6]

- The states of Uttar Pradesh and Manipur have been under President's Rule the most, namely ten times each. Jammu and Kashmir and Punjab have experienced President's Rule nine and eight times, respectively.
- The maximum number of times President's Rule was imposed in a year was in 1977, when the Janata Party government led by Morarji Desai dismissed fourteen state governments, nine among them ruled by the Congress.
- In 1980, when Indira Gandhi's Congress came to power, the same nine Opposition-ruled states were put under President's Rule.
- The year 1992 saw six states come under President's Rule as they witnessed communal violence in the aftermath of the Babri Masjid demolition. Among them were Uttar Pradesh, Rajasthan, Himachal Pradesh and Madhya Pradesh.
- In 2019, Maharashtra faced a political crisis following the assembly elections. The role of the governor at that time came under severe criticism over hurriedly administering oath of office to Devendra Fadnavis and Ajit Pawar as chief minister and deputy chief minister, respectively, despite the fact that the numbers did not add up.[7]

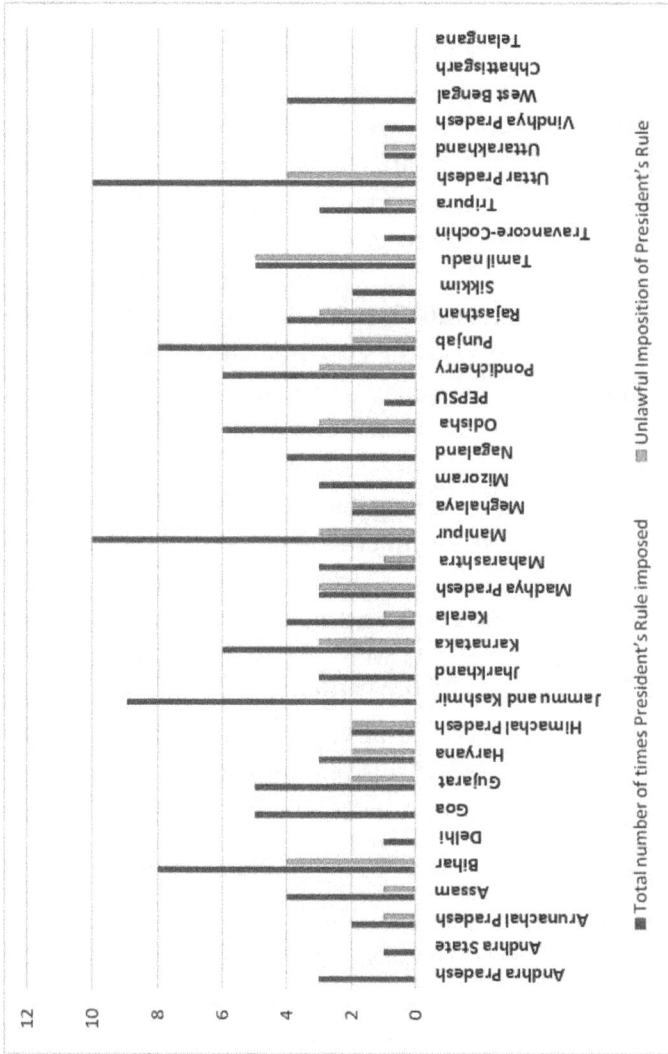

Figure 5.1: Number of times President's Rule imposed in Indian states, compared with unconstitutional imposition, since 1950[8]

In an article published in the *Hindustan Times* on
11 March 2024, four scholars, Shruti Rajagopalan,
Abishek Choutagunta, Christian Bjørnskov and Stefan
Voigt, highlighted the main points of their study titled
'President's Rule in India: State Emergency or Political
Capture?'[9] Referring to the Sarkaria Commission's
findings in 1988 that at least one-third of all cases of
President's Rule were politically motivated, the scholars
zeroed in on the reason: 'Once dismissed, it was much
harder for that government or party to get re-elected. Our
study [...] finds that of the 123 instances of President's
Rule in states (1952–2019), the dismissed CM [Chief
Minister] continued only in 24 cases, and the dismissed
party formed the government again in only 44 instances.
The then-dominant Congress represents 29 of these 44
instances.'

In the course of analysing the legislative figures of the
Union and all state governments between 1952 and 2019,
the scholars found that 'the primary driver for imposing
President's Rule is political arithmetic'. They pointed out
that coalition governments were 'three times more likely
to experience President's Rule' than a government formed
by a single party. The political vacuum created by, say, the
death of a chief minister in office, 'increases the likelihood
of President's Rule by 37 times'. Simply put, 'the strength
of the state's political majority determines the likelihood of
President's Rule'.

There are other ways, too, in which governors invite
criticism. For instance, after the 2021 West Bengal assembly
elections, in which the Trinamool Congress (TMC)
emerged victorious, the then Governor faced criticism
for his alleged partisan approach. He was accused of
interfering in the functioning of the state government,
making politically biased statements, and exceeding his

constitutional mandate. This led to strained relations between the governor and the state government.

The Sarkaria Commission had dwelt on the role of the governor. In its report it mentioned the oft-cited responses of state governments and a cross-section of the public to their questionnaires[10]:

> 4.6.01 In all the evidence before us, a common thread is that much of the criticism against governors could have been avoided if their selection had been made on correct principles to ensure appointment of right type of persons as governors. Even the most critical of the witnesses agree that if the proper person is chosen there will be little cause of complaint.

> 4.6.02 Most of the replies to our questionnaire received from a cross-section of the public are critical of the qualities and standards of some of the persons appointed as governors. To summarize their comments:

> - Discarded and disgruntled politicians from the party in power in the Union, who cannot be accommodated elsewhere, get appointed. Such persons, while in office, tend to function as agents of the Union government rather than as impartial constitutional functionaries.
> - The number of governors who have displayed the qualities of ability, integrity, impartiality and statesmanship has been declining. A state government has cited recent instances of persons who had to resign from office as ministers following judicial strictures being subsequently appointed as governors. It has also quoted instances of governors who returned to active politics.

The commission recommended that the person chosen for the position of governor 'should be eminent in some walk of life', be from 'outside the state', and not 'too intimately connected with the local politics of the state'. Not only that, they 'should be a person who has not taken too great a part in politics generally, and particularly in the recent past'. Importantly, 'it is desirable that a politician from the ruling party at the Union is not appointed as governor of a state which is being run by some other party or a combination of other parties.'

However, the culture of appointing as governors individuals with a background in active party politics affiliated to the ruling party at the Centre has only gained ground. Successive Union governments have used the gubernatorial office in partisan ways to promote their political interests. Not surprisingly, frequent run-ins between elected governments in states and governors have been common.

CURRENT STATUS OF THE FEDERAL ARCHITECTURE

There are arguments, both for and against, to revisit the Seventh Schedule in light of constitutional intent, taking into consideration the historical background of the current scheme of distribution of powers, owing to developments in the decades following its adoption. While the Constitution of India has been amended multiple times since its enactment, the Seventh Schedule has never been comprehensively reviewed. At the same time, the practical experience of federalism may make us reconsider the appropriateness of allocation of particular legislative powers. Here's a quick look at the Union, State and Concurrent Lists, which give the lay of the land:

- Originally, the Union List had 97 subjects, the State List had 66 subjects and the Concurrent List had 47 subjects.[11]
- The number of subjects in the Union List has gone up to 100.[12] Among them are foreign affairs, defence, banks, currency and coinage, telecommunications, plus any item not mentioned in the State and Concurrent Lists.
- The number of subjects in the State List has reduced to 61 subjects such as public order and police, public health and sanitation, land, among others.
- The number of subjects in the Concurrent List, over which both the Union and state governments have powers, has risen to 52 following the enactment of the 42nd Amendment in 1976, during the Emergency. Five subjects were moved from the State List to the Concurrent List—education, forests, protection of wild animals and birds, administration of justice, and weights and measures.
- The 42nd Amendment also gave the Union government the power to deploy armed forces in a state.

Former Union Cabinet Secretary B.K. Chaturvedi points out that over the years, with the reduction in the State List and expansion of the Union List, the legislative competence of states has been restricted.

He explains how the 'deployment of large Central funds in areas which are essentially of states further encroaches on their power. The division of legislative powers is now getting blurred.'[13] Transferring the funds to the states and letting them design the scheme would be more suitable, for they are in a better position to deliver services at the grassroots on account of proximity. Such a move would also be in keeping with the spirit of federalism. But that may not always happen because political calculations of governments often influence such decisions.

Again, when it comes to financial relations between the Union government and the states, it can safely be said that the instinct for centralization has only strengthened with time. While many say it is only natural for the Centre to have the upper hand in financial relations vis-à-vis the states because it also has to think of overall growth for the country, it has led to a vertical fiscal imbalance.

- While the Union government has a larger share of revenue, states have greater responsibilities, especially in the economic and social sectors.
- While states incur over 60 per cent of the total government expenditure, their share in revenue collection is about 40 per cent.

As envisaged by the Constitution, the vertical fiscal imbalance was to be addressed in two ways: through the distribution of certain Central taxes between the Centre and the states by the Finance Commission, and through planned grants from the Centre.

Many better-performing states argue that they account for a far higher share of revenue collections of Central taxes but they receive much lower, barely a third, from the divisible tax pool via Finance Commission transfers. A recent article by former Tamil Nadu Finance Minister P. Thiagarajan brought out the contrast between Tamil Nadu and Uttar Pradesh in this context. The southern states of Kerala, Tamil Nadu and Karnataka have argued that they are being penalized for achieving higher growth, better human development indices and a stable population, the last being the criterion for share of transfer. The more populous states in the north get a larger share of the Finance Commission tax devolution. Yet, as Thiagarajan's report points out, the gap between per capita incomes of the southern states and the more populous northern states has only increased.

This simmering issue has the potential to assume a bigger dimension if not addressed so that fiscal federalism works.

Moreover, the rising trend of Union governments levying cesses means a decrease in the states' share of the divisible pool of gross tax revenue, for cesses are not shared with states. As far as grants are concerned, with the discontinuation of the Planning Commission and five-year plans, the grants given by the commission to states have also stopped. What is worrisome is that Finance Commission grants now comprise about 20 per cent of the grants given to states. Discretionary grants by Central ministries are the order of the day. As political compulsions largely shape Union–state relations, the overall dynamic between the Centre and a state government is bound to come into play.

These aspects have to be considered against a larger backdrop. The passing of the Fiscal Responsibility and Budget Management [FRBM] Act, with all the states forced to fall in line, the GST Act with the GST Council holding the controlling lever, and the existence of a multi-tier fiscal system following the Constitution (Seventy-third Amendment) Act, 1992, and the Constitution (Seventy-fourth Amendment) Act, 1992, have changed India's fiscal landscape, intensifying centralizing tendencies.

There are other flashpoints too. The Centre's proposed delimitation of parliamentary constituencies and the defiant attitude of Opposition-ruled states, which do not bode well for Centre–state relations.

EDUCATION AS A GROUND FOR CENTRE–STATE DUELS

The decision to place education in the Concurrent List, too, has drawn severe criticism. For a long time, educationists have pointed out that the administration of education from a government in Delhi is counterproductive to the aim of designing it in a way that it not only reflects the diversity found at the local level but also across different states.

States such as Tamil Nadu have argued that Union governments have used this provision to enact policies such as the three-language formula, National Education Policy (NEP, 2020) and introduction of the National Eligibility-cum-Entrance Test (NEET) for undergraduate medical courses without the concurrence of the states.

Another area that has been a site of contestation between governors and state governments is that of state universities. The role of chancellorship for governors, which dates back to the 'Despatch of 1854 on the General Education in India' under colonial rule, continues to cast a shadow on the administration of state universities in the country.

The pre-Independence rule of 1854 recommended that the universities consist of a chancellor, vice chancellor and fellows, who would constitute a senate. It stated further that the 'offices of chancellor and vice chancellor will naturally be filled by persons of high station, who have shown an interest in the cause of education'.[14] Given the change of circumstances, there is a widespread view, both in academic and administrative circles, that governors essaying the role of chancellors in this day and age is an anachronism.

Starting from 1967, when the Congress Party lost power for the first time in multiple states, governors began to have frequent run-ins with Opposition-ruled state governments, which often extended to the arena of state universities.

They have sometimes been accused of arbitrarily removing vice chancellors from their positions without proper justifications or due process. For instance, in February 2024, the governor of Kerala sacked two vice chancellors. These actions have been criticized as political interference in the autonomy of universities.

There have been instances where governors have delayed or stalled the appointment of vice chancellors, leading to prolonged vacancies in university leadership positions. These allegations were recently made in Opposition-ruled states of West Bengal, Tamil Nadu and Kerala.[15] This has affected the smooth functioning and decision-making processes of state universities. Apart from this, governors have also faced allegations of appointing individuals with political affiliations or personal connections to key positions within universities, bypassing established selection procedures and compromising the principles of meritocracy and academic excellence. Recently, the West Bengal government came down heavily on its governor over appointing an interim vice chancellor without its consent, and over appointing officiating vice chancellors allegedly without consulting the state government.[16]

Some governors have been criticized for excessive interference in the day-to-day affairs of universities, including academic matters, administration and financial decisions. More importantly, they have also been involved in making policy decisions for universities that have courted controversy, such as making changes in admission criteria, syllabi, examination patterns or administrative regulations, leading to concerns about the impact on academic standards and institutional autonomy.[17]

Due to the increasing politicization of the role of governors as chancellors, several states, among them West Bengal, Tamil Nadu, Maharashtra and Kerala, have enacted laws stripping governors of their powers as chancellors.[18]

As the matter of governors as chancellors continues to stoke controversy, it is pertinent to ask why such a system is needed in the first place when there are far better models, such as the system of the academic senate followed in democracies such as the United States, Germany, United Kingdom, among others.

Basically, the academic senate is a representative body of faculty, students and other academic staff members that either has a direct or advisory role in decision-making on academic matters, curriculum development, faculty appointments and policies. Working with the administration, the academic senate provides a valuable model of shared governance.

In the Indian context, the administration of education gets mired in politics, preventing a true spirit of federalism from emerging, whereby state governments can think of more inclusive models of governance in universities that provides the right ambience for pursuits of education.

◆

When we look at the way the distribution of legislative, executive and fiscal powers between the Union and states as laid down by the Constitution has worked out, it is clear that due to hard political considerations, centralizing tendencies have gained ground. They have prevented the federal architecture from taking strong root. In the Indian context, effective governance requires responding to diversity at the grassroots, which states are in the best position to do—which the federal architecture was meant to facilitate. The bottom line is that the federal architecture will work if there is an intent to make it work by respecting the distribution of powers between the Centre and the states.

This tension also plays out in the socially-charged field of reservation quotas and is, once again, driven by political compulsions. The Centre governs reservations in central services and institutions, whilst states promote categories and communities with local influence. Each may have a different agenda and, in the next chapter, we investigate how successive governments, regardless of political affiliation, have handled this very emotional subject.

6

RESERVATIONS: NOT A MAGIC BULLET TO RESOLVE BACKWARDNESS

The mere utterance of the terms 'reservations' or 'quota' in today's India is bound to invite polarizing reactions from people. Such is the sensitivity of the issue that there is invariably a vertical divide along the lines of those who support the idea and those who vehemently oppose it. But the issue is no longer as simple as envisaged by the framers of our Constitution. It has gained a life of its own.

In fact, it will not be an exaggeration to say that some caste or economic group holds some protest in some corner of the country almost every day demanding reservation on account of their 'backwardness'.

What does India's Constitution say about reservations? Does the reservation policy square with the ideals of the framers of the Constitution? When state governments carve out more slices from the same pie of reservations or expand the reservation pie, what does it mean? Is this expansion of reservations based on any real and tangible reasons? Or are they being designed based only on electoral considerations?

The idea behind instituting reservations in India was to address the historical injustice faced by certain communities on account of their caste in accessing social, economic, political and cultural opportunities. The idea was that through reservations these hitherto disadvantaged communities would get access to education, government jobs and political power.

There is another aspect to consider. Although the Constitution enunciates the right to equality, the makers of the Constitution took note of the fact that formal equality, where everyone competes on an equal footing, is inadequate to tackle entrenched inequalities and inherent disadvantages of the less well-to-do sections. Therefore, the Constitution framers and also courts on a number of occasions have come to recognize the idea of 'substantive equality' or 'positive discrimination',[1] which is necessary to bring about a level playing field in a caste-ridden society. Looked at through the perspective of substantive equality, the idea of reservations is not an exception to the equality rule but a facet of the norm of equality itself.

Initially, reservations were extended only to the Scheduled Castes (SCs) and Scheduled Tribes (STs)—15 per cent for the former and 7.5 per cent for the latter at an all-India level—for direct recruitment than by open competition. However, over the decades, successive governments have extended reservations to several other groups. Based on the Mandal Commission report in 1990, the scope of reservations was further widened to include OBCs, 27 per cent at an all-India level, which resulted in the total percentage of reservation going up to 49.5 per cent. Despite that, there are caste groups today who are not necessarily oppressed but are demanding reservations.

S.C. Kashyap, who had met Ambedkar in person, has been quoted in a report of *The Hindu* as saying that Ambedkar never wanted Parliament to have the power to extend reservation by law.

'Dr Ambedkar did not spell out too many things but on the point of reservation for SC and ST, he had said that 10 years is too short a period and it should be 40 years, but

thereafter the Parliament should have no power to extend
reservation by law. He was against reservation in perpetuity.
He had said: "I would not want that symbol to continue in
Indian society forever",' says Kashyap.[2]

Referring to the father of the Indian Constitution,
Kashyap added, 'It would have pained him to see that
people are increasingly wanting more reservations for their
castes. The reservation for SC and ST was agreed by the
Constituent Assembly on the condition that it will not be
extended to any other group of people. He repeatedly said
he was for a casteless and classless society.'

Today, the situation is such that many states, such as
Haryana, Tamil Nadu, Telangana, Andhra Pradesh, Madhya
Pradesh, Uttar Pradesh, Rajasthan, Chhattisgarh and
Maharashtra, have passed laws pegging reservations at over
50 per cent in education and jobs, that is, more than what is
available in the open category,[3] as detailed in Table 6.1.

- In Bihar and Jharkhand, the figure has reached
  60 per cent after including the latest 10 per cent
  quota for the economically weaker sections (EWS).
- In Gujarat, reservations are pegged at 58 per cent
  after including the 10 per cent EWS quota.
- Kerala has a reservation policy of 60 per cent in
  government jobs.
- Tamil Nadu, which has 69 per cent reservations in
  education and public employment, has refused to
  implement the 10 per cent quota saying that it goes
  against the idea of securing social justice for socially
  backward classes.
- There are several other states with similar examples.
  Often, these percentages change, but states come
  up with ingenious ways to reserve more than 50 per
  cent seats. Laws made by many of these states are
  facing legal challenges.

Table 6.1
Reservation for each state (%)[4]

State/UT	SC	ST	OBC	EWS	Other reservations	Total
Andaman and Nicobar Islands	—	12	38	—	—	50
Andhra Pradesh	15	6	29	10	—	60
Arunachal Pradesh	—	80	—	—	—	80
Assam	7	15	27	10	—	59
Bihar	16	1	33	10	—	60
Chandigarh	—	—	27	—	—	27
Chhattisgarh	13	32	14	10	—	69
Dadra and Nagar Haveli and Daman and Diu	3	9	27	—	—	39
Delhi	15	7	27	10	—	59
Goa	2	12	27	10	—	51
Gujarat	7	14	27	10	—	58
Haryana	20	—	23	10	—	53
Himachal Pradesh	25	4	20	10	—	59
Jharkhand	10	26	14	10	—	60
Karnataka	17	7	32	10	—	66
Kerala	8	2	40	10	—	60
Lakshadweep	—	100	—	—	—	100

State/UT	SC	ST	OBC	EWS	Other reservations	Total
Madhya Pradesh	16	20	14	10	—	60
Maharashtra	13	7	32	10	1 (Orphan)	63
Manipur	3	34	17	—	—	54
Meghalaya	—	80	—	—	—	80
Mizoram	—	80	—	—	—	80
Nagaland	—	80	—	—	—	80
Odisha	16	22	11	10	—	59
Puducherry	16	—	34	—	—	50
Punjab	29	—	12	10	—	51
Rajasthan	16	12	21	10	5 (Most backward classes)	64
Sikkim	7	18	40	—	20	85
Tamil Nadu	18	1	50	—	—	69
Telangana	15	10	29	10	—	64
Tripura	17	31	2	10	—	60
Uttar Pradesh	21	2	27	10	—	60
Uttarakhand	19	4	14	10	—	47
West Bengal	22	6	17	10	—	55

Over the years, the Supreme Court has dealt with the issue of reservations and the percentage of seats that can be reserved.[5] Some of these cases are *M.R. Balaji* v. *State of Mysore* (1962), *T. Devadasan* v. *Union of India* (1963), *State of Kerala* v. *N.M. Thomas* (1975), *K.C. Vasanth* v. *State of Karnataka* (1985) and *Indra Sawhney* v. *Union of India* (1992).

Even the courts are divided on the matter. However, the 1992 Indra Sawhney verdict, often quoted as a landmark verdict, laid down a ceiling limit within which reservations can be granted: More than 50 per cent of positions should not be reserved (the '50 per cent rule'). The court, however, said it can be breached but only in 'extraordinary situations'.

'It is relevant to point out that Dr Ambedkar himself contemplated reservation being "confined to a minority of seats",' the lead judgement said,[6] quoting a Constituent Assembly speech of B.R. Ambedkar, chairman of the Drafting Committee of the Constitution, in the context of reservations in jobs.

Yet, in 2019, the total share of the reserved category went up to 59.5 per cent when the Union government passed the Constitution (One Hundred and Third Amendment) Act, 2019, to enable reservations not exceeding 10 per cent in higher education and government jobs on the basis of economic criteria, in addition to existing quotas for disadvantaged castes and tribes. Before this, the total quota stood at 49.5 per cent: 15 per cent for SCs, 7.5 per cent for STs and 27 per cent for OBCs.

MAJOR MILESTONES IN THE EVOLUTION OF RESERVATIONS

Pre-Independence

- **1902:** On 26 July 1902, Chhatrapati Shahu Maharaj of Kolhapur (1894–1922) issued a proclamation to the effect that 50 per cent of the posts in the state's services would be reserved for the backward classes.[7] It was the beginning of what came to be called 'reservations'. The order read: 'His Highness orders that, of all the seats that go vacant from the date of this proclamation, 50 per cent should be filled with the backward classes.'[8]

- **1918:** On 23 August 1918, Maharaja Nalwadi Krishnaraja Wadiyar of the princely state of Mysore (now Mysuru) had formed a committee to examine the idea of reservations for non-Brahmin communities. The committee was headed by Sir Leslie Miller, the then Chief Judge of the Chief Court of Mysore. The princely state's order and intent was to ensure that other communities, too, were represented in the administration, which was dominated by Brahmins. To that end, changes in recruitment policy were also mentioned. According special status to deprived sections and a move to bolster their representation were among the measures cited.

- Bhagwan Das, who has recorded the journey of the reservation movement, writes, 'Some of [the] princely states were progressive and eager to modernize through the promotion of education and industry; and by maintaining unity among their own people. Mysore in south India and Baroda and Kolhapur in western India took considerable interest in the awakening and advancement of the minorities and deprived sections of society. It should not surprise us then that the very first records of implementing reservations policies are from these princely states.'[9]

- **1932:** The British government's Communal Award, also known as the MacDonald Award, was announced by the then prime minister Ramsay MacDonald in August 1932. The award provided separate electorates for minorities, including Muslims, Sikhs, Indian Christians, Anglo-Indians, women and the 'Depressed Classes', now referred to as SCs.

- **1932:** The Poona Pact, which resulted out of the Communal Award of 1932, was an agreement between

Mahatma Gandhi and Dr B.R. Ambedkar over the extent of representation of the Depressed Classes in Central and provincial legislatures and the manner in which it would be brought about, namely a joint electorate with reserved seats for the Depressed Classes. The Poona Pact provided for reservation of more seats than the Communal Award. The Poona Pact provisions shaped the political representation of the Depressed Classes.

- **1942:** Viceroy's Executive Council recommended 8.5 per cent reservation for SCs in civil services. Dr Ambedkar was a member of the Council.[10]

Post-Independence

- **1947:** In 1947, following Independence, the Constituent Assembly set up a committee with Ambedkar as chairman to draft the constitution of India. As Bhagwan Das writes, 'Some members [...] were opposed to the provision of reservations in favour of SCs. SC members, mostly belonging to the Congress, were worried about losing reservation because Sardar Vallabhbhai Patel, president of the minority committee, was opposed to reservations. They approached Ambedkar, who in turn advised them to speak to Mahatma Gandhi and remind him about the promise made in the Poona Pact. Provision was made in the Constitution of India for reservation in the legislature for 10 years ending in 1960.'[11] This has been extended every 10 years. The latest extension is valid until 2030.[12] Bhagwan Das adds, 'Provision was also made for reservation in public services. This has no time limit. Surprisingly, prime ministers, political leaders and journalists have been making speeches and writing articles giving the impression that it is reservations in public services which have been extended for ten years. Reservations made under Article 335 read together with Article 46 has no time limit prescribed under the Constitution.'[13]

- **1951:** The first amendment was made in the Constitution to empower the state to make provisions for reservations.
- **1990:** The Mandal Commission report recommending 27 per cent reservation for OBCs was implemented by the then Prime Minister V.P. Singh.
- **1992:** The Supreme Court (Indra Sawhney case) ordered a 50 per cent cap on caste-based reservation. It also struck down the P.V. Narasimha Rao government's move to reserve 10 per cent government jobs for the poor among the upper castes, stating that economic condition was not a criterion for reservations.
- **2019:** Parliament passed the Article 15 amendment bill allowing 10 per cent quota for the poor and EWS in higher education and jobs. The Constitution (One Hundred and Third Amendment) Act, 2019, was challenged in the Supreme Court.
- **2022:** In November 2022, the Supreme Court of India upheld the constitutional validity of the Constitution (One Hundred and Third Amendment) by a 3-2 majority decision. The amendment provides a 10 per cent reservation for EWS in education and public employment.

DIFFERENT EXPERIENCE IN NORTH AND SOUTH INDIA

A detailed report in *Frontline* magazine throws light on the very different trajectories taken on the issue of reservation in north and south India.[14]

In north India, the issue of reservations assumed centre stage in 1990, following the then prime minister's announcement about implementing the Mandal Commission recommendation of 27 per cent reservation for OBCs. As far as south India was concerned, reservations for OBCs in education and public service had been a reality for decades prior to that.

'The concept of reservation in education for historically oppressed sections of society took roots in south India over a century ago, along with the freedom movement,' states the report, which makes several points:

- The states of south India and Gujarat and Maharashtra have witnessed strong anti-caste movements that led to the formulation of reservation policies long before Independence. Veteran journalist and social analyst B.R.P. Bhaskar made an interesting point in the *Frontline* report, namely that this 'social reform lineage' was an important factor in creating a consciousness about the idea of reservation for social justice. Regions and societies with a history of anti-caste and social reform movements tended to comprehend and support the concept of reservation as opposed to regions and societies that had not witnessed any such movements.

- In Tamil Nadu, the social and political assertion of OBCs and other deprived sections led to the creation of the powerful Dravidian movement, which continues to shape the political landscape of the state to this day. In fact, the process of reservation was started by the colonial administration in 1831 in the Madras Presidency, a good deal of which falls under present-day Tamil Nadu. The decision was taken following petitions from various groups for reservation in education and public jobs. The provisions of reservation were worked upon over the following decades to smooth out the anomalies.

- After Independence, successive governments in Tamil Nadu followed the practice of reservation. In fact, the state had 69 per cent reservation in education and public service even before the Mandal Commission recommendation of 27 per cent OBC reservation became a reality in the 1990s. Moreover, Tamil Nadu's 69 per cent reservation is beyond judicial scrutiny as it comes under the Ninth Schedule of the Constitution. Central and state laws that fall under the purview of the Ninth Schedule cannot be subjected to a judicial review by the high courts or the Supreme Court.

- The southern states of Karnataka and Kerala, too, had a similar trajectory as Tamil Nadu. The princely states of Mysore, Cochin (now Kochi) and Travancore started implementing reservations in education in the late 19th century or early 20th century, which were modified over time. These measures received much popular support. In comparison, OBC reservations came much later to Andhra Pradesh, Maharashtra and Gujarat. In Andhra Pradesh, they were started in the 1970s. In Gujarat and Maharashtra, OBC reservations were put in place in the 1980s and 1990s, respectively.

Well-known political scientist Sudha Pai also puts the issue of reservations in context in an article in *The Hindu*.[15] Pointing out that assertion on the part of the Depressed Classes and SCs was a much later phenomenon in north India compared to the southern counterparts, Pai provides some examples from the colonial period such as the Veerashaiva movement in north Karnataka, with its anti-

Brahmin, anti-ritualistic outlook, and the anti-Brahmin movement in Tamil Nadu. However, in the Hindi heartland, not only did the Dalit movement start late, it was scattered as well. Ambedkar's influence, too, was felt later, says Pai, giving a reason for it. She explains that in the United Provinces, or present-day Uttar Pradesh, the SC movement started in the 1940s but dissipated after Independence. Similarly, the Republican Party of India, which was strong in the 1960s, faded because of the dominant position of the Congress, states the political scientist.

In the same article, K.K. Kailash, professor, political science, University of Hyderabad, makes a significant point: 'The primary distinction is that in the south, we had movements first and then electoral politics, whereas in the north, it was primarily only electoral politics.'

SHIFT FROM HISTORICAL SOCIAL DISCRIMINATION TO ECONOMIC CRITERIA

As is evident, the idea of reservation arose in the context of providing communities that faced institutional barriers such as caste. A shift can be seen with the recent Supreme Court judgement, which upheld the Constitution (One Hundred and Third Amendment) Act, 2019, reserving 10 per cent seats for EWS. The move from according reservations to a community to focusing on the individual is clear.

In its order dated 7 November 2022, the Supreme Court said, 'The observations of this Court in the past decisions that reservations cannot be claimed only on the economic criteria, apply only to class or classes covered by or seeking coverage under Articles 15(4) and/or 15(5) and/or 16(4); and else, this Court has not put a blanket ban on providing reservation for other sections who are disadvantaged due to economic conditions.'[16]

This means that economically weak individuals from the upper castes, too, can avail of this opportunity. In fact, in states like Kerala and Gujarat, Brahmins have been demanding reservation on account of their economic backwardness.

As Akhilesh Pillalamarri, international relations analyst, writer and journalist, writes, 'Since the 1990s, however, many of those from the upper castes initially opposed to reservations have instead begun to demand reservations for themselves, so that they too may partake in the division of the pie of government employment.'[17]

This is because 'India has a relatively weak private sector and a large informal economy, so government work or *sarkari naukri* is seen as a guaranteed source of income, stability and status', explains Pillalamarri. Hence the thinking, 'Those who get government jobs are set for life [...] The problem, according to many activists, was that poor members of the upper castes were suffering from a lack of access to government jobs.'[18]

Pillalamarri contextualizes a significant aspect of the reservation issue, namely that while according reservation to the most deprived castes in the highly stratified Indian society 'could be beneficial, India has come a long way from aspiring to be a meritocratic society with some concessions given for the purpose of correction of prior caste abuses to becoming a society where now almost all social groups— except religious minorities—can avail themselves of reservations'. This shows, he concludes, that 'economic growth and social change have not proceeded fast enough to make India a truly casteless society'.

The National Commission for Religious and Linguistic Minorities (also called Ranganath Misra Commission, which was constituted in 2004, with its final report being tabled in Parliament in 2009) had recommended the extension of quota to all religious minorities while advocating an overhaul of the reservation policy to make income the lone criterion for affirmative action. This report has not been accepted by the government.

THE SITUATION TODAY

Today, the situation is such that dominant castes in India are demanding that they be slotted as backward to ensure reservations in jobs and education.[19] Among them are the Marathas and Jats.

Here, it would be pertinent to mention a 2018 survey by the Lokniti research programme at the Delhi-based Centre for the Study of Developing Societies (CSDS).[20] According to the survey, the data suggests that the Marathas and Jats who are agitating 'fare just as well as upper castes in terms of affluence, but lag behind in education'.

Looking at the levels of education among dominant castes, the survey revealed some important findings:

- In Haryana, Jats have 33 per cent college-educated individuals as compared to 27 per cent among OBCs and 39 per cent among upper castes.
- The percentage of college-educated individuals among Marathas and OBCs in Maharashtra is the same at 34 per cent. Among upper castes, this figure is considerably higher, namely 51 per cent.

The survey notes, 'Apart from the gap in education, there is very little to differentiate the peasant castes from the upper castes. In some respects, these castes have traditionally enjoyed greater dominance than any other caste group in their respective states.'

According to sociologist D. Shyam Babu, this trend of better-off groups demanding reservations has been around since the 1950s.[21] He says numerically larger castes with social heft, who can articulate their demand strongly, can force the political establishment to give in to their demands. As a result, groups that are unable to project themselves as a strong social group capable of altering political arithmetic lose out on reservations. To use Shyam Babu's words, 'Wanna Be Weak? You Gotta Be Strong'.

For instance, the activist behind the Maratha quota stir, Manoj Jarange-Patil, sat on a fast for 17 days in September 2023 demanding reservations.[22] Consequently, on 20 February 2024 the Maharashtra assembly unanimously passed a bill granting 10 per cent reservation in education and government jobs to the Maratha community. This 10 per cent reservation is over and above the total of 52 per cent reservation in the state.

There is an apprehension among Marathas that the Supreme Court may strike down the above bill as unconstitutional, as it had done earlier when previous state governments had tried to bring about a similar law. The result is that Marathas want the government to carve out another slice from the OBC quota pie in the state. However, OBCs in the state are not ready for this, given that they lose out on their share of reservation.

The question is, why do socially better-off groups demand reservations? An IndiaSpend analysis of February 2016 tries to answer this question by looking at the employment figures as well as the aspirations of young Jats.[23] Its finding: Underlying their demand for reservations in education and public jobs is the reality of India's 'slow, inadequate job-creation and a failing education system creating thousands of "unemployable" graduates'.

According to the analysis, 'This disconnect between education, aspirations and jobs explains similar demands to be classified as "backward" and "OBC" by socially powerful caste groups—Gujjars (Rajasthan), Marathas (Maharashtra), Patels (Gujarat) and Kapus (Andhra Pradesh), among others—struggling to find satisfactory employment.'

DATA ON UNEMPLOYMENT

Over the last 10 years at least, educated unemployment has worsened sharply. For graduates, the unemployment rate rose from 19.2 per cent to 35.8 per cent; and for postgraduates from 21.3 per cent to 36.2 per cent, according to the National Sample Survey Office's (NSSO) Periodic Labour Force Survey (PLFS).[24]

According to the *India Skills Report 2021,* nearly half of India's graduates are unemployable—education quality in our colleges and universities has deteriorated sharply, most noticeably after the massification of higher education in the last two decades.

In an insightful article, 'Reservations can help, but hurt too', M.V. Nadkarni, author and professor at the Institute for Social and Economic Change, puts forth his views[25]:

- The policy of 50 per cent reservation (positive discrimination) while keeping 50 per cent for the merit and open category has worked well.
- The new claimants are from dominant castes that are 'politically more potent' due to their numerical preponderance.
- There is a need to realize that the reservation policy only distributes available opportunities in education and jobs. It is more important to increase these opportunities. Nadkarni writes, 'An obsession with reservations as the only or main solution to the problem of poverty and unemployment diverts

our attention from the pertinent issue of economic development.'

- In the author's words, the reservation policy in India has led to an 'incidental but unfortunate side effect', namely a rise in caste consciousness. This can have a very divisive impact on society.

- According to the author, one way of addressing this rise in caste consciousness is to adopt the practice of exclusion of the creamy layers, defined as members of a backward caste who are relatively more affluent, better educated and more socially advanced. These members are considered the forward section of the backward class and could be, therefore, excluded from reservation benefits to ensure that the benefits reach the most disadvantaged.

◆

As things stand today, whether it is the groups who have access to reservations or those who do not, there is a general sense of dissatisfaction about how the reservation system has panned out in the country. While many who have availed of reservations are not entirely satisfied with the extent of change in their social circumstances, those outside the reservations feel they have been robbed of genuine opportunities that they deserve.

The question now is who has really benefitted from reservations. Without addressing this question, the political class wants the country to believe that for reservation to be effective, more reservations are needed. What gets lost in such a political discourse is the question of opportunities. Reservations are possible only from the pool of opportunities.

With no commensurate increase in seats in educational institutes and jobs in line with increase in population, no form of reservation will work in alleviating the distress being felt by large sections of the population. Unless opportunities for growth are created and democratized, the reservation policy as it exists today is bound to deepen the fissures in our society. The time is right for a dispassionate and holistic review of the reservation system in the country in the interests of growth of individuals, communities and the nation.

PART II

∿

The previous part focused on the architecture of governance, as mandated by the Indian Constitution. To complete the picture, this part examines the quality of governance as reflected in sectors such as agriculture, education, public health and nurturing human capital, which are vital for the well-being and development of India. Importantly, it also looks at collecting up-to-date data, which is crucial to the formulation of polices for effective governance.

7

INDIAN AGRICULTURE: SPUTTERING ALONG

In the past few decades India has sought to be counted among the leading industrial economies in the world, pursuing strategies to that end. However, despite the increase in urbanization over the decades, much of India still lives in its villages, with agriculture providing livelihoods to two-thirds of India's population. It is also the single most important sector that has held back India's development, and for that reason, needs the attention of our planners in the future.

The arc of Indian agriculture goes back thousands of years, boasting a long and richly diverse history. The cultivation of land made fertile by bountiful monsoons and silt-laden rivers yielded a wide variety of crops that contributed substantially to India's reputation of a prosperous land. Take the evidence gathered by historians like Irfan Habib, Percival Spear and Ashok Desai that per capita agricultural output and standards of consumption in 17th century Mughal India were equal to 17th century Europe and even early 20th-century British India.[1]

When India gained independence in 1947, Indian agriculture presented a somewhat different story. For almost two centuries the farm sector had stagnated under an exploitative colonial administration. The zamindari system put in place by the British for the sole purpose of extraction of rent had ensured that landownership was concentrated in the hands of a select group of Savarna, or upper-caste, families. Millions of tillers, landless farmers, worked on the farms without any security of tenure. Many of the feudal zamindar families were absentee landlords with little to no interest in agriculture, let alone improving the lot of the peasants.

With Independence dawned the hope that after centuries of exploitation and neglect the lot of Indian farmers would improve. The sector was beset with problems: the exploitative stranglehold of the local zamindars, fragmentation of small landholdings and low productivity caused by complete dependence on monsoons.

There was an urgent need for land reform measures such as giving land to tillers, large investments, and access to technology and the latest farming practices to lift agriculture out of the morass of stagnation.

A new government, a progressive prime minister who laid emphasis on the cultivation of a scientific temper as the springboard to development, and the adoption of a planned economy gave rise to optimism that the agriculture sector would experience a much-needed revival.[2]

Prime Minister Jawaharlal Nehru's First Five Year Plan [FYP] (1951–56) diagnosed the problem correctly and prescribed the right remedies.

'The pattern of priorities', enumerated in chapter 2 of the First FYP document, puts it well: '[F]or the immediate five year period, agriculture, including irrigation and power, must in our view have the topmost priority [...] We are convinced that without a substantial increase in the production of food and of raw materials needed for industry, it would be impossible to sustain a higher tempo of industrial development...'

The plan allocated almost a third of the ₹1,960 crore budget to the farming sector.[3] For instance, recognizing that Indian farmers were far too dependent on the vagaries of nature, the plan focused on bringing new land areas—14 million acres—under irrigation. Additionally, the government also reclaimed and brought an additional 12 million acres of land under cultivation. Further, in order to enhance India's farm practices after centuries of stagnation, the government introduced the Japanese method of rice cultivation, which reduced wastage and improved yields.

These initiatives began to show results almost immediately. By the end of the plan period India seemed to have achieved self-sufficiency as a variety of crops from foodgrains and oilseeds to sugarcane and cotton exceeded production targets by 1.0 per cent to 4.2 per cent. Reflecting this buoyancy in supplies, the price index for farm goods, which was 100 during 1952–53, fell to 92.8.[4] In fact, India hovered at the cusp of an economic miracle, albeit for a brief period.

SHIFTING FOCUS: BAD NEWS FOR AGRICULTURE

However, these early successes lulled the government into complacency. Those who helmed the FYPs, mostly respected economists from an urban, elite background, had little first-hand experience of agriculture. Assuming that the crisis in Indian farming had been solved and that the sector was now placed on a long-term growth trajectory, the government turned its attention to heavy industries as encapsulated in the 'Temples of Modern India' strategy.[5]

In fact, this shift in priorities was reflected in subsequent plan allocations for agriculture: from 31 per cent under the First FYP, the agriculture budget, at ₹1,050 crore, was reduced to 20 per cent of the total budget.[6] The reasoning behind the focus on heavy industries was that it would soon pay dividends by creating new job opportunities, thus drawing a considerable number of Indians away from their dependence on farming. The fact that this mistaken reasoning did not bear fruit and has worked to the detriment of agriculture ever since is known now. At that time, there was a sense of exhilaration at the initial successes in agriculture after such a long time of inertness.

The initial euphoria about strides made in agriculture dissipated by the mid-1960s. The shortcomings of the Second and Third FYPs with regard to agriculture led to a fall in food production, a situation exacerbated by successive droughts in 1965 and 1966. The average inflation rate, which was touching a high of 13.36 per cent in 1964,[7] caused widespread discontent.

The respected economic writer Swaminathan S. Anklesaria Aiyar put it succinctly in one of his columns: 'Even in the bumper monsoon year of 1964–65, food aid totalled 7 million tonnes, over one-tenth of domestic production. Then India was hit by twin droughts in 1965 and 1966. Grain production crashed by one-fifth.'[8]

By this time, India was receiving and subsisting on massive American wheat shipments, which had begun in the early 1950s and reached 4.3 million tonnes by 1963 under a scheme called Public Loan 480 (PL480).[9] These shipments gave India a negative image as a country that lived from ship-to-mouth.[10]

A DECISIVE TURN: THE GREEN REVOLUTION

In the early 1960s, a new dwarf wheat variety developed in Mexico was sent to the Indian Agricultural Research Institute for testing. The results were encouraging and when the report reached the then Food and Agriculture Minister Chidambaram Subramaniam, he realized that this new wheat variety could help India attain self-sufficiency in the production of foodgrains.

Shedding the administrative apathy that had marked the government's approach to agriculture since the end of the first plan period, and under the leadership of noted agronomist and geneticist M.S. Swaminathan, India imported 16,000 tonnes of seeds as well as large quantities of fertilizers to bring about a transformation in the Indian agricultural sector. In 1971, the Government of India declared India self-sufficient in foodgrain production.[11] The Green Revolution, as this approach to farming was termed, was hailed as a success story.

TRAJECTORY OF AGRICULTURAL GROWTH

As Professor Ramesh Chand, Member, NITI Aayog, stated in his presentation, the Indian Council for Agricultural Research (ICAR) Lecture Series #29 (24 September 2021), agriculture has gone through four distinct stages of growth since Independence.[12] The respective figures have been provided in Table 7.1.

- The first phase, from 1950–51 to 1964–65, marked the beginning of active policymaking on aspects such as access to irrigation, land reforms and expansion of the total area under agriculture. This phase was bookended by the setting of priorities with regard to agriculture in the First FYP and the relatively less importance given to the agricultural sector in the following two plans.
- The second phase, from 1967–68 to 1990–91, followed two successive years of severe droughts in 1965 and 1966. This phase saw the revival of agricultural growth, driven primarily by the Green Revolution and the widespread use of technology

Table 7.1
Growth in gross value added (GVA) and terms of trade in different periods[13]

Subsector	Trend growth rate (%)			
	1950–51 to 1964–65	1967–68 to 1990–91	1990–91 to 2004–05	2004–05 to 2020–21
Agriculture and allied	2.54	2.53	2.74	3.56
Non-agriculture	5.86	5.31	7.39	6.90
Human population	2.03	2.22	1.88	1.38
Bovine population	0.93	0.91	0.18	0.20
Crops	2.66	2.75	2.71	2.40
Livestock	2.64	2.69	2.73	6.88
Fishing and aquaculture	4.79	3.66	4.40	6.72

Note: 1965–66 and 1966–67 were very serious drought years, which brought down agri output drastically (–12.5%).

and modern practices that put the sector on an upward trajectory.

- The third phase, from 1990–91 to 2004–05, coincided with the liberalization of the Indian economy and saw a slight acceleration of the agricultural growth rate. The focus shifted to rural development and income generation. While market-oriented reforms were introduced, public investment in agriculture declined, leading to rising costs, farmer indebtedness and stagnating productivity in some areas.

- The fourth phase, from 2004–05 to 2020–21, was primarily driven by demand and price. The growth rate of agriculture accelerated further and prepared the sector for a demand-driven transformation. Further, new opportunities emerged through digital technologies, precision farming and agri-startups. Policy initiatives like Pradhan Mantri Kisan Samman Nidhi (PM-KISAN), Electronic National Agriculture Market (eNAM), and the push for organic and sustainable farming aimed to enhance farmer incomes and resilience. Yet, the sector continued to grapple with structural issues requiring comprehensive reforms.

THE CURRENT PHASE: AGRICULTURE DOGGED BY LEGACY ISSUES

The numbers say it all: in 1947, agriculture accounted for more than 50 per cent of India's gross domestic product (GDP). That figure fell progressively over the decades, plummeting to 15 per cent in 2022–23.[14] Notably, this decline was brought about essentially by a rapid expansion in industrial and services sector GVA.

The falling share of agriculture in India's economic pie belies its importance as 45.76 per cent of the country's workforce and two-thirds of its population still depend heavily on this sector for livelihood, giving it a salience disproportionate to its relative size.[15]

These figures camouflage a deeper truth about the Indian economy, namely that two-thirds of Indians are surviving on less than one-sixth of the national income. It is important to state that there is a systemic reason for this. As mentioned above, the urban bias of Indian planners and the government's early focus on heavy industry to the detriment of agriculture have led to a neglect of the concerns of rural India. Moreover, these figures also underline the urgent need for drawing people away from farming into industry. Unfortunately, Indian policy planners have not been able to adequately address this issue.

For instance, although India is now self-sufficient in foodgrain production and has emerged as a net exporter of food,[16] the agricultural sector as a whole continues to suffer from falling productivity levels and rising farmer distress as a result of inadequate policy responses. These issues have been exacerbated over time by challenges like erratic rainfall, inadequate irrigation facilities, massive soil degradation in large parts of the country, unscientific and outdated farming techniques, and falling groundwater levels. The ongoing crisis in the agricultural sector is proving to be a drag on the overall economic development of the country.

THE FARMERS WORLD: A LONELY EXISTENCE, PERSISTING CHALLENGES

Left to their own devices, farmers continue to face persistent problems. Contrary to the unnuanced Bollywood frames of lush green fields, bountiful harvests and uniformly happy villagers, life in Indian villages is full of challenges. From unviable farm sizes and difficulties in sourcing high quality seeds to the lack of adequate irrigation facilities and the absence of sufficient post-harvest facilities, farmers face problems that have a direct bearing on the productivity of Indian farms. Just listing them gives a sense of the depth of the problems.

Small and fragmented landholdings: According to the 10th Agricultural Census in 2015–16, the total operational landholding in India was 146.45 million hectares.[17] Of this, as much as 86.2 per cent of the land was held by small and marginal farmers with farm sizes of 0–2 hectares. This resulted in suboptimal yields and inadequate incomes. Importantly, such smallholdings force farmers to practise monocropping[18] and engage in other agricultural practices that lead to a deterioration in the quality of land and yield poor returns to farmers, leaving little surplus for investment in soil regeneration. High production costs and low productivity characterize this sector.

Lack of mechanization: A vast majority of Indian farms continue the practice of manual labour as the primary input for tasks such as ploughing, harvesting, threshing and irrigation. Mechanical ploughs, automated threshers, as well as seeding and weeding machines are available, but relatively few farmers have the means and the scale to use them. This inhibits productivity gains and the possibility of higher profitability.

Soil fertility depletion: Indiscriminate use of chemical fertilizers, in the wake of the success of the Green Revolution in the 1960s, has led to an alarming depletion in soil fertility. The dependence on chemical fertilizers, particularly the excessive use of urea, has led to reduced organic matter content in the soil, which in turn has reduced soil fertility. In 2022–23, for instance, urea accounted for 58 per cent of fertilizer production and 56 per cent of total fertilizer consumption.[19] Moreover, increased pest attacks and the altering of soil pH has further led to low productivity. Besides, unscientific agricultural practices, such as monocropping (over 47 per cent of total cropped area in 2015–16), have also contributed significantly to soil quality depletion.

Poor irrigation facilities: As of 2022–23, only 55 per cent of Indian farms had access to irrigation facilities, whereas in 1950–51 this figure was at 17.5 per cent (22.6 million hectare out of 129 million hectare).[20] Despite the increase, about half of Indian farms are left to the vagaries of the monsoon for their sustenance. The apathetic attitude of Indian planners and a paucity of funds have combined to leave Indian farmers at the mercy of nature.

Lack of marketing and storage facilities: The Food and Agricultural Organization (FAO) estimates that 40 per cent of food produced by India is wasted.[21] Other estimates say about 16 per cent of fruits and vegetables, 10 per cent of oilseeds, 9 per cent of pulses and 6 per cent of cereals produced by Indian farmers are being wasted every year due to lack of proper storage facilities and cold storage chains.[22] These wastages effectively compel farmers to sell their produce soon after the harvest regardless of the price, which is often less than remunerative. Furthermore, poorly developed agricultural marketing facilities— transportation costs, inadequate market infrastructure, price fluctuation, lack of proper market information and the role of exploitative local traders and middlemen—combine to ensure that farmers get inadequate returns for their labour.

Price volatility: Indian farmers also have to face a high degree of volatility in the price of their produce. These fluctuations do not necessarily reflect market fundamentals, and are usually the result of manipulations and restrictive practices by traders as well as the official government machinery. They reflect both a failure of proper price discovery mechanisms as well as a robust regulatory regime, and lead to incorrect decisions by farmers. Moreover, volatility can result in unremunerative prices for farmers while simultaneously generating large speculative gains for middlemen, wholesalers and retailers. Hence, while the end customer continues to pay a high price for farm produce, the small farmer receives an unsatisfactory compensation for his labour. Therefore, both ends of the spectrum suffer from excessive volatility, and this tends to lead to suboptimal investment decisions by the farming community over the long term.

Credit availability: More than ₹20 lakh crore ($250 billion) was earmarked for agricultural credit in the Union Budget of 2023–24.[23] Considering that the average farmholding is 1.08 hectares, with 86 per cent of the country's farmers owning less than 2 hectares of farmland,[24] ensuring that millions of farmers get their share of farm credit to buy modern inputs like seeds, fertilizers, pesticides and machinery is a humungous task. But without this critical link in the agricultural value chain, feeding India's 1.4 billion people would not be possible. In their seminal study, Ashok Gulati and Ritika Juneja state: '[T]he share of institutional credit to farming households in overall credit increased from about 10 per cent in 1951 to 63 per cent in 1981. But since then, it has hovered around that level until 2013, the latest year for which this information is available from All India Debt and Investment Survey.'[25]

In fact, even today, small and marginal farmers find it difficult to access institutional credit. This forces them to approach local moneylenders who provide the funds at exorbitant interest rates. While their influence and power have been curtailed, some rural pockets continue to be in their thrall. Therefore, streamlining credit delivery mechanisms and enhancing financial literacy among farmers is imperative for a seamless supply of credit to strengthen the Indian agricultural sector.

Inadequate access to crop insurance schemes: Adequate and quality access to crop insurance remains a major institutional challenge for the farming community, especially small and marginal farmers who lack proper awareness of such schemes. This results in inadequate coverage of insurance schemes, non-payment and/or delayed settlement of claims and even lack of ways to estimate the extent of damage caused by crop losses.

The risks farmers face are many, from unpredictable weather conditions and pest attacks to price fluctuations and market access. Given this, crop insurance plays a crucial role in ensuring fair returns for farmers by offering a safety net in the form of financial protection. Despite significant progress over the past few decades in improving the reach of insurance across the length and breadth of the country, its coverage, particularly in rural India, has been less than adequate, and a significant section of farmers still remains vulnerable.

The 2013–14 Situational Assessment Survey by the NSSO revealed that more than 60 per cent of Indian farmers were unaware of crop insurance schemes. Moreover, the cost of crop insurance deters many small and marginal farmers from subscribing to such schemes. Although the government does offer several subsidies to reduce farmers' burden, the actual cost remains a significant barrier to a more widespread adoption of crop insurance covers.

Addressing these challenges, raising awareness of the benefits of crop insurance, simplification of the procedures and providing innovative financing schemes are necessary and imperative to increase insurance coverage in the farming sector.

Poor training and extension facilities: Proper training and extension services are absolutely necessary for providing farmers with the skills they need to improve productivity and adapt to evolving challenges such as climate change and market dynamics. Unfortunately, agricultural extension services, which provide technical aid and essential inputs and services to farmers, are marred by numerous shortcomings. For instance, lack of adequate infrastructure and limited funding have resulted in a shortage of trained personnel, agriculture experts and demonstration farms, thereby constraining the reach and effectiveness of extension programmes.

Extension services in India have historically relied on lectures and pamphlets, a one-way communication that may not always discuss the challenges that farmers face on the ground. Consequently, extension services often fail to find favour with Indian farmers. There is an urgent need to conceptualize interactive programmes that are relevant to the needs of the Indian farming community, benefitting from farmers' experiences when creating their content.

To provide proper training in extension facilities, all the stakeholders, that is, government agencies, research institutions, NGOs, private sector participants and interested individuals, have to come together to increase investment, leverage technology and make it financially viable for professionals to enter this field and provide services that appeal to farmers.

Limited spending on R&D by government: In the 2024–25 budget the Indian government had allocated only about 0.4 per cent of GDP on research and development (R&D) in agriculture. This translated to a monetary allocation of ₹9,941 crore, which was far below the levels of China, Brazil and Israel.[26] China, for instance, spent 2.1 per cent of GDP in 2015,[27] which is slightly lower than the Organisation for Economic Co-operation and Development (OECD) average of 2.4 per cent. By and large, experts advocate a farm R&D spend of at least 1 per cent of GDP. The low level of spending is, therefore, a significant barrier to innovation, sustainability and progress. Research and innovation play a pivotal role in driving agricultural productivity, enhancing crop resilience and developing sustainable farming practices tailored to the diverse agro-climatic zones of India. The farmers who invest their sweat and toil on their land need the support of scientists and technical institutions to unlock their full potential. That is the only way to ensure food security and sustainable livelihoods for millions of Indians across the country.

Impact of climate change: The Indian farmer is still overwhelmingly dependent on the monsoon rains for a bountiful harvest. As we have seen above, as much as 45 per cent of Indian farms have no access to irrigation facilities, and are, therefore, fully at the mercy of the weather gods. Rising temperatures and other erratic weather patterns, such as unpredictable rainfall, droughts, cyclones and floods, wreak havoc with cropping cycles, reducing yields and leading to water scarcity. Small farmers, who, as stated earlier, account for 86 per cent of the Indian farming community, are particularly vulnerable to disruptions caused by climate change, owing to their limited resources. The government has to take the lead in helping them adopt resilient farming practices such as growing climate-resilient crop varieties and better water management techniques. Additionally, research institutions in the public and private sectors have to come together with large farmer bodies, along with NGOs and civil society, to chart out long-term measures to combat the impact of climate change on agriculture.

Support for Indian farmers on all these fronts is crucial for their success. It is also essential for the future development of India—without progress in rural India, where the bulk of the farming community resides, India's progress will remain unequal and that does not bode well for it. With an improved rural economy through agriculture, aspects such as education and public health in rural India will also receive a much-needed boost.

LEARNING LESSONS FROM CHINA

In this regard, Ashok Gulati and Sakshi Gupta, writing in the *Financial Express* in 2019, enumerated three lessons that India could draw from China[28]:

Lesson one: China has focused on agricultural knowledge and innovation systems (AKIS), which also includes R&D and education. In 2018–19, China spent $7.8 billion in this area, which was 5.6 times more than the amount spent by India. Significantly, according to a study by Ashok Gulati and Prerna Terway (2018), investments in agricultural research and education (R&E) have the highest impact on agri-GDP growth and poverty alleviation compared to other inputs: every rupee spent on agri R&E added ₹11.2 to agri-GDP, and 328 people were brought out of poverty for every million rupees spent on agri-R&E.[29]

Gulati and Gupta's article of 2019 had interesting details: the then investment of India in agri R&D and extension constituted 0.35 per cent of its agri-GVA. In contrast, China was spending 0.8 per cent. The authors' remedy: increase the expenditure on agri R&E, with ICAR being 'accountable for targeted deliveries'.

Carrying the comparison further with the help of World Bank estimates, the authors pointed out that in 2016 China utilized fertilizer to the tune of 503 kg per hectare, whereas India's figure was 166 kg per hectare. 'No wonder, China's productivity in most crops is 50 per cent to 100 per cent higher than India's,' they commented.[30]

Lesson two: China's incentive structure, as measured by producer support estimates (PSE), is far superior to India's.

Put simply, PSE, developed by OECD, 'measures the output prices that farmers get in relation to free trade scenario, as well as input subsidies received by them'. Mentioning that the idea of PSE was in use in 52 countries 'that produce more than three-fourths of global agri-output', the authors presented one telling statistic—the PSE for Chinese farmers came to 15.3 per cent of gross farm receipts during the triennium average ending 2018–19, while the PSE for Indian farmers during that period was (–)5.7 per cent.[31] What it meant was that despite receiving a higher amount of subsidies Indian farmers were 'net taxed, not subsidized'. The reason for this was the 'restrictive marketing, and trade policies that do not allow Indian farmers to get free trade prices for their outputs'. In such circumstances, the 'negative market price support is so strong that it exceeds even the positive input subsidy support the government gives to farmers through low prices of fertilizers, power, irrigation, agri-credit, crop insurance, etc.'[32]

However, as pointed out by the authors, instead of turning towards reforms in agri-marketing (such as the Agricultural Produce Market Committee [APMC] and the Essential Commodities Act), the government has been moving in the opposite direction, namely attempting to raise the minimum support prices (MSP) for 23 crops.

The authors further suggested that India could consider the example of China, which 'dropped the price support scheme for corn' and gradually reduced 'support prices for wheat and rice'. India, they proposed, should consider reducing the number of crops that come under the MSP system, and therefore keep prices below international levels. As things stand, farmer groups have forced the Indian government to move in the opposite direction.

Lesson three: China has focused on direct income support schemes. China, wrote Gulati and Gupta, had put the various significant subsidies for inputs into one scheme based on 'direct payment to farmers on a per hectare basis'. In 2018–19, China spent $20.7 billion through this scheme. The inputs don't come cheap, they are accessible at market rates, which instils the idea of optimal use of resources. Compared to China's $20.7 billion direct income support scheme of 2018–19, wrote the authors, India spent only $3 billion under its direct income scheme, PM-KISAN, during that period. However, it spent $27 billion 'on heavily subsidizing fertilizers, power, irrigation, insurance and credit. This leads to large inefficiencies in their use and has also created environmental problems'.[33]

Gulati and Gupta concluded that 'it may be better for India to also consolidate all its input subsidies and give them directly to farmers on a per hectare basis, and free up their prices from all controls'. The scheme would go a long way in making Indian agriculture more efficient and productive.

These lessons are worth pondering if Indian agriculture is to be directed towards a high-growth trajectory.

TAKING CUES FROM ISRAEL'S SUCCESS

Apart from China, the other country from which India can imbibe valuable lessons is Israel. In fact, Israel is acknowledged the world over for its remarkable success in:

- transforming a desert into a flourishing agricultural area that yields high-value crops, such as olives and citrus fruits, for its export sector.
- perfecting a high level of efficiency in water management through techniques such as drip irrigation, and utilizing various sources of water for agricultural purposes, such as recycled wastewater and desalinated water.

Water management is a crucial issue for India in more ways than one. According to NITI Aayog's 'Composite Water Management Index 2018' (CWMI), India, with a 1.4 billion population, 'is facing the worst water crisis in its history'. The report points out that 'currently, 600 million Indians face high to extreme water stress, and about two lakh people die annually due to inadequate access to safe water'. Sounding a dire warning, the report says that by 2030, the demand for water in India will be double the supply.[34]

That is not all. CWMI 2019 states that 'about 74 per cent of the area under wheat cultivation and 65 per cent of the area under rice cultivation faces significant levels of water scarcity.'[35] Juxtapose this with the 2022 figures provided by the Central Ground Water Board (CGWB) that 87 per cent of groundwater extracted annually was for agricultural purposes, and the crisis becomes clearer.[36]

In all these aspects, Israel leads by innovation. According to a 2023 *Times of Israel* report, desalinated water now provides 60 per cent to 80 per cent of Israel's drinking water, and Israel has reached 'almost 100 per cent reuse' of treated wastewater, with 90 per cent of it going to agriculture.[37] Now, compare this with India's figure of only 30 per cent of urban wastewater being recycled.[38] While desalination holds out hope for India's cities on the coast, more efficient wastewater treatment for utilization in agriculture will take the pressure off groundwater.

No wonder that high-level delegations of government officials as well as various companies from around the world visit Israel to study the practices adopted by them with a view to adopting these in their own countries. From India, too, prime ministerial and chief ministerial delegations have visited Israel. Interestingly, in a 2021 article in *The Financial Express*, Ashok Gulati points out that the delegations return with the mantra of saving water and using each drop judiciously. However, when he meets Israeli experts, they tell him just one thing: unless India puts a stop to the policy of giving free power to agriculture, farmers will not have any incentive to save water. The biggest worry, writes Gulati, is the depleting groundwater table.[39]

Keeping these issues in mind, the Indo-Israel Agriculture Cooperation Project was launched in 2008 as part of bilateral cooperation between India and Israel, and implemented by India's Union Ministry of Agriculture and Israel's Agency for International Development Cooperation (MASHAV). The main goal of the project's three-year action plans (there have been five thus far) is clear: 'Establish centres of excellence in agriculture to demonstrate best practices and new technologies to increase crop diversity, productivity and water use efficiency.' The centres provide a space for the demonstration and transfer of 'Israeli agro-technologies adapted to the local conditions and requirements of the farmers'.[40]

As many as 43 such centres of excellence have been established across India so far to familiarize farmers with greenhouse technologies and soilless agriculture, drip irrigation and automation technologies to meet local requirements. All these measures have helped Israel introduce precision into its agricultural activities.

Drip irrigation, conceived through necessity by Israel, has transformed their agriculture. Through a network of pipes, water and nutrients are released directly to the root in a gradual manner, thus avoiding the pitfalls of wastage that occur in flood irrigation, reducing water usage by '20 per cent to 60 per cent when compared to conventional flood irrigation methods'[41] as well as increasing yield. A report mentions pilot projects in Maharashtra that have shown positive results: sugarcane farmers said that water wastage was 40 per cent less and the crop yield was 20 per cent more.[42]

Drip irrigation in areas cultivating water-intensive crops, such as sugarcane, rice and cotton, holds a great deal of potential.

Another area in which Indo-Israel cooperation can be beneficial is in furthering the use of unmanned aerial vehicle (UAV) or drone technology in Indian agriculture to overcome labour shortages and low levels of mechanization. Drones can perform so many functions: map the fields, evaluate damage to the crop, and spray seeds, fertilisers and pesticides.

An Observer Research Foundation (ORF) report mentions a pilot project by an Israeli firm that employs drones for tasks like picking apples, which requires both time and labour—an ideal option for farmers facing labour shortage. The report also writes about a memorandum of understanding (MoU) signed by a Chennai startup and an Israeli firm to build an advanced drone for the task of large-scale surveying and mapping of Indian villages under the Swamitva Scheme.[43]

In April 2025, India signed a significant agriculture agreement with Israel to strengthen bilateral cooperation in key areas such as modernizing farm practices and addressing the challenges of climate change and population growth to enhance productivity and move towards sustainability.

The agreement 'focuses on a range of crucial areas, including soil and water management, horticultural and agricultural production, post-harvest and processing technology, agriculture mechanization, animal husbandry, and research and development'.[44]

An important aspect of the talks between the two countries 'was the exploration of a five-year seed improvement plan aimed at developing high-quality and high-yielding seed varieties to boost agricultural productivity and ensure food security.'[45]

The two countries agreed on setting up a joint working group to enable an ongoing dialogue and help develop a roadmap with clear targets and timelines, focusing on 'specific areas of cooperation, including market access, agricultural research and the expansion of the centres of excellence.'[46]

An Effective Ecosystem

It is crucial for India to understand the nature of efforts that have made Israel a world leader in agriculture and water management that it is today. Credit is due to Israel's extensive ecosystem of R&D, based on the collaboration between government, academia and private enterprises.

Indian policymakers would benefit from encouraging such collaborations by providing incentives for working on innovations that could power agriculture, promoting public–private partnerships and putting in place a supportive regulatory environment. That's not all; extension services in Israel bridge the gap between research institutions and farmers, for the practitioners are at the centre of the country's R&D ecosystem. The extension services ensure that innovative solutions are rapidly adopted by farmers. India would do well to emulate this model of enhancing the effectiveness of its agricultural extension services and investing in the continuous education and training of farmers.

SOME ENCOURAGING NEW TRENDS IN INDIAN AGRICULTURE

The Statistical Yearbook of the Ministry of Statistics and Programme Implementation[47] has revealed some interesting trends.

Shift Towards High-Value Agriculture

'[A] structural shift in consumption patterns away from cereals to high value agricultural commodities, both in rural and urban areas, has been observed in the last two decades. A relatively strong and growing domestic demand for livestock products and fruits and vegetables in both rural and urban areas and increased trade in these commodities has spurred a shift towards production of high value commodities in agriculture. During the 2000s, the growth rate in value of exports of rice, sugar, marine products, tea, etc., declined, while high-value exports (fruits and vegetables, floriculture, meat, processed fruit juices) grew by about 18 per cent annually.'

Marching Towards an ICT Revolution

'Since Independence, India has witnessed significant increase in foodgrain production (green revolution), oilseeds (yellow revolution), milk (white revolution), fish (blue revolution) and fruits and vegetables (golden revolution). Now, India is marching towards what is called [an] ICT Revolution in agriculture. Most of the earlier revolutions were with the single objective of increasing production. The extension activities were limited to providing physical inputs, viz. fertilizers, seed, pesticides, among others. However, all this is undergoing a change. The extension efforts are now directed towards providing farmers with the knowledge of the market conditions, so as to enable them to decide what to produce, how and how much to produce, when and where to sell. Farmers can now also avail information regarding the weather conditions and decide their farm operations. The use of Geographic Information System (GIS) is also being promoted in a big way.'[48]

Additionally, there is a new focus on this sector through a digital revolution. The Union Cabinet recently approved the revamping of the Digital Agricultural Mission and approved an outlay of ₹2,817 crore for it. This mission envisages the setting up of extensive digital infrastructure that is expected to transform almost every aspect of rural life and the economy. According to a PIB release, 'These comprehensive approaches leverage digital technologies to enhance productivity, efficiency and sustainability in India's agricultural sector, potentially transforming the lives of millions of farmers across the country. By extending the digital revolution to agriculture, India aims to further solidify its position as a global leader in innovative, technology-driven solutions for critical sectors of the economy.'[49]

NEW PERSPECTIVE NEEDED ON FARM LOAN WAIVERS

An important question is whether this new thinking on reviving agriculture can succeed without addressing the harsh reality of financial distress faced by this sector. It is a reality that is not hidden from view, for there is no dearth of heart-wrenching reports of farmers dying by suicide across the country. In a large number of cases, indebtedness and the inability to repay loans is the primary cause of their distress. The political class has taken recourse to loan waivers as their preferred instrument to address this endemic problem. Since 2012, more than a dozen states have taken the route of farm loan waivers. The farm loan waiver scheme has seen a rise in frequency and scale in the past decade. However, this is a politically expedient but expensive and shortsighted remedy. The fundamental question is, how effective are loan waivers? And do they mitigate the crisis they set out to address?

Several studies by organizations such as the SBI and the National Bank for Agriculture and Rural Development (NABARD) as well as experts have put forth the view that implementing loan waivers without addressing the underlying problems is like applying Band-Aid to a life-threatening injury. A report titled 'Farm Loan Waivers in India: Assessing Impact and Looking Ahead', by Shweta Saini, Siraj Hussain and Pulkit Khatri, stated that paying off outstanding debts 'while leaving distress due to income instability and unpredictability in production unaddressed, governments appear to be treating only a symptom, i.e., indebtedness, of a much more complex problem'.[50] This assessment is right because it captures the conceptual weakness of the loan waiver argument. By writing off a farmer's past dues, and providing them access to fresh credit, governments try to reduce farmers' distress. But it offers only a short-term palliative while leaving the crux of the issue of farm distress, namely the cyclical nature of debt, unaddressed. In other words, it means that the beneficiary farmer is likely to become indebted once again and would need another round of loan waivers to provide relief.

However, this is not to say that farm loan waivers are ineffective in all circumstances. They are an effective instrument for providing relief in situations like droughts, floods and famines. But a NABARD report had this to say: 'by increasing the frequency of waivers and by universalizing its distribution for reasons mostly unconnected to levels of farmer distress, the benevolent purpose of the scheme appears to have been diluted, leading to worsening credit culture in the country.'

Another significant problem is to do with the loan waiver scheme architecture, that is, loan waivers do not necessarily address the needs of those who need them most. A study by SBI highlighted that only about half of the intended beneficiaries of farm loan waivers announced by nine states since 2014 have actually received debt write-offs. In fact, several large states have recorded much poorer performances, as can be seen in Table 7.2.[51]

Table 7.2
Status of various farm loan waivers[52]

State	Year of loan waiver	Amount of loan waiver (₹ crore)	Eligible farmers (in lakh)	Farmers loan waiver received (till Mar '22) (%)
Telangana	2014	17,000	51	5
Madhya Pradesh	2018	36,500	48	12
Jharkhand	2020	—	9	13
Punjab	2018	10,000	8	24
Karnataka	2018	44,000	50	38
Uttar Pradesh	2017	36,000	39	52
Maharashtra	2017	34,000	67	68
Andhra Pradesh	2014	24,000	42	92
Chhattisgarh	2018	6,100	9	100

The SBI report cited several reasons for the poor performance of the scheme. These included rejection of farmers' claims by state governments, limited or low fiscal capability to meet promises, and a change of government. Apart from benefits not reaching the targeted farmers, the SBI report also flagged concerns about whether they helped farmers in genuine distress. The report noted: 'Of the total accounts eligible for farm loan waiver, most of the accounts (more than 80 per cent in some states) were in standard category, defined as loan accounts that are not in distress, begging a question: Whose interest rampant waivers actually serve?'

The report concluded that 'loan waivers destroy the credit culture which may harm the farmers' interest in the medium to long term and also squeeze the fiscal space of governments to increase productive investment in agriculture infrastructure'.

Former RBI Governor Shaktikanta Das stated that loan waivers are credit negative, and thereby undermine the credit culture of the country. Further, he said that such loan write-offs affect farmers' ability to access loans in the following season. Despite these obvious drawbacks, political parties are unlikely to eschew this measure as they are seen as an easy way to win over 70 per cent of the electorate.

BAD ECONOMICS, GOOD POLITICS

Unfortunately for India, bad economics continues to be considered good politics, ignoring crucial expenditures that are bound to put agriculture on the right track. For instance, the government's expenditure on agriculture continues to be far behind India's peer nations. In the interim budget of 2024–25, the government allocated ₹1.27 lakh crore to the Ministry of Agriculture & Farmers Welfare. In contrast, China, which has a comparable populace, but only about 70 per cent of the area under cultivation in India, spent more than double this amount on agriculture, forestry and water resources in 2023.[53]

In addition to the budgetary allocation, the Indian government also provided direct financial assistance to 118 million farmers. Despite this, small and marginal farmers, who constitute about 86 per cent of the farmer population, continue to face challenges in accessing credit. On the other hand, the bigger and relatively better-off farmers are the main beneficiaries on the basis of their access to the disbursing agencies, political clout and better creditworthiness.

The fact is that barring a brief period during the First FYP (1951–56), agriculture has suffered a serious deficit of attention from Indian policymakers. Consequently, although the sector has grown in absolute terms, and has transformed India from a food-deficit country to a net exporter of farm produce, it has not kept pace with the productivity gains and advancements witnessed in China, East Asia and Southeast Asia. An RBI report on currency and finance in 2022 pointed out that the sector suffers from low capital formation, declining R&D, low crop yields, inadequate crop diversity and intensity, with excessive dependence on subsidies and price support schemes.

The Union Budget for 2024–25, which made a provision of ₹1.52 lakh crore for agriculture, sought to address the issue of improving the productivity and resilience of agriculture. The budget proposed the following[54]:

- A comprehensive review of the agricultural research set-up to focus on raising productivity and developing climate-resilient varieties of crops.
- The release of 109 new high-yielding and climate-resilient varieties of 32 field and horticultural crops for cultivation by farmers.
- Initiating 1 crore farmers across the country into natural farming, supported by certification and branding over the next two years.
- Establishing 10,000 need-based bio-input resource centres.

- Developing large-scale clusters for vegetable production closer to major consumption centres.
- Facilitating financing for shrimp farming, processing and export through NABARD.
- Undertaking a digital crop survey in 400 districts.

It was an ambitious to-do list, with a lot hinging on execution. The 2025–26 Union Budget roughly has the same allocation as the previous budget.

◆

Experience tells us that it may not be possible for the state machinery alone to implement all of the above and resolve the legacy issues hobbling the Indian agricultural sector. It is imperative that the private sector, too, comes on board to ensure a holistic economic development of agriculture in India. Further, given the critical importance of the agricultural sector, the government could consider setting up a specialized central service on the lines of the IAS and Indian Police Service (IPS) to administer all farm-related activities in the country. Members of this service would need exposure to and possibly representation from the farming community, particularly from among the small farmers, in order to provide inputs that translate into effective policies.

Clearly, with regard to the agricultural sector, there is no time to lose if India has to make up for lost time. What better way than to be on a steep learning curve, with education and skills development providing the edge required for higher productivity, resilience and growth.

8

A DEEPLY UNJUST
EDUCATION SYSTEM

The first census that independent India conducted, in 1951, mirrored some sobering findings on the population of the country and its literacy rate: a nation with a population of about 361 million had a literacy rate of 18.32 per cent.[1] This meant that more than 81 per cent of the country's population, or 295 million Indian citizens, was illiterate.

Sixty years hence, the 2011 census recorded that India's population had risen to 1.121 billion and it had a literacy rate of 72.98 per cent, 80.88 for males and 64.63 for females.[2] Even after six decades, while there had been an increase in literacy in the country, the number of illiterate people was about 327 million. Since then, the population has risen to about 1.4 billion, and the literacy rate has inched closer to 80 per cent.[3]

However, as a nation, we still have the world's largest unlettered population. A United Nations Educational, Scientific and Cultural Organization (UNESCO) report of 2015 stated that India was home to a staggering 35 per cent of the world's illiterate populace.[4] It is important to keep in mind the considerable rural–urban divide as well, as presented in Table 8.1. According to the 2011 census, the overall rural literacy rate was 66.77 per cent, as against 84.11 per cent in urban India. The literacy rate among males in

Table 8.1

Trend in literacy rates in post-independence India (%)[5]

Year	Rural			Urban			Combined		
	Female	Male	Total	Female	Male	Total	Female	Male	Total
1951	4.87	19.02	12.10	22.33	45.60	34.59	8.86	27.15	18.32
1961	10.10	34.30	22.50	40.50	66.00	54.40	15.35	40.40	28.31
1971	15.50	48.60	27.90	48.80	69.80	60.20	21.97	45.96	34.45
1981	21.70	49.60	36.00	56.30	76.70	67.20	29.76	56.38	43.57
1991	30.17	56.96	36.00	64.05	81.09	67.20	39.29	64.13	52.21
2001	46.70	71.40	59.40	73.20	86.70	80.30	53.67	75.26	64.83
2011	57.93	77.15	66.77	79.11	88.76	84.11	64.63	80.88	72.98
% Increase in 2011 over 2001	24	8	12	8	2	5	20	7	13

rural India was 77.15 per cent, as against 88.76 per cent in urban India, while among women the literacy rate in rural India was 57.93 per cent, compared to 79.11 per cent in urban India.[6]

Considering that almost two-thirds of the Indian population continues to live in rural India, the importance of providing quality education to children in rural India is starkly evident. The role of education for all-round development, and for the creation of a skilled workforce with the capacity to energize not only the agricultural sector but also other sectors, cannot be over-emphasized.

Indian planners would do well to recall the profound words of American economist and diplomat John Kenneth Galbraith: 'One must always have in mind one simple fact—there is no literate population in the world that is poor, and there is no illiterate population that is anything but poor.'[7]

Education is universally recognized as the real differentiator; in a world beset with stark inequalities, a good quality education has the potential to bring about a positive turnaround in the fortunes of an individual, a community, a society and an entire nation. Quality education results in the creation of a more responsive and aware citizenry, the results of which can be seen across all aspects of life. Education is commonly acknowledged as the most potent force to fight poverty, inequality and discrimination. Therefore, denial of a quality education is tantamount to injustice to the citizens of India as it goes against the democratic principles of offering every Indian an equal opportunity to progress.

THE MAGNITUDE OF THE CHALLENGE

Pre-Independence, there were very few schools in rural India where 85 per cent of the population resided, according to the 1951 census. One of the most pressing tasks was to provide schools across vast swathes of our country.

In the absence of private interest, the government stepped in to fill this gap after Independence. This was the natural and right thing to do for any young government.

Today the Indian education system has become one of the largest in the world in terms of size: there are more than 1.5 million schools and 8.5 million teachers. At any given time, a total of 250 million children from different socio-economic backgrounds are part of the Indian school system. These are estimates for the year 2017–18 as per the Government of India.[8]

However, this was done without proper planning; we prioritized expansion and quantity over quality—which proved to be a grave mistake over the years, exacerbated by an ostrich-like attitude to all manner of critiques.

Some things stick in the mind. One still remembers the sense of shock at reading about India's dismal display in the Program for International Student Assessment (PISA) in 2009. Conceptualized by OECD and first conducted in 2000, PISA 'tests the skills and knowledge of 15-year-old students in mathematics, reading and science' and how well they can apply those skills to real situations. In the 2009 PISA edition, India occupied the 72nd position out of 74 countries.[9]

Instead of taking this as a wake-up call, the Indian authorities went into denial mode. The institutional responses were all too familiar—'the process was unfair to Indians, there was a sociocultural disconnect', etc. Indian planners stuck their collective heads in the sand, and refused to participate again.[10]

For a country that believed in the mantra of globalization, interdependence and integration, this was a shortsighted reaction. In 2021, the government announced its decision to participate in the 2021 field trials but abruptly pulled out citing the Covid pandemic. As a country with a large demographic dividend and aspiring for high economic growth, India would have benefited from a rigorous approach to addressing the problem.

Besides, the PISA results would not have come as a surprise to Indian bureaucrats and politicians had they been paying attention. Numerous warning signs had been flashing long before the PISA results.

For instance, the 1997 World Bank Report on Primary Education in India stated that teachers in Madhya Pradesh failed the very same tests that were meant for students. The Annual Status of Education Report (ASER), 2017, found that India's learning deficit was worsening year on year. The 2023 ASER on the status of foundational skills for youth in the age group 14–18 years revealed some more disturbing facts[11]:

- About 25 per cent of this age group still could not read a Std II-level text fluently in their regional language.
- More than half struggled with division (3-digit by 1-digit) problems. Only 43.3 per cent of 14–18-year-olds were able to solve such problems correctly. This skill is usually expected in Std III or IV.
- A little over half (57.3 per cent) could read sentences in English. Of those who could do so, only three-quarters (73.5 per cent) were able to tell their meanings.
- Across enrolment categories, females (76 per cent) did better than males (70.9 per cent) in reading a Std II-level text in their regional language. In contrast, males did better than their female counterparts in arithmetic and English reading.

ASER 2017 had cautioned that the learning deficit that
had been visible in elementary school children was starting
to show amongst young adults as well. Bill Gates, in an
article in *The Times of India,* had echoed a similar sentiment
around that time, stating that 'my biggest disappointment
with India is the state of its education'.

EDUCATION NEGLECTED BY PLANNERS

Indeed, largely indifferent planning and a lack of political
will on the part of successive governments have combined
to deny a vast majority of Indians access to education that
could have made a positive difference to their lives.

It was not that there was no awareness of the problem
among the political class. India's first prime minister
Jawaharlal Nehru wrote in *Discovery of India*: 'Of our
millions, how few get any education at all, how many live
on the verge of starvation; of even those who get some
education how many have nothing to look forward to but a
clerkship in some office...'

Further, 'If life opened its gates to them and offered
them food and healthy conditions of living and education
and opportunities of growth, how many among these
millions would be eminent scientists, educationists,
technicians, industrialists, writers and artists, helping to
build a new India and a new world?'

So, what accounts for the indifference of successive
governments towards the education sector? Reputed
educationist Professor Krishna Kumar, former director
of the National Council for Educational Research and
Training (NCERT), indicated an important reason in an
interview published by The Hindu Centre for Politics and
Public Policy in 2017. He made two significant points: the
portfolio of education 'has never been considered a high-

status portfolio for a powerful politician to aspire for, right from independence onwards'. Moreover, education was not perceived by the Indian state as 'a matter of national concern or a national interest, like Defence is a subject of national interest'.[12]

As governments settled down to the task of governance in the years following Independence and set developmental goals, priority was given to sectors like industry, agriculture and infrastructure. Education as a strong enabler was not taken into account and hence lacked necessary investment.

In the First, Second and Third FYPs, education received allocations of between 5.9 per cent and 7.9 per cent of plan funds, which was about one-third to half of what was allocated to sectors such as agriculture, industry and communications.[13] Overall, successive governments have spent much less on education than suggested by experts.

This is indicative of a certain lack of understanding of the potential of education, in a developing country intent on forging ahead, as countries of East and Southeast Asia have demonstrated to good effect.

Still, as in the case of agriculture, India made a reasonably good start in the First FYP by signalling a focus on strengthening the grassroots. As much as 58 per cent of the education budget was allocated to primary education. The thrust was on creating a network of primary schools in rural areas.

However, in the second plan, the share of funds for primary education went down to 35 per cent of the education budget.[14] Attention shifted to immediate goals such as employment generation, rapid industrialization, population control and reducing caste discrimination.

NOT AN EITHER–OR SITUATION: WITNESS THE EAST ASIAN TIGERS

A greater focus on education could have helped India achieve its developmental goals. There were ready examples to be found from the 1960s onwards: the East Asian Tiger economies had leveraged their excellent primary education system to delay marriage, reduce fertility rates and improve child health.[15] Educated workers enabled businesses in these countries to swiftly scale up the level of technology absorption and become an important part of the global supply chain. In India's case, education could have loosened the stranglehold of caste, which possibly could have helped in reordering the terms of sociocultural and economic engagement between various social groups. But the failure to focus on education overall, and primary education in particular, signifies a lost opportunity for what could have been in terms of transforming the terms of engagement among its citizens.

Notwithstanding the larger scenario, there have been islands of excellence in several parts of the country. In his book *India is Broken* economist Ashoka Mody highlighted how Kerala, which was spending double the amount on average per primary school student compared to Uttar Pradesh in the 1960s, had a literacy rate of 70 per cent in 1970 as against Uttar Pradesh's literacy rate of 22 per cent.[16] As happened with India's Asian neighbours, a higher literacy rate led to increased social awareness and compelled the Kerala government to invest more on health facilities and social infrastructure, leading to a higher Human Development Index (HDI) overall.

FOCUS ON QUANTITY, NOT QUALITY

The number of government schools have ballooned exponentially over time. Not only has this been in response to our rapidly growing populace, it has also been driven by political expediency. Still, measures such as schools within 1 km of habitation have led to some notable successes. Since 1980, the proportion of Indian teenagers who have had no schooling has fallen from about half to one in ten. That is a significant, if belated, success for a country with over 250 million children of schoolgoing age—more than in any other country on the planet.[17] Yes, literacy levels and enrolment figures have gone up significantly over the past few decades. The gross enrolment ratio (GER) for primary education has increased over the years, indicating that more children are attending school. According to the District Information System for Education 2019–20, the overall GER at the primary level was 99.8 per cent.

However, despite the substantial financial investment on the part of state governments in infrastructure in the form of new schools, the quality of education has remained poor. This was predictable, because in any sudden ramping up of production of services or physical products, let alone education, a clear focus on quality is critical. However, by driving expansion with poorly trained, low-calibre teachers and poor infrastructure, we ignored this fact at substantial cost to our collective future. While ensuring that there was a school within a short walk of 1 km for every rural child was a well-intended measure, a single-teacher school simply cannot meet the essential need for good instruction. In 2016, the World Economic Forum (WEF) ranked India 104th out of 140 countries on the basis of the quality of its school education.

A 2004 report by the Azim Premji Foundation titled 'Status of Learning Achievements in India: A Review of Empirical Research' stated that despite the high enrolment rate, learning outcomes are poor, and the dropout rate is alarmingly high:

- From 30.5 million children in Std I to only 3.5 million in Std XII 'reflects low learning in the system since most children are not completing grades for which they are enrolled'.[18]
- The non-detention policy at the primary level pushes children up the grades irrespective of how much they are learning. 'Findings from a number of studies reveal that Class III or IV children are not able to read and write even simple sentences. Thus, something is surely wrong with the learning outcomes of children.'[19]
- The curriculum load, too, affects learning levels as children find it hard to cope with the ever-increasing barrage of information. While many opt for private tuitions, first-generation learners from poor families are the hardest hit for there is no help at home, nor are there resources for tuitions. 'Schools have lost sight of kindling creativity, developing a critical mindset in children, and inculcating a value system based on our Constitution.'[20]

Nevertheless, it would be unfair to say that no attempts have been made to address these issues in nearly eight-odd decades of independence. The first of these was the Education Commission, headed by D.S. Kothari in 1964, which was tasked with studying the inadequacies of the education system and making recommendations for its improvement at the primary and higher education levels. The members of the Kothari Commission were leading educationists from India and abroad. The report was submitted in 1966. It was circulated to state governments, universities and other interested groups, following which extensive discussions were held. The report was also discussed in both houses of Parliament.

The recommendations of the Kothari Commission laid the foundation for the government's National Policy on Education (1968), with a clear programme of action. In essence, the Kothari Commission report stated: '[I]t becomes evident that the present system of education, designed to meet the needs of an imperial administration with the limitations set by a feudal and traditional society, will need radical changes if it is to meet the purposes of a modern democratic and socialistic society—changes in objectives, in content, in teaching methods, in programmes, in the size and composition of the student body, in the selection and professional preparation of teachers, and in organization.'

The report made one thing clear: 'In fact, what is needed, is a revolution in education, which in turn will set in motion the much desired social economic and cultural revolutions.' Providing free and compulsory education till the age of 14, focusing on quality training of teachers to enhance their capacities and standing, emphasizing the three-language formula as a way of developing Indian languages and fostering unity, and the study of mathematics and science were some of the recommendations.

The National Policy on Education of 1968 was ambitious in its scope; however, it was implemented poorly, because of an unaccountable organization, amongst others.

In 1979, there was a further attempt to make certain changes to the original draft of 1968, but nothing came of it. The second National Policy on Education was adopted by Parliament in May 1986. Several review committees were subsequently set up, and reams of reports and recommendations were issued, resulting finally in an endorsement by the Central Advisory Board of Education (CABE) in May 1992.

The most recent NEP was framed in 2020. According to the Union Ministry of Education, 'It envisions a massive transformation in education through "an education system rooted in Indian ethos that contributes directly to transforming India, that is Bharat, sustainably into an equitable and vibrant knowledge society, by providing high quality education to all, thereby making India a global knowledge superpower". The NEP 2020 is founded on the five guiding pillars of Access, Equity, Quality, Affordability and Accountability.'

Unfortunately, the actual educational developments in the country have varied markedly from the recommendations of the Kothari Commission. There can be several explanations for this: either the recommendations were inadequate or unsound; or, even if they were sound, they were either ignored or modified in such a way as to render them useless; or, they were accepted, but only implemented imperfectly—and this seems to be the most likely. After all, the successful implementation of the recommendations required a strong political authority to drive them to effective completion, ideally against a background of favourable socio-economic conditions.

It is worth noting that members of the Education Commission comprised primarily educationists. However, from a management point of view, to be truly effective, any commission should also include representatives with the power to make decisions (politicians), as well as those who would be implementing them in practice (bureaucrats). This would have enabled inputs from and interactions between all interested parties and made the recommendations more practical and actionable. Because it is only by successful implementation that we are able to achieve the right results for the efforts we put in.

When the Education Commission met with Dr Zakir Husain (eminent educationist and third President of India, 1967–69) to seek his advice about the report, he summed it up perfectly with just three words, 'Implement, implement and implement'.

In 2000, a report on a Policy Framework for Reforms in Education by Mukesh Ambani and Kumar Mangalam Birla echoed the spirit of the Kothari Commission when it stated: 'This is not a time for just reforms. It is a time for a revolution—a knowledge revolution.' Elaborating further, the report states, 'The green revolution in agriculture ushered in high productivity and prosperity through technology, education of farmers and field extension activities. Likewise, a revolution in education that embraces information technology (IT), fosters freedom and innovation and induces a market competitive environment is vital for our future. The need of the hour is for bold steps, not incremental and tentative ones.'

The Right to Education Act (RTE) of 2009, which sought to guarantee 'good education' to all Indian children between the ages of 6 and 14, was one such bold step. But, as many commentators, among them Professor Geeta Kingdon, pointed out, it has gone completely off-track. While enrolment has improved, actual learning has gradually deteriorated.

PERSISTING CHALLENGES

Clearly, despite its vast scale and spread, the Indian education system continues to face a slew of significant challenges.

Huge disparities in quality of education: There is considerable disparity in the quality of education dispensed in different regions of India. Generally speaking, urban areas across India have better equipped schools and more qualified teachers than schools located in rural areas. This has created an urban–rural divide, which is reflected in socio-economic differences. Within urban areas, too, schools run by the private sector or by missionary organizations are by and large considered better than government-run schools.

English versus Indian languages as medium of instruction: A related issue flowing from the difference in quality is the debate over the medium of education, where English is pitted against the vernacular Indian languages. It is a fact, one that perhaps reflects our colonized past, that fluency in and a sound knowledge of English equips individuals with several socio-economic advantages: it provides greater access to influential sections of society, affords better employment opportunities, including international jobs, and facilitates the path to higher education. Also, most English medium schools and colleges have better infrastructure, teaching staff and pedagogical outcomes than those that impart education in Indian languages.

Outdated syllabi, teaching methods: Barring a relatively small number of schools, the Indian education system largely encourages learning by rote, which privileges memorization over critical thinking. This hinders the development of critical problem-solving skills in students. The syllabus, too, is often not changed for years, with the result that students are made to learn outdated concepts and theories. Students' ability to adapt to a world of fast-evolving socio-economic challenges is compromised from the very outset.

Shortage of qualified teachers: The country may have 8.5 million teachers on record, but many of them are ghost teachers who exist only in official records. Many of the teachers lack adequate training and qualification to teach. This problem is particularly acute in rural areas. UNESCO's State of Education Report, 2021 pointed out that 11.16 lakh positions of teachers were lying vacant in government schools across the country. This number has been on the rise, which is a troubling fact. There are government schools in the country with just one teacher for different classes. Other surveys have shown that on any given day, 25 per cent of teachers in government schools in India are absent from work. It gets worse: only 60 per cent of the teachers who are present are actually teaching.[21]

In a July 2017 judgement, Justice Adarsh Kumar Goel and Justice Uday Umesh Lalit of the Supreme Court said: 'To make the right to education meaningful, a qualified teacher undoubtedly has a significant role.' According to a United Nations International Children's Emergency Fund (UNICEF) report, the percentage of trained teachers in India increased from 53.5 per cent in 2014 to 69.5 per cent in 2019. However, the quality of training and support provided to teachers leaves much to be desired. Perhaps one should go further to stress that more than 'qualified teachers', the country needs 'quality teachers'. Many who become teachers do have the necessary qualifications, but the reality is that they lack quality.

Here it is imperative to ask a crucial question: certainly, the RTE is in place, but how much difference will it make without quality education? This implies that the right to quality education has a direct correlation to the right to quality teachers. Unless quality teachers are provided, the RTE Act does remain a law without the potency to show tangible results on the ground. Part of the blame must fall on successive governments over the years, for utilizing teachers for non-academic work. In many instances, governments use teachers in villages for rolling out and implementing various government welfare schemes and programmes, and updating of electoral rolls. During elections, teachers are drafted into the task of working in polling stations. All this diverts teachers from their core responsibility of teaching and school administration.

Therefore, it is not surprising that many bright and talented youth do not opt for teaching as a career. Not only is it not remunerative, but teaching positions also often offer little scope for personal and professional growth for individuals who want to take up teaching. Therefore, high pupil–teacher ratios, coupled with insufficient professional development opportunities, compromise teaching quality and student learning outcomes.

Research carried out by various government and non-governmental organizations has highlighted the poor quality of teachers and learning environment, which can have a negative impact on a child's development. The majority of teachers lack the knowledge, skills, attitude and passion to teach and connect with the new generation. Many, still cast in the old mould, resort to corporal punishment in spite of the fact that it is prohibited under the RTE Act, 2009. Apart from bodily trauma, corporal punishment leaves a psychological scar on children's minds for they associate scholastic endeavours with pain and punishment.

Deficient infrastructure: Another area of concern pertains to the lack of essential facilities for imparting quality education. Not only are facilities such as libraries, laboratories and functional toilets missing in many a government school across India, essential teaching aids like textbooks, blackboards and even classrooms are conspicuous by their absence. This obviously hinders effective teaching and learning. The absence of the requisite infrastructure impedes academic progress, and also compromises students' health and well-being.

Socio-economic barriers: Students from poor families belonging to historically disadvantaged groups and other marginalized communities face major sociocultural and economic barriers to accessing quality education. Children from such backgrounds find it doubly difficult to overcome the educational inequities that perpetuate poverty and social exclusion.

Indicating that he was aware of this problem, Nehru, in a message to the Hindustani Talimi Sangh, in 1957, expressed himself eloquently: 'In the final analysis, no subject is of greater importance than that of education. It is men and women of a country that make and build a nation, and it is education that is supposed to make and build those men and women.'[22]

The failure of the education system has consequences that go beyond the realm of education. It has economic implications as well. A poorly educated population undermines India's ability to fully leverage the potential of its demographic dividend. It hampers the ability of the country to compete on equal terms with peer nations, as a poorly educated workforce limits productivity, technology absorption and innovation; these, in turn, impede the country's growth potential and impact its long-term prosperity.

ONE OF THE FEW SILVER LININGS: PUTTING TECHNICAL EDUCATION IN PLACE

Even though the Indian government, post-Independence, failed to nurture a sound primary education system in the country, it did succeed in putting in place a system of technical education that trained a tiny sliver of the country's educated population, and equipped it to compete on equal terms with the best in the world.

The IITs are the standard bearers of this elitist education system; but there are other institutions of comparable quality. They include the Indian Institutes of Management (IIMs) and private sector bodies such as the Indian Institute of Science (IISc), which predates the IITs and IIMs, the Tata Institute of Social Sciences (TISS), Birla Institute of Technology and Science (BITS), Manipal Institute of Technology, XLRI, Indian School of Business (ISB), and a few others. There are also several traditional universities such as the University of Delhi, the University of Mumbai, and the University of Calcutta, and others like Jawaharlal Nehru University, Ashoka University and Jadavpur University that have built well-deserved reputations for imparting quality education.

Commenting on Nehru's views about the role of education, Nobel Laureate Amartya Sen said: 'Although Nehru had the understanding of primary education, and was committed to it, in terms of channelling resources, priorities or planning, there was a big failure. His attitude to primary education was deeply lamentable in my view, but he did understand one thing—the importance of technical education.'[23]

In 1950, following the Nalini Ranjan Sarkar report that recommended the setting up of technical institutes in India on the lines of the Massachusetts Institute of Technology (MIT), the Government of India set up the first IIT at Kharagpur in West Bengal in 1951. A total of 210 students were admitted in the first batch. The plan was to increase admissions to 1,320 over the next five years. Four more IITs opened during Nehru's helmsmanship, in Delhi, Bombay (now Mumbai), Kanpur and Madras (now

Chennai). This pioneering and visionary move set the stage for the emergence of arguably the best-known Indian brand globally. It gladdens my heart to be connected to this brand: as mentioned in the Preface, I studied in Roorkee University, independent India's first engineering university. Established in 1847 as Roorkee College, it was designated an IIT in 2001.

The IITs have produced some of the most successful entrepreneurs, scientists, technocrats and corporate leaders who have stamped their presence not only on the Indian landscape but across the world. The list of IIT alumni reads like a who's who across the spectrum: Sundar Pichai, CEO of Alphabet; Vinod Khosla, co-founder of Sun Microsystems; and Arvind Krishna, CEO of IBM, among several others. Within India, the IITs have produced pioneering entrepreneurs like Infosys co-founders N.R. Narayana Murthy and Nandan Nilekani, Flipkart co-founder Sachin Bansal, and Zomato co-founder Deepinder Goyal. These institutions have played a big role in India's emergence as a technology powerhouse. For this, we have to thank the vision and foresight of India's first prime minister and his fascination with science.

THE CONSEQUENCES OF INDIA'S LOPSIDED EDUCATION SYSTEM

The focus on elite institutions to the exclusion of primary and secondary education has led to a skewed situation: below the thin layer of some excellent colleges and technical education institutions is a sprawling bottom of the rest of the education system in which the quality of learning outcomes is far below acceptable standards. In effect it means that barring a few thousand graduates of the IITs and a few other institutions, the vast majority of Indians are denied the opportunity of acquiring quality education that can improve their chances of social mobility.

Over decades, the success of a handful of higher-education institutions, juxtaposed with the failure of mass education, has created a class of well-educated Indians at home both in India and the world at large. In absolute terms they may number in the millions, but given India's population, they form a small percentage, like the proverbial drop in the ocean. Some of them become civil servants, others join the corporate sector, and yet others become academics. Together, they have comprised the ruling class of the country for a long time.

Below this thin layer of well-educated people is the vast, chaotic mass of India comprising poorly educated or uneducated citizens lacking basic facilities and unable to access the fruits of development or leverage available opportunities to fulfil their own potential.

THE NEXT STEPS

What is the remedy for this unforgivable disparity? The irony is that every now and then there have been moments when the problems of the education system have been acknowledged, but not worked upon in a decisive manner.

Four decades ago, in 1985, the Ministry of Education, in a report titled 'Challenge of Education', rightly pointed out: '[M]any studies have shown that in the field of education, investments in elementary education yield the highest rate of returns and have a significant impact on productivity and general well-being of the masses.' It was an unerring diagnosis.

The report clearly stated, 'The analysis of developments over the last two decades makes it clear that desired improvements have not materialized because neither the resources nor the measures for restructuring were commensurate with the imaginative and purposeful thrust of the education policy adopted in 1968.'

The reference was to the years of Indira Gandhi's prime ministership, when there was seemingly a recognition of the problems of the education system, but little willingness to invest the desired political capital, effort and money required to overhaul the country's primary education system.

The 1985 report, which spoke of the National Policy on Education that was in the works, did demonstrate a sense of occasion, considering Rajiv Gandhi's refrain of looking ahead and preparing to step into the 21st century. 'Education is concerned essentially with the future. It has a holistic character. Therefore, everyone capable of contributing to it has a duty [...] to do so.' Further, 'If the new generation entering the 21st century finds itself ill-equipped, it will hold the present generation responsible for its inadequacies [...] Education is a national responsibility.' But, 40 years after the report was prepared, we are still talking about the inadequacies of the Indian education system at the grassroots.

To address the long-term shortcomings in the Indian education system, and to prepare Indians for the ongoing knowledge revolution, the government of India unveiled NEP 2024 in an endeavour to update NEP 2020 by adding operational elements. It seeks to achieve an ambitious overhaul of the education system at various levels, from early childhood care and education to vocational training from Std VI, the use of technology to improve teaching and learning, and restructuring higher education. The aim is to create a modern education system that arms Indian students with the knowledge tools needed to navigate the knowledge economy. Its key features include:

Vocational training: Providing internships, vocational training and on-the-job-learning programmes that have been integrated into the NEP to enable students to develop skills that equip them for the job market, and also prepare them for self-employment and entrepreneurship. On 7 February 2025, the Union Cabinet chaired by Prime Minister Modi approved funding worth ₹8,800 crore for the continuation of the Skill India Programme (which commenced in 2022–23) till 2026.

Competency-based assessment: Abandoning the principle of rote learning, NEP 2024 lays emphasis on competency-based assessments that focus on understanding and applying knowledge.

Global exposure: The new policy attempts to give students an international exposure in their respective fields of study by encouraging partnerships with foreign institutions, and facilitating exchange programmes.

Choice-based credit system: In place of the one-size-fits-all courses that have been the norm in India, the new policy provides for a choice-based credit system (CBCS) in higher education. Students can now choose courses from a wide menu of options in line with their interests and professional ambitions.

Holistic learning: The policy focuses on holistic learning, digital literacy and skill development.

Research opportunities: The policy places a strong emphasis on improving the quality of academic research within the country's higher education institutions and encourages establishment of research-intensive universities. The idea behind these institutions is that they should be well equipped, armed with cutting-edge technology, with a commitment to constant innovation.

Like the national policies on education in 1968 and 1986, NEPs 2020 and 2024 attempt to modernize the education system so that Indians can hold their place with the best in the world in a fast-expanding knowledge economy. Of course, their success will depend on effective implementation.

COMPREHENSIVE REFORMS NEEDED FOR A MODERN EDUCATION SYSTEM

As to what extent a policy translates on the ground depends on the kind of ecosystem it is introduced in. Catering to the needs of the world's largest student population is a challenging task. It would require a comprehensive approach and initiatives across the board to make the Indian education system ready for the challenges of the 21st century, such as policy reforms, fashioning a holistic approach to education, and community involvement, among others.

Three important policy decisions need to be considered to provide a robust framework for the Indian education system.

- An increase in financial allocation for a grossly underfunded Indian education system is a must. At present, the government spends about 3 per cent of GDP on education, as against the requirement of 6 per cent prescribed by the National Policy on Education 1968, the National Policy on Education 1986, and the NEP 2020.[24]
- Decentralized decision-making is the need of the hour. A top-down administration makes the education system dysfunctional, particularly in rural areas. Local school authorities have little power to adjust to local needs. Decentralization would, in

contrast, enable operating staff to be in continuous touch with local communities and consequently make changes to suit local circumstances. A bottom-up approach to education in place of the current top-down approach is likely to lead to better utilization of resources as well. Further, there should be a clear division of responsibility between the Centre and state while shaping the education system.

- In a fast-changing world, a specialized bureaucracy of educationists is better than generalists is a widely accepted opinion across the globe. In a well-written and insightful paper, 'The Case for an Indian Education Service', Dileep Ranjekar and S. Giridhar made a compelling point when they noted, 'India can become a developed nation only if it addresses the quality and scale of education in a manner such that it becomes a leader in knowledge creation and management.'

Reforming the education system to make it contemporary is absolutely essential if we are to work towards better learning outcomes. This requires changes in four significant areas—from curriculum and teacher training to technology adoption as well as community engagement:

Revamping the Curriculum

It is important to move beyond the method of rote learning and create a curriculum that encourages critical thinking, creativity, problem-solving and life skills—in short, an approach that engenders a holistic development of students. The curriculum should reflect:

i. **An accent on vocational training:** Employers often complain that the Indian education system does not produce people with employable skills. Thus, there is an urgent need to integrate vocational training and skill development programmes into the education curriculum to enhance employability in students.

ii. **An awareness of cultural sensitivity:** Living in the midst of incredible cultural diversity, Indian students need to learn to respect it. In the present-day context, a curriculum needs to be sensitive to issues of environmental sustainability as well, apart from reflecting the ethical values that enable the development of a well-rounded personality with an awareness of social responsibility.

Enhanced Teacher Training

Teachers trained in the latest teaching methods are critical for energizing students and inculcating a joy of learning in them. To create a pool of such teachers involves the following:

- **Continuous professional development:** Implementing continuous professional development programmes for teachers to enhance their pedagogical skills, subject knowledge and use of technology in teaching is important for desirable learning outcomes.
- **Recruitment and retention:** Strengthening teacher recruitment processes by paying competitive salaries and providing benefits and career advancement opportunities to ensure retention and high morale is critical for attracting talented individuals.
- **Emphasis on pedagogy:** Emphasizing innovative pedagogical approaches such as active learning, project-based learning and experiential learning will make classrooms more engaging and interactive.

Adopting New Technologies

For any education system to align with the requirements of fast-changing societies in today's world, engaging with and adopting technology in a constructive manner is imperative if the goal is to enhance learning outcomes. To achieve that:

- **Investing in ICT infrastructure is necessary:** This will facilitate digital learning, and help overcome geographical barriers, particularly in remote and underserved areas.
- **Digital content development is crucial:** It is necessary to leverage technology to develop high quality digital content, including multimedia resources, educational apps and online courses, to supplement traditional teaching methods and cater to diverse learning needs.
- **Enabling teachers to be tech-savvy:** Teachers must be trained to effectively integrate technology into their teaching methods. These include the use of educational software, online collaboration tools and learning management systems.

Ensuring Community Engagement

The community has a crucial stake in seeing that the education system works well. Accordingly, regular interaction between the education system and the society it serves is desirable. To ensure this, there must be:

- **Parental involvement:** Teachers must be encouraged to actively involve parents and guardians in the education of their children through regular meetings, workshops and outreach programmes.
- **Collaborations with civil society:** The education system must partner with NGOs, civil society

organizations and community leaders to address educational challenges, promote literacy campaigns and support marginalized groups.

- **Collaboration with industry:** There must be a systematic method whereby industry partners provide internships and mentorship programmes to bridge the gap between what students learn in the classroom and the skills they require at the workplace.

HITS AND MISSES

Some positives have been revealed in ASER 2024:

- Enrolment in the age group 3–5 years in pre-primary institutions has improved across the country between 2018 and 2024. The enrolment of 3-year-olds rose from 68.1 per cent in 2018 to 77.4 per cent in 2024, of 4-year-olds from 76 per cent in 2018 to 83.3 per cent in 2024; and of 5-year-olds from 58.5 per cent in 2018 to 71.4 per cent in 2024.
- Across all states enrolment in the elementary age group 6–14 years is above 95 per cent.
- Since 2022, there has been an improvement in the reading levels of children in government schools at the all-India level across all elementary grades (Std I–VIII).
- Nationwide, basic arithmetic levels of children in elementary grades (Std III, V, VIII) reached the highest level in over a decade both in government and private schools.

But it is not a uniformly cheery picture. As expressed by Dhir Jhingran in an article in *The Indian Express* on 6 February 2025, 'These gains can, however, only offer some temporary satisfaction. We have a huge mountain to climb.

He points out that ASER reflects that 'learning gains are mainly at the primary stage. The Grade VIII results are not encouraging.'[25] Reason: the middle school (Std VI–VIII) curriculum is heavy, and availability of subject teachers for science, mathematics and English is a problem that needs focusing on, he adds.

That is not all. There is another serious takeaway, as demonstrated in ASER 2024: 'Learning improvements […] have been small over the past two decades. At this rate, we will take another 20–25 years to achieve the goal of at least 80 per cent of children mastering FLN [foundational literacy and numeracy] skills.'

◆

The conclusion is inescapable. Although the Indian education system has come a long way since Independence, notching up some hits and many more misses, the challenges of creating an inclusive, equitable and quality education system in a rapidly evolving world are immense. At a media conference, Dr Amartya Sen summed up the Indian education system by pointing out that while a small group of privileged people are well trained, 'our educational system remains deeply unjust'.[26]

It is time to prove that we are equal to the challenge of creating an education system in which every child is valued, and students are enabled to engage with the demands and opportunities of the 21st century, in the process taking their country to greater heights.

Educated individuals can make better-informed choices about various aspects of their life, including healthcare. Education and public healthcare constitute the bedrock of social and economic growth. Having shone a light on the state of India's education system, it is necessary to examine the state of our public health system as well.

9

PUBLIC HEALTH: IN NEED OF REVITALIZATION

India poses a conundrum on the health front: it is the fourth largest economy in the world, poised to be the third largest in a few years, next only to the US and China, but it has a relatively low per capita income and possibly the lowest health spend to GDP ratio compared to most emerging economies in Asia. India's economic narrative is about a growth surge powered by intent and policy, but its public health system tells a markedly different story of disparities, one that continues to be plagued by a lack of vision and ownership. The disparities are many: between rural and urban, government and private, rich and poor, and gender and caste as well.

It's a truth that has been tested by all nations that have ascended the economic scale, from the Western world to Southeast Asia: investing in the health and well-being of citizens is not only vital to increased productivity and inclusive growth; it results in the long-term health of the nation. This is particularly so when health is defined as 'a state of complete physical, mental and social well-being and not merely the absence of disease or infirmity'.[1] Over the decades, a comprehensive approach to health has emerged, based on the understanding that health is not about medical care alone. It is as much about nutrition, clean water, good sanitation and mental well-being, among others.

India's health system presents a confusing reality: a large majority of its population resides in rural areas, but nearly all major medical resources are in urban areas. In a country boasting one of the world's largest economies, access to healthcare services is still not easy for the vulnerable sections of society. Stories of indebtedness caused by out-of-pocket expenditure on healthcare are too common. According to experts, almost two-thirds of health expenditure is at the initial stage of doctor visits, drugs and diagnostics, even before hospitalization.

At the same time, there have been instances of significant success in some aspects of public health as well, be it the drive to eradicate smallpox and polio or the HIV/AIDS programme that resulted in HIV incidence coming down by 50 per cent in the first decade of the 21st century.

EVOLUTION, ROLE AND QUALITY OF THE PUBLIC HEALTH SECTOR IN INDIA

Clearly, the public health sector presents a complex landscape.

As for the distortions and disparities across the health system, we need to look at its evolution post-Independence. The fledgling new nation adopted the Bhore Committee (1946) recommendations as the basis for developing its public health system. The central idea was that the state would finance and provide health services to all citizens regardless of their paying capacity, with primary healthcare being the most important point of access for the community. Every level of the three-tier structure—primary, secondary and tertiary—would be characterized by the integration of preventive, curative and promotive care. It was hoped that the system would be in place in three or four decades.

A combination of circumstances decided otherwise. The clutch of issues facing the newly independent nation were enormous. Health services, which had to joust with the pressing demands of many other sectors in the FYPs, received less-than-adequate outlays. Moreover, the urgency to deal with the debilitating impact of infectious diseases was such that over time the public health system became a vehicle for vertical disease control programmes, or centrally driven programmes with the objective of eradicating a particular disease. '[T]he thinking that rural areas can do with [only] a few public health and disease control interventions while urban areas would need [comprehensive] medical care took root at this time, resulting in the fragmented approach to the building of the health system,' observes former Union Health Secretary Sujatha K. Rao in her well articulated book *Do We Care? India's Health System.*[2] As the idea of the primary healthcare integrating preventive and curative medicine took a back seat, the private sector stepped in to occupy the curative slot. One consequence was the rising graph of out-of-pocket expenses, and a growing disparity in the ability to access healthcare services.

Describing India's 'mixed' health system as having evolved by default and not by design, K. Srinath Reddy states, 'We have several disconnected pieces in our health architecture which we now need to build into a cohesive whole [...] We need to prioritize primary healthcare as we do so. Rural primary care [...] needs more financial and human resources and improved public health management systems. Urban primary care, long ignored, needs to step off the starting block...'[3]

In India's federal framework, public health and hospitals are a state subject, but the Centre has concurrent powers on subjects like drugs, medical education, food security, prevention of infectious diseases, among others. This has led to a position where the states have to depend on the Centre for funds. The Centre has always decided the health agenda, say experts. It gives state governments financial and technical support to fortify their healthcare services.

The quality and effectiveness of public health programmes, which aim to improve the availability of and access to quality healthcare, especially for those living in rural areas, have come in for their share of criticism. Public health infrastructure, including primary health centres (PHCs) and district hospitals, often grapples with chronic issues like understaffing, inadequate resources and subpar facilities. These serious drawbacks hinder the delivery of comprehensive healthcare services, and jeopardize the quality of care.

Notwithstanding these systemic weaknesses, India has achieved success in some aspects of public health:

- The average life expectancy of Indians, which was only 32 years in 1947, has more than doubled to 70.8 years, according to the World Health Organization's (WHO) World Health Statistics 2021.[4]
- The maternal mortality rate has been brought down from 2,000 per 1,00,000 live births at the time of Independence to 97 in 2018–2020.[5]
- The infant mortality rate (IMR) improved to 28 per 1,000 births in 2022 as compared to 81 per 1,000 births in the 1990s, according to WHO and 146 per 1,000 in 1951.[6]

LOOMING CHALLENGES

India is undergoing a demographic and environmental transition, and these factors are adding to communicable, non-communicable and emerging infectious diseases. Even as India struggles to cope with and overcome long-existing conditions like malnutrition and infectious diseases like tuberculosis (TB) among the poorer strata of society, it faces the challenge of combating diabetes, heart ailments, addictions and mental health conditions among other sections of society.

The only way to effectively address these is through an 'efficient, equitable and empathetic' health system.[7] For that it is critical that issues of low public expenditure on healthcare, lack of adequate number of public health institutions in the country and official apathy are addressed.

CONSTITUTIONAL AND POLICY FRAMEWORK

While health is included in the Indian Constitution's Directive Principles of State Policy, the right to health has been read into the right to life guaranteed under Article 21 of the Constitution in several judicial pronouncements. However, the reach of healthcare to the marginalized and underserved communities remains a critical issue.

Several official committees have reviewed and recommended improvements to the public health system, starting with the Bhore Committee in 1946, with primary healthcare at the core of the public health system. This gave rise to an infrastructure of PHCs, community health centres (CHCs) and subcentres in the country. There have been about 25 expert committees over nearly eight decades,[8] among them the oft-quoted Mudaliar Committee (1959), which was the first to flag the issue of inadequate outlays by the state for setting up PHCs and having the required personnel strength.

The National Health Policy (NHP) of 1983 was framed in the wake of WHO's seminal Alma-Ata Declaration (1978) of 'Health for All by 2000'. The policy accepted that health was at the centre of development and acknowledged the importance of non-medical interventions (nutrition, clean air, water and sanitation) as well as preventive interventions for improved healthcare. Action points included focusing on creating a good network of comprehensive primary healthcare services providing integrated healthcare within a specified time frame.

The 2002 NHP, coming a decade after the push for liberalization of the economy, and two years after the Millennium Development Goals [MDG] Summit, aimed for 'an acceptable standard of good health amongst the general population of the country'. It mentioned expansion of healthcare infrastructure to neglected areas and groups, and greater investment in healthcare on the part of the Union government, fixing 55 per cent of the health allocation to primary-level healthcare services. At the same time, NHP 2002 also saw a role for the private sector, especially in secondary and tertiary care, which was not affordable for the majority of the population. The policy suggested health insurance as a way out. In that sense the idea of universal healthcare was diluted.

In 2005, the then government at the Centre launched the National Rural Health Mission (NRHM) to shore up the public health system, which had weakened in the decade following liberalization. As Rao notes, the NRHM put in place some 'processes for people's participation and widened access to basic healthcare'.[9] It also sought to encourage states to participate. The former Union Health Secretary noted that a threefold increase in the budget provided resources to recruit community health workers, and 0.15 million personnel for healthcare facilities. 'Since

2005, institutional deliveries have increased from 47 per cent to 68 per cent, doubling the rate of decline in maternal and infant mortality compared to the period prior to NRHM.'[10] Immunization was also stepped up. Still, as she notes, the NRHM's focus was limited to securing some essential services only.

After a long gap, NHP 2017 was framed, with an accent on access, affordability and accountability.

NHP 2017 lays emphasis on allocating a major share of the healthcare expenditure to primary healthcare, creating patient-centric institutions and laying down standards for treatment quality. The policy envisaged augmenting the health infrastructure and providing free drugs and diagnostics, and essential healthcare in all public hospitals. The NHP's key goal was to raise the life expectancy at birth from 67.5 years to 70 years by 2025 and reduce infant mortality to 28 by 2018.

AYUSHMAN BHARAT: A COMPREHENSIVE LOOK AT PUBLIC HEALTHCARE

To actualize NHP 2017's theme of universal health coverage, in 2018, the Union government announced its flagship scheme, Ayushman Bharat. The scheme has attempted to move away from a segmented approach on health service delivery to a comprehensive need-based healthcare service. The initiative proposes to help the government in meeting the United Nations' Sustainable Development Goals (SDGs), along with its underlining commitment, which is to leave no one behind.

Ayushman Bharat's aim is to holistically address the healthcare system at the primary, secondary and tertiary levels. It has two interrelated components. The first consists of transforming 1.5 lakh existing sub-centres and PHCs into health and wellness centres (HWCs) that would deliver comprehensive primary healthcare or a range of services, thus bringing healthcare closer to the citizens. Moreover, the emphasis is on health promotion and prevention by encouraging people to choose healthy practices that reduce the risk of contracting diseases.

The second component of Ayushman Bharat is the Pradhan Mantri Jan Arogya Yojana or PM-JAY, a scheme that provides a health cover of ₹5 lakh per family per year for secondary and tertiary care hospitalization to over 12 crore poor and vulnerable households and covers about 55 crore beneficiaries who account for the bottom 40 per cent of the Indian population. The scheme is free of cost for the beneficiaries, and is fully government-funded, with the central and participating state governments sharing the cost of its implementation. PM-JAY provides cashless access to healthcare services, and is designed to mitigate the burden of expensive medical treatment, which pushes nearly 6 crore Indians into poverty every year and covers up to three days of pre-hospitalization and 15 days post-hospitalization expenses such as diagnostics and medicines.[11] While the scheme has contributed to strengthening both public and private healthcare infrastructure, a range of challenges continues to exist.

BUDGETARY PROVISIONS OF NHP 2017 AND COMPARISON WITH PEERS

NHP 2017 made one important commitment: 'raising public health expenditure progressively to 2.5 per cent of the GDP by 2025'[12] from 1.2 per cent of GDP in 2019–20. This would include expenditure by the Union government as well as state governments.

A report on the PIB website showed the progression

in the health spend in the previous years: 'in keeping with this objective, central and state governments' budgeted expenditure on the health sector reached 2.1 per cent of GDP in FY23 (budget estimate) and 2.2 per cent in FY22 (revised estimate), against 1.6 per cent in FY21.'[13]

Even though this is an improvement over India's historically low spending on healthcare, it still lags behind neighbouring nations in Asia. In 2022, China spent 7.05 per cent of its GDP on health, while Sri Lanka spent 4.07 per cent of its GDP on this count in 2021.[14]

MENTAL HEALTH IN FOCUS

In a move to bring public healthcare in India in line with global standards, the National Mental Health Policy (2014) was framed to provide for mental healthcare services for persons suffering from mental illness. Promoting de-stigmatization of mental illnesses, providing accessible, affordable and quality treatment with a view to their socio-economic inclusion is an important aspect of the policy.

To bring mental healthcare within the reach of many more people, the Union government launched the National Tele Mental Health Programme (NTMHP) in 2022 to improve access to quality mental health counselling and related services. As on 23 July 2024, 36 states and UTs had set up 53 Tele Cells for this purpose.

THE BURDEN OF DISEASE

Even as there are attempts to view healthcare more comprehensively, a long-standing issue such as the burden of diseases remains a major concern:

- Despite the strides made in recent decades, India remains the TB capital of the world, accounting for 2.9 million of the 10.6 million TB cases that occur every year. India constitutes over 28 per cent of the global case load.[15]
- It is estimated that 2.5 million Indians are HIV infected: about 7.6 per cent of the global case load of 33 million.[16]
- On average, 1.5 million Indians are afflicted by malaria every year.[17]
- About 41 per cent of the world's filarial disease patients are found in India.[18]
- In 2007, India accounted for nearly half the world's leprosy cases.[19]
- As many as 35 million Indians carry viral hepatitis B.[20]
- India sees more than 300 million cases of acute diarrhoea every year in children below 5 years. It ranks as the third highest cause of infant mortality in India.[21]

These and other communicable diseases result in high morbidity rates. However, non-communicable diseases are the biggest killer, causing 42 per cent of all deaths in the country.[22] According to a report in *The Times of India* dated 19 February 2024, the 10 leading causes of death in India are:

1. Ischemic heart disease
2. Stroke
3. Chronic obstructive pulmonary disease
4. Lower respiratory infections
5. Diarrhoeal diseases
6. TB
7. Diabetes
8. Neonatal disorders
9. Chronic kidney disease
10. Liver disease

In addition, India is home to the highest number of blind people in the world; and 2–2.5 million Indians suffer from cancer.[23] In such circumstances the lack of an efficient public health system becomes all too evident.

Here, it is important to mention India's handling of the Covid-19 caseloads and minimizing viral spread. It showed that the country's health system can rise to the occasion when faced with a once-in-a-lifetime crisis. Initially, when the pandemic struck, India seemed ill-prepared to face the onslaught of this new virus. At that point, India had the world's second largest population and a healthcare sector whose functioning left a lot to be desired. The initial prognosis was not encouraging, following which there was an apprehension of millions of deaths in many quarters. But that did not come to pass thanks to a concerted attempt by the country's political leadership, scientific community, healthcare professionals and civil society. From the development of a vaccine to the administration of 2 billion doses to the adult population, an exercise coordinated through CoWIN, the digital platform created for the exercise, the process spoke for itself. India was also among the first to introduce rapid antigen tests, along with RT-PCR tests. Ironically, while this strategy was initially criticized, it was later adopted by WHO.

However, as experts point out, a health system needs to be functional at all times, capable of carrying out all its activities along with the priority task at hand. That is the measure of an efficient health system.

GLOBAL RANKING: A MEDIOCRE REPORT CARD

In the 2021 Global Health Security [GHS] Index prepared by the Johns Hopkins Centre for Health Security, India ranked 66th out of 195 countries. The index assesses countries on the basis of their performance in six categories: prevention, detection and reporting, rapid response, health system, compliance with international norms, and risk environment. The performance in each category is judged on the basis of 37 key indicators and 171 questions. The latter includes queries relevant to the country being assessed. As compared to India's 66th rank, China, Sri Lanka and the UK were ranked 52nd, 105th and 7th, respectively. A perusal of India's performance in each category would be instructive[24]:

Prevention: In this category, India scored an undistinguished 29.7, as can be seen in Figure 9.1, and was ranked 85th out of 195 countries. India's ability to track and monitor anti-microbial resistance, which is a constituent of this category, was found unsatisfactory. However, the GHS website did make the point that 'the global average for the prevention of the emergence or release of pathogens is 28.4 out of 100, making it the lowest-scoring category within the GHS Index'.[25]

Detection and reporting: India fared better in this particular category with an overall rank of 51 in the GHS Index. More importantly, the strength and quality indicators of India's laboratory system were ranked first in the world for their capacity to detect diseases, especially WHO-defined core tests. That and India's capacity for testing during public health emergencies positioned it at the top of the list on this parameter. However, India's poor laboratory supply chains and its projected inability to scale up its transport system to deal with public health emergencies have brought its overall score down on this parameter.[26]

Rapid response: The GHS Index defines this category as 'rapid response to and mitigation of the spread of an epidemic'. Indicators in this category assess emergency preparedness and response planning, exercising response plans, emergency response operation, linking public health and security authorities, risk communication, access to communications infrastructure, and trade and travel restrictions. No country 'scored in the top tier [...] with 58 per cent of countries scoring below average'. India stood 139th in the rankings.[27]

Health system: India's rank of 56 appears commendable at first sight considering its large populace, low per capita income, and large gaps in its healthcare delivery infrastructure, which makes accessibility difficult. In fact, it would have ranked much higher, but for the abysmal 193rd rank on parameters such as access to primary health services and constitutional guarantee for the right to medical care. Paradoxically, India was ranked right on top on 'communications with healthcare workers during a public health emergency, infection control practices and availability of equipment'.[28]

Compliance with international norms: To be placed 92nd in this category indicates a poor overall performance, but within this section, India bagged the top spot on international commitments, and the 12th spot in its commitment to Sharing of Genetic and Biological Data and Specimens. However, it was placed 137th on cross-border agreements on public health and animal health emergency.[29]

Risk environment: India was placed 73rd in overall risk environment and country vulnerability to biological threats. However, within the respond category, it was ranked 51st on early detection and reporting epidemics of potential international concern. This suggests that the country needs a law to deal with such exigencies in the future.

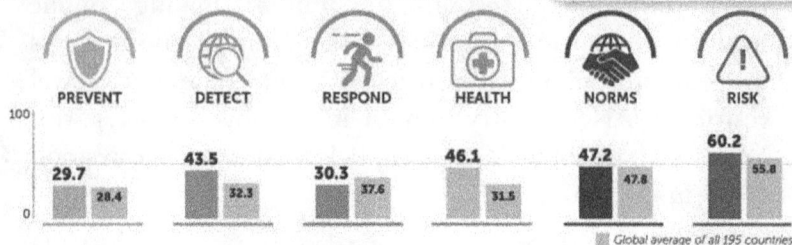

India — 42.8 Index Score — 66/195

	2019 SCORE	2021 SCORE	2021 GLOBAL AVERAGE
PREVENTION	**29.7**	**29.7**	**28.4**
Antimicrobial resistance (AMR)	50	50	45.3
Zoonotic disease	29.5	29.3	19.8
Biosecurity	24	24	18.7
Biosafety	0	0	20.9
Dual-use research and culture of responsible science	0	0	2.6
Immunization	75	75	63.3
DETECTION AND REPORTING	**37.2**	**43.5**	**32.3**
Laboratory systems strength and quality	75	87.5	44.9
Laboratory supply chains	0	0	15.9
Real-time surveillance and reporting	75	75	34.6
Surveillance data accessibility and transparency	23.3	23.3	34.7
Case-based investigation	0	25	16.9
Epidemiology workforce	50	50	46.5
RAPID RESPONSE	**42.1**	**30.3**	**37.6**
Emergency preparedness and response planning	41.7	41.7	30.4
Exercising response plans	12.5	25	21.1
Emergency response operation	33.3	33.3	27
Linking public health and security authorities	0	0	22.1
Risk communication	58.3	70.8	57.9
Access to communications infrastructure	48.6	41.2	65.7
Trade and travel restrictions	100	0	39

Scores are normalized (0-100, where 100 = most favorable)

	2019 SCORE	2021 SCORE	2021 GLOBAL AVERAGE
HEALTH SYSTEM	**46.1**	**46.1**	**31.5**
Health capacity in clinics, hospitals, and community care centers	37.1	36.9	30
Supply chain for health system and healthcare workers	16.7	16.7	28.5
Medical countermeasures and personnel deployment	0	0	10.3
Healthcare access	19.2	19.2	55.2
Communications with healthcare workers during a public health emergency	100	100	10.8
Infection control practices	100	100	40.5
Capacity to test and approve new medical countermeasures	50	50	45.1
COMPLIANCE WITH INTERNATIONAL NORMS	**47.2**	**47.2**	**47.8**
IHR reporting compliance and disaster risk reduction	50	50	58.5
Cross-border agreements on public and health emergency response	0	0	50
International commitments	100	100	56.1
JEE and PVS	25	25	18.7
Financing	41.7	41.7	35.2
Commitment to sharing of genetic and biological data and specimens	66.7	66.7	68.4
RISK ENVIRONMENT	**59.1**	**60.2**	**55.8**
Political and security risk	65.5	58.3	58.1
Socio-economic resilience	71.5	71.9	60.9
Infrastructure adequacy	33.3	50	50.2
Environmental risks	65.3	59.6	54.7
Public health vulnerabilities	59.9	61	55.3

Figure 9.1: Scores for India across the six categories of the GHS Index 2021[30]

THE ACHIEVEMENTS WORTH MENTIONING

While India's rank on the GHS Index might lend itself to reflection, there are achievements in the sphere of public health that need no reiteration. Despite the heavy burden of diseases, fund shortages and inadequate health infrastructure in India:

- Diseases like smallpox, yaws and guinea worm have been completely eradicated.
- India was certified polio-free by the Regional Polio Certification Commission on 27 March 2014.[31] The country completed 12 polio-free years on 13 January 2023.
- Appreciable progress has been made in the detection and treatment of TB. The Global TB Report released on 7 November 2023 revealed that:
  - Treatment coverage in India has improved to 80 per cent of estimated TB cases, marking an increase of 19 per cent over the previous year.
  - India's efforts have resulted in the reduction of TB incidence by 16 per cent in 2022 (from 2015), which is almost double the pace at which the incidence of TB has been declining globally (8.7 per cent).
  - TB mortality has also reduced by 18 per cent during the same period (2015–22), both in India and globally. WHO has made a downward revision of India's TB mortality rates from 4.94 lakh in 2021 to 3.31 lakh in 2022, a reduction of over 34 per cent.[32]

These achievements point to the success of the public health system's continued focus on infectious disease control in the last almost eight decades.

INADEQUATE INFRASTRUCTURE

Notwithstanding these accomplishments, the poor quality of overall healthcare provided by India's public health system is too glaring to be ignored. A 2023 report by Knight Frank, the global real estate consultancy, stated that India faces a deficit of 2 billion square feet of healthcare space. Currently, India has a bed-to-population ratio of 1.3 per 1,000 people, private and public hospitals combined, well short of the accepted global ratio of 3 beds per 1,000, and a lot less than that of US, UK, China and Japan, as can be seen in Table 9.1. Knight Frank estimated that overall this works out to a shortage of 2.4 million hospital beds across India.[33] NHP 2017 envisaged the availability of 2 beds per 1,000 people, which was well short of the required figure.

Table 9.1

Existing bed-to-population ratio
and doctors-to-population ratio[34]

	No. of beds (per 1,000 people)	No. of doctors (per 1,000 people)
US	2.9	2.6
UK	2.5	5.8
China	4.3	2.0
Japan	13.0	2.5
India	1.3	0.9

QUALITY OF THE HEALTH WORKFORCE

One of the biggest strengths of any health system is its workforce. It is an aspect of the health system in the country that is problematic. India produces 70,000–80,000 medical graduates every year.[35] Barring a handful of institutions, the general quality of medical education and the challenges faced by medical graduates is cause for concern.

India's medical education curriculum has often been criticized for being outdated and excessively theoretical, with limited emphasis on practical skills. Furthermore, there is a severe shortage of postgraduate medical seats, resulting in intense competition. Allegations of admission irregularities in many a private college muddy the situation and raise concerns about the safety of patients.[36]

The government has been taking steps to address the problem of inadequate numbers of medical personnel in India. It has increased the number of medical colleges as well, primarily to bolster the number of MBBS seats:

- There has been an increase of 82 per cent in medical colleges from 387 before 2014 to 706 as on 12 December 2023.
- This has resulted in an increase of 112 per cent in MBBS seats from 51,348 before 2014 to 1,08,940 in 2023 and a 127 per cent rise in the number of postgraduate seats from 31,185 before 2014 to 70,674 in 2023.[37]

Augmenting the number of medical colleges is not enough; it is equally necessary to overhaul the system of medical education in India. As in many other fields of study, in medical studies, too, rote learning is prioritized over practical knowledge. Examinations test a student's ability to memorize and regurgitate textbook knowledge. Thus, their actual clinical and surgical skills are not tested till they begin working as doctors. Moreover, the medical syllabus in India is not updated regularly to include the latest breakthroughs in the discipline. The mode of education makes far less use of technology than in the developed countries.

As for the health workers in health centres and hospitals, poor pay and unsatisfactory working conditions pose a major impediment to improving the quality of public health delivery in India. To remedy this situation, the authorities must make concerted efforts to improve the efficiency of the recruitment process, fill vacant positions, focus on upskilling and reskilling of existing staff by providing timely and adequate training, provide career growth opportunities for the staff, and create an enabling environment that includes comfortable facilities for the workforce to live and work, particularly in rural areas.

RURAL–URBAN HEALTH DISPARITIES

One of the most pressing issues in India's public health sector is the alarming shortage of trained medical personnel, especially in rural areas.

According to WHO's 2018 data on India, the country had one of the lowest densities of health workers in the world:

- The density of physicians was 1:1428, and that of nurses 1: 584.
- The nurse-to-physician ratio in India was 0.6:1.

As per the government's December 2022 data, the nation has a doctor–population ratio of 1:834, better than the WHO-recommended norm of 1:1000, and a nurse–population ratio of 1:476.[38] However, the concentration of healthcare professionals in urban India, home to about 36 per cent of the country's populace, leaves the rural areas woefully underserved, resulting in delayed or inadequate medical care, and culminating in compromised health outcomes.[39] As is evident, this is a very significant constraint in the delivery of public health services in India, particularly in rural areas. Furthermore, government spending accounted for only 29 per cent of total expenditure on healthcare in India in 2014–15.[40] Of this, only a small percentage is spent in rural India.

A study titled Bharat Health Index 2023 by PayNearby found that only 25 per cent of India's rural and semi-rural population have access to modern medical facilities within their localities.[41] A report in *Business Standard* dated 11 August 2023 quoted Anand Kumar Bajaj, managing director and chief executive officer, PayNearby, as saying: 'Over 70 per cent of India resides in rural and semi-rural regions. More than 80 per cent of doctors, 75 per cent of dispensaries, 60 per cent of hospitals are concentrated in urban India, leaving [the] marginalized population to fend for themselves.'[42]

The same study found that 90 per cent of the people in rural India had to travel to different locations for specialized treatment, of whom 5 per cent reported losing a loved one because of the non-availability of doctors locally.

Another report titled 'Healthcare Access in Rural Communities in India' by Ballard Brief, a student-led social issue research library dedicated to publishing original analysis of relevant social issues, stated, 'In rural areas, primary health services are provided through sub-centres, PHCs, and CHCs meant to handle health needs at the most basic level for populations of 3,000–5,000 individuals.' Further, 'When compared to the Indian government's defined standards, India is 16 per cent below the number of PHCs and approximately 50 per cent below the number of CHCs it should have.' The report concluded that lower health indicators in rural communities were a direct reflection of the poor access to healthcare. It found that:

- About 86 per cent of medical visits in India are from individuals living in rural areas, whether to government or private medical facilities.
- The majority undertake a journey of over 100 km to access healthcare facilities where 70–80 per cent of the cost is paid out-of-pocket. Although poverty already has a negative effect on health, poverty in rural areas has been shown to have even greater negative effects than poverty in urban areas.
- Additionally, many measures of disease prevalence are underreported because of the difficulty associated with collecting data in rural areas, and because impoverished individuals are less likely to report things they perceive as negative about themselves. This fact suggests routine underdiagnosis and underreporting among India's poor, when compared to diagnostic or standard methods of measurement.[43]

The divide between rural and urban healthcare in India shows a huge contrast, reflecting the reality of inadequate healthcare infrastructure, a severe shortage of medical personnel, and limited access to essential medicines in rural India. This is all the more worrisome considering that rural health faces issues such as malnutrition, high maternal mortality rates, and restricted access to clean water and sanitation facilities, among others. These glaring disparities underscore the urgent need for targeted interventions to bridge the rural–urban healthcare gap, and thereby ensure equitable healthcare access.

Now, the problem of insufficient infrastructure is made worse by unfilled vacancies. As per *The Lancet* report in 2015[44]:

- Out of the 25,300 PHCs in the country, 8 per cent had no doctors, 38 per cent had no lab technicians and 22 per cent had no pharmacists.
- There were 83 per cent vacancies for surgeons, 76 per cent for gynaecologists, 83 per cent for physicians and 82 per cent for paediatricians in CHCs.[45]

Another serious issue is the number of informal healthcare providers with varied levels of education and training; they outnumber those with proper medical qualifications. A study, 'Healthcare Access in Rural Communities in India', in Ballard Briefs found that

- As many as 67 per cent of such 'informal' healthcare providers reported no medical qualifications.[46]
- Not surprisingly, 'correct diagnoses were rare' and incorrect treatments 'widely prescribed'.
- At several places, private clinics were found to be better than public ones across all quality metrics. So, even though these informal healthcare providers play an important role in providing last-mile medical care, especially in rural India, wrong treatment and incorrect prescriptions of drugs are common.[47]

A STARK CONTRAST

On the one hand there are rural health centres languishing for want of staff or suffering the consequences of being staffed by informal and untrained healthcare providers; on the other hand, healthcare facilities in some of the bigger cities and urban centres are at par with the best in the world. An estimated 7.3 million medical tourists were expected to visit India in 2024, according to credit rating agency Crisil. This segment of the Indian healthcare sector was valued at $7.69 billion in 2024, and is projected to touch $14.31 billion by 2029.[48]

A 2019 report by the global consultancy firm EY, along with the Federation of Indian Chambers of Commerce and Industry (FICCI), stated that the majority of medical tourists to India come from the SAARC region, Southeast Asia, West Asia and Africa.[49] Notably, patients from Australia, Canada, China, Russia, the United Kingdom and the United States are also increasingly visiting India for complex medical procedures.[50]

AN OVERHAUL OF PUBLIC INFRASTRUCTURE

For the various reasons discussed above, an efficient and equitable public health system is essential. Key indicators such as nutrition, infant mortality, life expectancy and maternal mortality offer important insights into the well-being of any society. However, India's health system is characterized by stark divides: between rural and urban, rich and poor, and government and private healthcare. The question is, what needs to be done to create a public health system that is in sync with the needs of the populace? Generally speaking, India's political leadership has never been fully invested in the subject of health, more specifically the public health system. That needs to change, for it is now understood that health and well-being are drivers of growth.

Increasing health spend: As a first step, the issue of increasing health spend to GDP ratio needs to be addressed. The target of NHP 2017 to reach the level of 2.5 per cent of India's GDP by 2025 remains unfulfilled. A recent study found only a marginal increase in public health expenditure, from 0.9 per cent to 1.6 per cent of GDP, which is well below the NHP's target.[51] As former bureaucrat Amarjeet Sinha observed: 'The National Health Mission, started in 2005 [then called NRHM], demonstrated how even from a little below to a little above 1 per cent of GDP public expenditure brought down IMR from 60 to 28, while the maternal mortality rate dipped from 406 to 97.' Further, he wrote, 'For us to reach the levels of the developed world, the centre and states need to provide that additional financial support to make a real difference...'[52]

A data-driven approach is important: A comprehensive database on diseases and a rigorous analysis of the data would provide timely pointers, or evidence, for urgent areas of focus and research. Excellence would be achieved by putting in place monitoring and evaluation mechanisms to ensure that the healthcare service being provided is responsive, effective and efficient in meeting specific needs. For instance, Sinha points out that out-of-pocket-expenditure happens to be the lowest in Tamil Nadu as the government has a 'robust system of generic drug supply through the Tamil Nadu Medical Services Corporation.' That is made possible because their 'digitized databases are linked to every district warehouse from where primary units and hospitals can indent and collect medicines through their passbooks'.[53]

Leveraging technology: It would be an important way of filling some of the infrastructure and resource gaps that have plagued the public health sector all these years. The adoption of telemedicine and video-conferencing facilities can help connect doctors and technical personnel in urban areas to patients in the rural hinterland. In fact, the national telemedicine platform eSanjeevani, which was launched in 2019, played an important role in enabling people to access doctors remotely during the Covid-19 pandemic, which had virtually paralysed the healthcare system.

Nikshay, the web-based system used by health workers around the country to register TB patients and monitor them, is yet another example of harnessing technology to bolster the health system. Launched in 2012 as part of the National TB Elimination Programme of the Ministry of Health and Family Welfare, Nikshay is not just a system to manage patients, it also provides timely data to the government. In 2018, the government launched the Nikshay Poshan Yojana. Under this programme, TB patients registered through Nikshay got a direct benefit transfer of ₹500 a month for their nutritional requirements. Leveraging technology for public healthcare is indeed a step in the right direction.

A public health cadre is essential: Tamil Nadu was one of the first states to introduce a distinctive public health cadre, putting the public health system on a solid footing. In fact, several expert committees have stated the importance of a public health cadre to manage the specific demands of a public health system that is multisectoral in nature. Public health managers, Rao points out, need to be able to 'integrate and converge health with other social determinants, community surveillance of diseases, building an environment of public participation, and a capability to enforce public health laws while effectively monitoring required skills in data management and analysis'.[54] Their training has to be in accordance with all of this.

Implementation is key: This is essential for shoring up the public health system. To give an instance, in 2022, Rajasthan became the first state in India to enact the Rajasthan Right to Health Act, 2022. However, a news report on 25 January 2025 revealed that the rules for the

Act had still not been framed. 'They said, as outlined in the Right to Health Act, a clear staffing policy should be implemented to ensure adequate deployment of qualified medical professionals, nurses and support staff in remote areas. Currently, hospitals in tribal regions face significant staffing shortages.'[55] The bottom line being that entrenched fault lines of inequality need to be addressed if India has to achieve its targets of inclusive growth.

In the federal set-up that informs our polity, this means that the Centre and states need to figure out how to work together. Often political calculations creep in, which affects public healthcare efforts. As always, it is the vulnerable who suffer. Avoiding excessive centralization and securing the community's involvement in the public health system is necessary.

◆

The current juncture is critical for India, for it seeks to join the select band of developed economies reigning on the growth chart. A country with a vast section of population that fares poorly on the health front is bound to have issues of instability.

The challenges India faces are substantial. It is the most populous country in the world today. India's population demographic is changing, too. It is true that the population growth rate is declining, but several million individuals are being added to the population every year. This will have an impact on the per capita availability of resources in crucial areas such as public health delivery.

Among other things, to prevent diarrhoeal deaths among children below five, clean water and good sanitation is a must. In a country where 35 out of 100 children are stunted,[56] providing nutrition becomes very important. All these social determinants mould individual and collective health and well-being, as do preventive interventions for maternal health and immunization. These along with medical care comprise a comprehensive package of public healthcare. Providing one at the expense of another will not work—those in a position to make a difference need to understand that.

The challenge of diseases on a broad scale is on the rise. Health experts are apprehensive about the possible outbreak of infectious diseases in the wake of climate change and its impact on the environment. Those who would be affected the most by these developments are the vulnerable and marginalized groups that the public health system ought to be reaching but is not. The problem is that every aspect of health mirrors a divide: between rural and urban, rich and poor; between states; and between caste and gender as well. Implementing a policy of health for all is the only way of creating conditions for a healthy and productive population that is equipped to face ever new challenges.

Public health also plays a vital role in shaping human capital, as a healthy population is essential for sustained productivity, learning and economic growth. Poor health outcomes such as malnutrition, high disease burden and inadequate access to healthcare limit individuals' ability to acquire education and skills, reducing the quality of the workforce. Thus, addressing public health challenges is crucial not just for individual well-being but also for unlocking precisely the kind of human capital that can be the tailwind in India's aspirations of global growth and development.

10

HUMAN CAPITAL: THE STORY OF INDIA'S WORKFORCE POTENTIAL

The present juncture could be the most interesting time to be an Indian, depending on the way things turn out over the next few decades.

For years the population explosion was described as a severe handicap to India's growth. However, for the past few decades, the idea that a large population can deliver a 'demographic dividend' of economic growth under certain circumstances has caught the world's attention.

A demographic dividend is made possible when, due to certain changes in the age composition of the population, those who are of working age (15–64) outnumber the non-working population (below 15 and above 64)—the calculation being that a society with a larger workforce and fewer dependants is well placed to achieve greater economic growth. The idea of a demographic dividend gained currency in the late 1990s 'to describe the interplay between changes in population age structure and fast economic growth in East Asia'.[1]

The good news is that India meets this basic condition of demographic transition. It is among the world's youngest countries: 52 per cent of its populace is aged 30 or below.[2] More importantly, the share of India's working-age population is poised to touch a high of 68.9 per cent by 2030. As for its dependency ratio, the proportion of individuals who are not in the labour force compared to those who are, it is the lowest ever at 31.2 per cent.[3] This ratio is used to gauge the pressure on the working-age population.

With a relatively young median age of 28.4 years, India can gain a competitive advantage in terms of its workforce as well as the consumption power of a young population. In that sense, it is perhaps the best time to be an Indian. However, it can only be the best time for Indians when the population has the human capital capable of creating economic value. OECD defines human capital 'as the stock of knowledge, skills and other personal characteristics embodied in people that helps them to be productive'.[4] According to the World Bank, human capital consists of 'the knowledge, skills and health that people invest in and accumulate throughout their lives, enabling them to realize their potential as productive members of society.'[5]

Therein lies the rub, for India faces an uphill challenge to overcome huge gaps in the education and skill sets of its burgeoning population. These negatives threaten to derail the country's development trajectory and dilute the demographic dividend of economic growth and prosperity promised by the presence of a large young population. Moreover, fast-moving AI-driven innovations, changes and disruptions, which are poised to upend global economic systems and supply chains, have created yet another level of difficulty for India, leading to very real fears of labour market disruptions on an unprecedented scale. India's quest for reaping the benefits of demographic dividend in an age of increasing automation and AI-driven processes will need to be driven by foresight, vision and strategic planning.

Economist and former governor of the RBI, Raghuram Rajan, aired his views on the subject at a conference titled 'Making India an Advanced Economy by 2047: What Will It

Take?' held at George Washington University in April 2024. 'I think we are in the midst of it [demographic dividend], but the problem is we are not reaping the benefits,' he stated.

Shakespeare described the juncture perfectly in Julius Caesar: 'There is a tide in the affairs of men, which, taken at the flood, leads on to fortune. Omitted, all the voyage of their lives is bound in shallows and in miseries. On such a full sea are we now afloat. And we must take the current when it serves or lose our ventures.'

India can ride this proverbial tide, and sail to a higher level of economic development if it can invest in and harness its human capital. Generally, in any society, the formation of human capital takes place as a result of investments in education and healthcare, on-the-job-training, and regular updating of workforce skills so as to keep abreast of new technologies that could keep the economy ahead of the curve.

As a World Bank document puts it, 'The main message of demographic dividend is that people are at the heart of development, but it is not automatic; prudent and timely policies are critical.'[6]

'Historically, demographic dividend has contributed up to 15 per cent of the overall growth of advanced economies.'[7] Demographic dividend helps in increasing the workforce, and there is rapid urbanization and industrialization. It leads to more investment in physical and human infrastructure. The productivity of a country's economy increases due to increased labour force. Demographic dividend will help create a massive move towards a middle-class society.

A considerable and concerted effort is required for that to happen. On the Human Capital Index (HCI) developed by the World Bank for its Human Capital Project, India ranks 116th out of 190 countries, while China ranks 45th.[8] The HCI, launched in 2018, measures contribution of health and education to the productivity of individuals and countries. The index, according to the institution, 'is a summary measure of the amount of human capital that a child born today can expect to acquire by age 18, given the risks of poor health and poor education that prevail in the country where she lives'.

According to the World Bank, the HCI is being used by countries 'to assess how much income they forgo because of human capital gaps, and how much faster they can turn these losses into gains if they act now'.[9]

India's low ranking on the HCI is owing to several factors, including challenges in health, education, and workforce inclusion. High child mortality rates, malnutrition, inadequate maternal and child healthcare, and stunting amongst children are some of the issues that plague the health sector. In terms of education, low quality education, poor learning outcomes, and gender and caste disparities in terms of access to education, particularly for girls and marginalized groups, need urgent attention. Finally, low levels of labour productivity, lesser number of women in the workforce, underinvestment in skill development and technology, and high unemployment and underemployment are perennial challenges as far as the workforce is concerned.

Chapters 8 and 9 have elaborated on the deficiencies of the country's education system and its public health system, respectively, showing that these sectors have not received serious attention from the political leadership even though they are critical to the nurturing of human capital. If anything, the education and health sectors have remained underfunded. Moreover, they continue to mirror the vast disparities that exist in the country: between rural and urban, rich and poor, government and private. This reduces the opportunities for social mobility.

Chapter 8 on the state of the education system states that according to the latest Annual State of Education Report, 2024, 50 per cent of Std V students are unable to read a Std II text, and fewer than 30 per cent of Std V students can solve a basic division problem. As for the Std VIII level, 45 per cent students are unable to do division, and 23 per cent can't do subtraction.[10]

The Indian education system is characterized by outdated curricula, a focus on rote learning rather than critical thinking and problem-solving skills, a lack of qualified teachers, and low investment in R&D.

Similarly, Chapter 9 reveals that decades of low spending, lack of well-trained healthcare professionals, inadequate infrastructure and poor working conditions have plagued the Indian health system. A large majority of the population lives in rural areas but the major medical resources are in urban areas. The marginalized who need public healthcare the most lack access to it. Decision-makers need to internalize the idea that healthcare is a combination of providing medical care, putting preventive health measures in place and addressing issues such as nutrition, sanitation, clean water. That is the way societies achieve health and well-being.

Now India is at a juncture where it has an opportunity to reap the demographic dividend. Chapters 8 and 9 illustrate the urgency of course correction in the education and health sectors. This chapter focuses on workforce inclusion and quality, skills and vocational training to tackle the challenges of new technologies, and an increase in participation of the female workforce. In a situation where millions of citizens still have to grapple with poverty and socio-economic disparities, the development of human capital becomes central to inclusive growth and economic empowerment.

AN INFLECTION POINT

India, which overtook China as the world's most populous nation recently, stands at a critical crossroads in its development journey. Armed with robust numbers with regard to its working-age population, it has a significant opportunity to achieve two interrelated goals of not only the country's economic growth but also individual betterment by nurturing its human capital. For the government, tackling the issues of poverty, illiteracy and unemployability is imperative. This will create an enabling environment of social mobility for those at the bottom rung of the socio-economic scale to move towards the ranks of the middle class.

UNDERSTANDING INDIA'S DEMOGRAPHY

However, it is important to get the lay of the land first. For instance, profound changes are taking place in India's demographic composition and they have a bearing on its development trajectory.

- According to the United Nations Population Fund's (UNFPA) State of the World Population Report, 2023, India's working-age population has risen to 68 per cent compared to 67.3 per cent in 2020, and 66 per cent in 2015. To put this in context, 69 per cent of China's population is in the working-age group, but the trendline there is falling: it was at 70.3 per cent in 2020 and 73 per cent in 2015.
- In 2023, India had a population of 1.428 billion compared to 1.425 billion for China.

- There is a wide variance in the status and pace of ageing in different states of India. For instance, the southern states are already ahead of the rest of the country in terms of demographic transition, and have a higher percentage of older people.
- This divergence in the age composition of different states points to different levels of development and health. Besides, they also reflect the different starting points of individual states at the start of the 2030 SDG Agenda. Addressing this variation in population statistics between states is a must.

A 2023 report by S&P Global Market Intelligence estimates that over the short term, India's economic growth would largely depend on its 678.6 million-strong workforce.[11] However, to fully unlock the potential of sustainable long-term growth, India would have to fulfil certain conditions. These include embarking on major labour reforms, training and upskilling its current workforce, so that it is ready to be a part of a global manufacturing hub—a dream that the current dispensation at the centre envisions—and encouraging more women to join the workforce.

WORLD'S LARGEST SUPPLIER OF WORKFORCE

By 2030, India's workforce would have grown to about 1.04 billion.[12] The country is expected to remain the world's largest supplier of workforce over the next decade, accounting for 24.3 per cent of the incremental global workforce.[13] In turn, this would give the country a significant advantage, as a rapidly ageing population in the developed world is expected to create various challenges for global supply chains. It is envisaged that the Indian population's relatively young median age of 28.4 years would effectively benefit from this trend.

The numbers speak for themselves. Today, about 26 per cent of the population is below 14 years of age, and about 67 per cent between 15 and 64 years. Only 7 per cent are above the age of 65.[14] In contrast, the 65-plus population in the US is about 17 per cent, and in Europe it is about 21 per cent.

These aspects align well with India's economic, strategic and geopolitical goals, but will translate into a positive outcome only when there is a strong focus on upskilling the labour force and improving women's participation in the workforce. The current government's flagship programme 'Make in India, Make for the World', aligns well with the labour advantage that India enjoys, and invites large multinational corporations to shift their manufacturing activities, along with parts of their supply chains, to India, leveraging the competitive advantage that the huge workforce provides. The current government has been trying to increase the share of manufacturing in the economy, which is service-oriented at present, with the service sector accounting for 30.7 per cent of the labour force, according to International Labour Organization (ILO) estimates.[15] However, raising the share of manufacturing is proving to be challenging in the absence of necessary reforms in land, labour and credit laws, collectively called factor reforms. Without these reforms and in the face of sagging consumer demand in the economy, the private sector seems unwilling to invest in increasing manufacturing capacity.

Despite the challenges, the global effort to diversify and de-risk supply chains from over dependence on China does present a wonderful opportunity for India to attract foreign direct investment (FDI) into the country, especially in the manufacturing sector, and provide employment to more of its army of young men and women.

A FINE EXAMPLE OF DEMOGRAPHIC DIVIDEND

One area in which India has shown its prowess is in the IT space; it is widely recognized as the world's back office. Over the last three decades, it has emerged as one of the leading exporters of IT and business process outsourcing (BPO) services.

Being able to produce the world's largest pool of English-speaking graduates in science, technology, engineering and mathematics (STEM) has given India a key competitive advantage over other countries. An estimated 21 lakh STEM graduates are being added to the pool every year, and of these, 47.4 per cent are women.[16]

This massive workforce provides a huge bank of talent capable of plugging shortages that may emerge within India and beyond. A well-trained workforce can give India the ability to address critical gaps in the global multi-nation supply chains that are critical to value chains in manufacturing across industries. Once these linkages are established, Indian talent will be able to benefit from global best practices and bring Indian expertise to the table.

Additionally, India has a massive pool of unskilled and semi-skilled workers. Sectors like construction, labour-intensive manufacturing, trade, transport, tourism, e-commerce logistics, etc., could absorb this section of the workforce. All this needs heavy investments on educating, training and upskilling.

THE DIVIDEND OF RISING PURCHASING POWER

Not only does India's young populace give it a competitive advantage in the manufacturing and service sectors, it also unleashes a virtuous cycle of consumption and increased demand. One just has to imagine a billion-strong populace spending on necessities and discretionary items. Young people typically spend more than older people (over their remaining lifespans) on assets like houses and cars, and on expenses such as children's education.

An EY report from April 2023 pointed out that rising consumption has driven economic growth over the past decade. Moreover, private final consumption expenditure (PFCE), which reflects consumer spending, has grown faster than GDP over the past decade, expanding at a compound annual growth rate (CAGR) of 11.3 per cent in nominal terms against a nominal GDP growth rate of 10.6 per cent. In fact, the ratio of PFCE to GDP has risen from 55 per cent to 60 per cent, states the report. Thus, with India expected to remain on a growth trajectory of 6–8 per cent over the next few years, consumption expenditure, too, is likely to grow in tandem with high macroeconomic growth rates and remain an important driver of economic expansion.

But this story of consumption expenditure would remain incomplete without a mention of its skewed nature. A report by Blume Ventures, a venture capital firm, states that only 130–140 million (13–14 crore) Indians out of a population of 1.4 billion comprise the 'consuming class'. Another 300 million (30 crore) Indians are 'aspirant' consumers who have started spending more money due to the ease of digital payments, while 1 billion lack the income needed for going beyond basic needs.[17]

CHALLENGES TO A DEMOGRAPHIC DIVIDEND

Further, there are some serious demographic challenges facing India:

- Unemployment is a major source of concern, with rates remaining high in both rural and urban India.

- Youth unemployment, between the ages of 15 and 29, is a big concern. It has been in double digits since 2017–18, when it touched 17.8 per cent.[18] Although it came down in 2023–24, it still remained in double digits.[19] If large numbers of young people cannot find gainful employment, the big positive of a large working-age population runs the risk of becoming the very opposite, with young people becoming restive. Hence, developing their skills to make them productive is crucial.
- Numerous studies have shown Indian graduates have a lower rate of employability.
- By 2031, the size of the working-age population would have fallen in 11 of the 22 major states. For instance, Kerala already has an ageing population, while in Bihar the working-age population would continue increasing till 2051.
- India ranks well below the global average in the United Nations Development Programme's (UNDP) HDI. The index was created to highlight that people and their capabilities—measured in terms of health and longevity, level of education, and their standard of living—should be the indication of a country's development. Unless we make significant progress in education, skill development, public health and economic welfare, these would remain major hindrances in India's quest to tap its demographic dividend.
- A disproportionately large section of India's workforce is engaged in agriculture, where disguised unemployment and underemployment are common.
- A large section of the workforce is employed in the unorganized sector, where workers are paid low wages, and are not given any social security benefits.

TRICKY ISSUE OF MANAGING HUMAN RESOURCES

Human resource management is a delicate task at most times, doubly so when it is affected by many a problem.

Growing population: Though the growth rate of India's population is declining, it is still adding several million people to its population every year. This reduces the per capita availability of resources, such as healthcare, education, food and nutrition, sanitation and employment, making it that much more difficult to equip every individual with the means to benefit optimally from growing economic opportunities.

Brain drain: As more and more talented and educated Indians settle abroad, the country loses their services. This brain drain is a major hindrance to human capital formation in India.

High poverty levels: A large proportion of India's populace still lives in poverty, lacking access to public goods such as healthcare, education and proper sanitation. Without the prerequisites to reach their potential, their prospects of growth are stunted.

UPS AND DOWNS OF FEMALE LABOUR PARTICIPATION

India's future economic growth could benefit from getting more women, who comprise approximately 50 per cent of the population, into productive employment. The participation of women in the labour force has been cause for concern. India's female labour force participation rate (FLFPR), which was 23.3 per cent in 2017–18, rose to 37 per cent in 2022–23, according to a PIB release dated 22 July 2024.[20] This was still well below the global average of 48.7 per cent.[21] The 2024–25 Economic Survey bore some encouraging news: the FLFPR has risen to 41 per cent (but much less than the global FLFPR, just over 50 per cent, according to the World Bank).[22]

On a positive note, women also accounted for almost 49 per cent of the total enrolment in higher education.[23] When these women graduate, they are expected to join the workforce. Therefore, India can expect a much higher rate of participation by women in its labour force in the years ahead.

The reasons for the low participation of women in the workforce are many, according to a report by the Directorate General of Employment. Domestic duties and providing care, both unpaid work; pervasiveness of social norms that are gender-biased; increase in household income 'which works as disincentive for female participation in [the] labour market'; and disparities in salaries and wages between males and females. The report mentions that a wide range of employment and gender discrimination issues act as big deterrents to more women joining the workforce.[24]

These issues have to be dealt with by the government at several levels so that women can participate in education and training and benefit from formalization of work. The Mission Shakti programme, for example, offers a safe haven for women who have been abused, creche services in the form of Palna Scheme, accommodation for working women and gap financing for women entrepreneurs. National Skill Training Institutes for Women impart vocational training to women of different age groups from different socio-economic strata. Such efforts need to be multiplied.

PLUGGING GAPS IN VOCATIONAL TRAINING: SKILLING, UPSKILLING, RESKILLING

In comparison with other countries, India has been lagging behind in vocational training. According to the WEF's

Human Capital Report 2020, India ranked 107th out of 133 countries in vocational and technical skills. This highlighted the need for India to improve its vocational education system to keep up with the demands of a rapidly changing job market.

The PLFS data reveals that 'there is a strong link between educational attainment, occupational roles and income levels'.[25] Hence, from 2014 onwards, the Indian government has invested heavily in vocational training programmes such as the Skill India Mission, the National Apprenticeship Promotion Scheme, and the Pradhan Mantri Kaushal Vikas Yojana. These initiatives envisage providing vocational training to individuals in various sectors, including manufacturing, healthcare and construction.

Demonstrating its determination to address the skills gap plaguing the country, the government established the Ministry of Skill Development and Entrepreneurship in 2014, with a clear mandate to coordinate nationwide efforts at skill development, and establish a national vocational and technical training framework. The following year, in 2015, the government launched the Skill India Mission with an ambitious remit of training 400 million Indians in various skills. Until 2022, 13.7 million people had received training under the Pradhan Mantri Kaushal Vikas Yojana but, as government data shows, only 18 per cent or 2.4 million were successfully placed in jobs.[26] The National Skill Development Corporation has taken this mission forward by setting up training centres in collaboration with training partners across different sectors. The 2025–26 budget has allocated ₹38,746.3 crore to the labour and skill development ministry as compared to ₹21,608 crore in the 2024–25 budget. The government has also outlined plans to spend ₹2 lakh crore over the next five years towards reinforcing the government's commitment to skill development and internship programmes.[27]

Now, according to the Human Development Report 2025, India ranked 130th out of 189 countries, up from 135th in 2019. It is too early to hazard a guess on the extent to which India's investment in vocational training has contributed to the marginal improvement in its position in the HDI. However, vocational training has the potential to contribute to India's economic growth by addressing the skills gap in the job market, and providing people with opportunities for employment and entrepreneurship.

It is crucial to identify skills gaps and provide training that meets the needs of employers. This effort needs to be complemented by greater investment in the requisite infrastructure and technology to improve the quality of training.

India's large pool of untapped labour is actually a source of long-term advantage, as marginal workers can be trained in skills needed in new-age industries. This slack is in sharp contrast to the shortages that many other economies are facing in their labour force.

It would help if the vocational education system were to be made more flexible and adaptable to the needs of learners. This can be achieved through modular and competency-based training, which allows learners to acquire skills at their own pace and flexibly.

Further, in sharp contrast to India's highly educated and skilled workforce in the service sector, the country's manufacturing sector still employs mostly unskilled and semi-skilled workers. The lower skill levels of Indian workers are reflected in the relatively low value added per worker compared to other countries. Improving their skills would go a long way in preparing a workforce that can make India a global manufacturing hub.

According to S&P Global Market Intelligence, every Indian worker added $8,076 on average in 2021. This is a small fraction of the average value added per worker in peer nations such as Malaysia, the Philippines, Thailand and Indonesia, as shown in Figure 10.1.[28] This is a key parameter that global investors take into account when they think about moving their supply chains to a new country, and India's poor performance on this count could jeopardize its bid to emerge as a major global centre of manufacturing. Further, a ManpowerGroup Employment Outlook Survey for the second quarter of 2023 found that employers had difficulties sourcing talent for their operations in India.[29] This is an indication of the depth of the challenges that India faces.

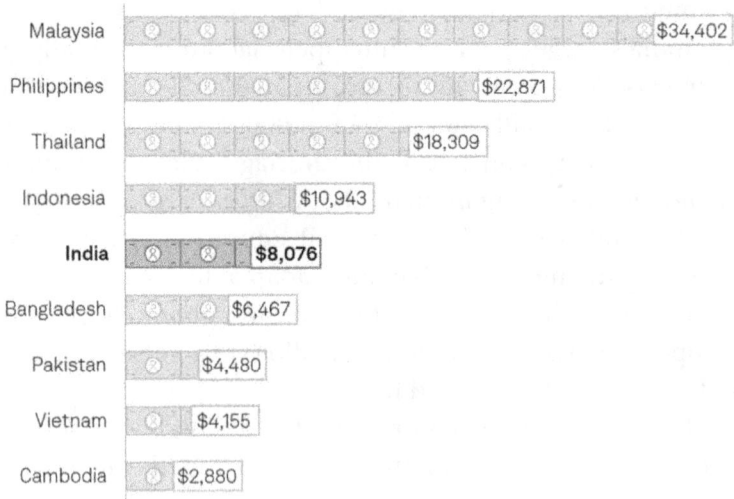

Malaysia	$34,402
Philippines	$22,871
Thailand	$18,309
Indonesia	$10,943
India	**$8,076**
Bangladesh	$6,467
Pakistan	$4,480
Vietnam	$4,155
Cambodia	$2,880

Figure 10.1: Real manufacturing value added per employed person ($)[30]

The bottom line is that it is important to create human capital by ensuring quality training that meets the demands of the job market, and for that it is necessary to improve

India's vocational education system. As the 2024–25 Economic Survey states, the government aims to establish 'a resilient and responsive skilled ecosystem to keep pace with emerging global trends such as automation, generative AI, digitalization and climate change'.[31]

With regard to the challenge posed by AI, the Economic Survey 2024–25 states, 'As India's workforce in low-skill and low-value-added services remains vulnerable to AI, robust enabling institutions are essential to help transition workers to medium- and high-skilled jobs, where AI can augment their efforts rather than replace them.' The Survey mentions an ILO study estimate that about 75 million jobs globally are threatened by automation due to rapid advancements in AI technology.[32]

The Economic Survey suggests that 'policymakers must balance innovation with societal costs, as AI driven shifts in the labour market could have lasting effects'. In such a situation, 'the corporate sector also must act responsibly, handling the introduction of AI with sensitivity to India's needs'. Further, it states that as 'AI is in its infancy, India is afforded the time necessary to address these challenges, strengthen its foundations and mobilize a nation-wide institutional response. For that, it concludes that a collaborative effort between government, private sector and academia is essential.'[33]

Further, the NEP 2020 envisages a framework to transform India's education system by 2030, focusing on foundational literacy and numeracy. This, along with vocational training initiatives, is expected to get millions of additional workers ready for the manufacturing and other sectors that are seeing rapid changes triggered by AI-driven interventions. This could help India attract more value-added and globalized jobs.

224   THE GOVERNANCE GAP

ARE THE YOUTH JOB-READY?

India's unemployment level is relatively high; as of February 2022, data from the Centre for Monitoring Indian Economy (CMIE) showed an unemployment rate of 6.9 per cent. However, this figure does not account for the large number of individuals who are underemployed or working in the informal sector. That could account for the difference in the unemployment rates arrived at by the World Bank and CMIE in 2022. The youth unemployment rate, as per the World Bank, was stated to be in double digits (10.2 per cent) in 2023–24.

Besides, a significant number of Indians lack the skills required to perform their jobs. As mentioned earlier in the chapter, India was ranked 107th out of 133 countries in vocational and technical skills in the WEF's Human Capital Report 2020. This indicates that there is a significant gap in India's vocational education system, and many workers do not possess the skills needed to succeed in the job market.

To put it succinctly, Indian youth are not job-ready. While there's a large pool of graduates, they lack the skills required for employment. A survey conducted by an employability assessment company, Aspiring Minds, in 2019 found that only 4.77 per cent of Indian engineering graduates were job-ready.[34] Similarly, a survey by staffing firm TeamLease Services found that only 22 per cent of Indian graduates were deemed employable in 2019.

Examples from other countries suggest that a strong emphasis on vocational training and skill development can have a positive impact on employment. Germany, for instance, has a well-established dual education system that combines classroom learning with on-the-job training. This has helped to reduce youth unemployment, and address the skills gap in the job market. Similarly, Switzerland has a strong vocational education system that provides learners with skills that are in high demand in the job market.

THE OPPORTUNITY FOR INDIA

- India has the youngest workforce in the world with a median age much lower than in China and the developed countries.
- The developed nations of the West are expected to face a worker shortage. Additionally, other peer nations such as China and Southeast Asia would also have a lower proportion of their populace in the working age, as opposed to India.
- There is an opportunity for Indian workers to fill this workforce gap, both within the country and beyond, which in turn would lead to higher economic growth.
- Periods of demographic dividend typically lead to higher levels of personal savings. This results in greater purchasing power for many more people; and their collective spending leads to a virtuous cycle of consumption, demand and growth, which propels fast economic expansion for the entire country.

STEPS REQUIRED TO TAP INDIA'S DEMOGRAPHIC DIVIDEND

To create conditions to benefit from a demographic dividend, the government, the private sector and civil society need to come together so that there is a greater investment in education and healthcare, along with R&D. The focus areas would be as follows:

- Enhancing investment on programmes concerning early childhood care and education. A UNESCO report dated 7 October 2024 stated: 'Investing in early childhood care and education yields lifelong benefits. Research shows that 90 per cent of a child's brain development occurs by the age of five, with the period between ages one and three being particularly crucial for cognitive growth.'

- The quality of education in schools and colleges, especially those outside the big urban centres, has to be improved. Education is widely recognized as the most potent tool for empowerment and socio-economic mobility. In India, there are wide disparities in the quality of education between urban and rural areas. There is also a wide gulf in the quality of education imparted in private schools compared to those run by the government. Quality primary and secondary education lays the foundation for cognitive development, critical thinking and lifelong education. Moreover, as observed thus far, higher education and vocational training play a major role in equipping individuals with specialized skills essential for finding employment in a rapidly evolving, technology-intensive economy. Addressing these disparities in the quality of education and ensuring universal access is key to nurturing human capital and benefitting from the demographic dividend.
- The reach of rural water supply and sanitation services has to be increased and improved. This has a direct impact on the health and hygiene standards of people and helps reduce the spread of many diseases.
- Delivery of quality health services would have to be ensured, especially in rural and remote areas of the country. A healthy population is crucial not only as far as the well-being of individuals is concerned but

also for the economic resilience and productivity of society. Despite some successes in this field, Indians continue to face challenges relating to affordability, access and quality. Therefore, there is an urgent need to invest more on preventive healthcare measures, and primary healthcare services. Ensuring access to affordable and quality healthcare services would empower Indians to mitigate the debilitating impact of diseases, enhance their productivity and foster better-equipped human capital that can fuel economic growth.

- Schemes such as Beti Bachao Beti Padao, Ayushman Bharat, Mission Shakti, etc., that have a direct impact on the health, well-being and development of individuals, would have to be further improved.

- India is increasingly becoming part of global supply chains, and it is critical to ensure that skill development and vocational training programmes as well as apprenticeship schemes focus on bridging the gap between education and industry requirements of new technology-enhanced labour practices. Investing in such focused initiatives would enable India to unleash the full potential of its population, drive the spirit of entrepreneurship and innovation, generate jobs in keeping with new industry demands and thus contribute to economic growth.

- While the government of the day undoubtedly needs to lead from the front in formulating and implementing policies, and allocating resources primarily aimed at developing the country's human capital, the private sector too, is a key stakeholder in this process, and does have the responsibility of investing in employee training, R&D, and community development initiatives. Therefore, more public–

private partnerships facilitating collaborations across sectors would be an ideal way to tackle the challenges therein.

◆

Ultimately, investing in India's human capital is not only a moral imperative but also a strategic necessity for lifting people out of extreme poverty and fostering the growth of a resilient middle class. It would enable India to set in motion a virtuous cycle of prosperity, equity, equality and social progress, and lay the foundation for a more inclusive future. That would be a real demographic dividend.

There is a foundational element for all policy decisions, be they in agriculture, education, public health or human capital development, and that is the need for up-to-date data. If the data is not accurate, then policy decisions can be flawed and the development outcomes less than desirable. Let us now take a look at how this important aspect of data has impacted governance.

11

CRITICALITY OF DATA IN DECISION-MAKING

Almost two decades ago, British mathematician Clive Humby used a phrase that seems to have become a leitmotif for our times. Data is the new oil, he declared. That comparison has been internalized by everyone from the political class to policymakers and business leaders to drive home a singular point—data, like oil, is the fuel of our times; it spells power, and whoever controls data and uses it to gather insights for decision-making is bound to have the upper hand in a fast-changing and complex world.

How can any policy or strategy about the present be made in the absence of data? It goes without saying that for data to be of use in matters of governance, the process of collecting it has to be rigorous, transparent and verifiable. The data source and methods are important for that would allow for authentication of the data; the lack of it can obfuscate realities. A sound grasp of boundaries within which data about people can be collected by the state and by private organizations is necessary, and so is understanding the criticality of data security. Last but not least, the significance of having up-to-date data cannot be overemphasized.

All this talk about data could give one the mistaken impression that data is an invention of our times. Needless to say, that is not so. According to the Census of India website, the Rig Veda, which is believed to have been

composed in the second millennium BCE, speaks about
the importance of maintaining a tally of the population.[1]
Kautilya's *Arthashastra*, written around 321–296 BCE, states
that having a census is an essential part of state policy for
taxation purposes.[2] Ancient Rome, too, conducted censuses
for the purpose of taxation.

Mughal emperor Akbar did the same. The *Ain-e-
Akbari*, written during his reign, included comprehensive
data on population, industry and wealth, among others.[3]
Data collection was an integral part of the British colonial
government's reign. The national census, as we know it, was
first conducted in 1881.

Post-Independence, the task of data collection has
carried on. The state has been undertaking this exercise
for various purposes. The decadal census, the National
Family Health Survey (NFHS), the PLFS and the Household
Consumption Expenditure Survey are some examples
of data collection to aid policymaking. Private sector
companies, too, have been conducting market surveys to
gauge the public response to their goods and services. These
are exercises that started in the pre-digital era, so to speak.

The digital age is very different. In the last few decades
we have been practically swimming in data, which is the
reason we sometimes imagine that data is an invention
of our times. However, it is a fact that digital data on the
internet has come to occupy centrestage in every field—
from government affairs and academia to industry, sports,
entertainment and more. A lot more data is now available
to both the government and the private sector. Additionally,
the availability of high-speed networks and broadband
across the length and breadth of the country has resulted in
the generation of billions of terabytes of data in real time,
facilitating the roll-out of several significant government
initiatives.

To cite an example, one of the most important data-driven interventions by the Government of India in recent times is the Jan Dhan Yojana (JDY), which aims to be the world's largest financial inclusion scheme by providing universal access to banking facilities. Former Prime Minister Rajiv Gandhi had lamented that for every rupee the government allocated for the poor, only 15 paise reached the intended beneficiary. The rest was lost to leakage, inefficiency and theft.[4] To correctly identify beneficiaries and plug the leakages in the government's financial outreach initiatives aimed at the weaker sections of society, the Government of India launched the JDY in 2014, which highlights the importance of up-to-date data.

By using three modes of identification, namely the JDY, Aadhaar and the registered mobile number, commonly referred to as the JAM trinity, the government has successfully implemented an ambitious reform scheme for direct payments, but challenges in the transfer of subsidies and other benefits to the intended beneficiaries still remain. Importantly, the Aadhaar database was critical in ensuring that there was no duplication.

PMJDY Accounts (in crore)

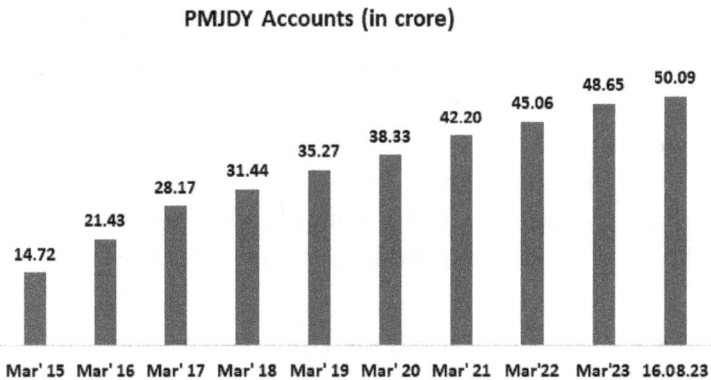

Figure 11.1: Pradhan Mantri Jan Dhan Yojana accounts (crore)[5]

Official figures put the number of individuals across the country with first-time bank accounts at 50 crore until August 2023, as can be seen in Figure 11.1. Of these account holders, 56 per cent are women, and around 67 per cent of these accounts are in rural and semi-urban areas.[6] However, exact figures on the extent of savings are not available.

HOW POOR DATA CONSTRAINS GOOD DECISION-MAKING

Whether it is a matter of good governance through targeted delivery of public goods, focused marketing strategies, or corporate plans for innovation and growth, what is of utmost importance is the reliability of the data being used.

The reality is that while data can be a big help to decision-makers, it can do the opposite too. Decisions based on faulty or poor quality data can lead to significantly inefficient outcomes, leading to the wastage of precious resources, along with reputational damage.

For instance, the Indian NSSO is responsible for conducting large-scale sample surveys to collect data at a national level. Recently, a member of the prime minister's Economic Advisory Council claimed that national surveys like the National Sample Survey (NSS), NFHS and the PLFS are based on faulty sampling; consequently, they underestimate the country's progress in various areas.[7] Prominent economists and analysts have also questioned data presented by these abovementioned bodies with regard to figures of poverty and distress. The question is, how effective would policy interventions based on questionable data be?

DATA AS THE BACKBONE OF DECISION-MAKING

The fact is that the internet has led to an explosion of data generation and collection of every conceivable kind. Its analysis and dissemination has given birth to a global multi-billion-dollar digital industry that promises to change the way the world makes its decisions.

The availability of huge amounts of data forms the backbone of cutting-edge applications, such as AI and machine learning (ML). The data explosion that we see today has, in turn, given rise to many new businesses that collect, collate and analyse the information available, and come up with actionable insights; in the process, giving themselves and their clients a key advantage while arriving at decisions.

Take the Indian governments over time. Traditionally, governments have collected data through the census, along with other surveys, using tried-and-tested methodologies. The findings from these surveys have helped the authorities design new policies, plan new programmes and formulate new schemes. Such surveys have also played an important role in the preparation of the national, state and departmental budgets.

Now governments have the facility of harnessing the power of data by leveraging latest technologies. The launch of the Digital India programme in 2015 signalled the government's intent to make extensive use of data for formulating, implementing and monitoring various flagship programmes such as the Pradhan Mantri Ujjwala Yojana, Housing for All, Swachh Bharat Mission and One Nation One Ration Card. It is worth mentioning that in-house tools developed by the National Informatics Centre (NIC) have proved helpful. For instance, Darpan extracts data from various IT systems, creating dashboards and insights that have helped several ministries and governments. Another tool, Prayas, monitors the progress of the government's flagship programmes based on defined key performance indicators (KPIs).

The government is making extensive use of data across all its programmes. Data is key to the formulation of poverty alleviation initiatives, such as schemes for subsidy distribution to farmers, pensions for senior citizens and scholarships for students. Data analytics is also used to identify the beneficiaries for schemes such as MGNREGA using technology solutions for timely dissemination of benefits to millions.

Data has many uses. It enables the country's criminal justice system to analyse crime patterns. The government, individual banks and large private financial services employ data to detect fraudulent activities. In fact, many organizations are trying to integrate fraud detection modules into their management information systems.

Further, the government made extensive use of data during the Covid-19 pandemic for contact tracing and trends analysis. This allowed the authorities to take appropriate measures to curb the spread of the virus. Data was also used for the management of hospitals, along with the supply of essential medicines and goods to citizens. In fact, the Indian government administered 2 billion vaccination doses to all eligible citizens.[8] CoWIN, the digital backbone set up for the purpose of coordinating the mammoth vaccination exercise, enabled registration, appointment scheduling, identity verification, vaccination and certification of each vaccinated member. The vaccination certification was made available on the same platform. This entire exercise was made possible due to the availability of up-to-date data.

It is not just the government or industry that is making use of data. Citizens, civil society organizations and society at large are also benefitting from the democratization of data, which is now available to many more people than before. This is enabling them to build inclusive solutions for the development of society.

QUESTION MARK OVER DATA

Despite these strides made by India in the fields of data analysis and management, there have been persistent questions about the quality of official data that the government relies on while formulating policies. So much so that some foreign agencies like Bloomberg have gone so far as to say that India 'has a serious data problem'.[9] In fact, in a report dated 14 July 2023, it said: '[F]or years, the South Asian nation has relied on outdated surveys to quantify everything from GDP to inflation. Most of India's economic data is based on numbers collected more than a decade ago, when smartphones were rare and apps like Uber or Zomato had not yet revolutionized the way Indians travel, eat and shop.'[10] The report was referring to the fact that the official figures are from the 2011 census.

This is a recurring problem, specifically in the Indian context, as the quality of data at the state level is poor. Consequently, experts have recommended frequent changes in sampling frames and base year, among others, to correctly capture consumption, employment and other patterns. India's chief statistician G.P. Samanta has admitted: 'What we cannot measure we cannot manage.'[11] For example, there is a school of thought that the Consumer Price Index (CPI)—the RBI's benchmark for setting repo and reverse repo rates, which in turn influence the retail lending rates of commercial banks—does not fully reflect the new realities of the Indian economy due to a lack of data. Among other things, it still includes the prices of audio cassettes, which are almost obsolete today. This makes it extremely difficult for economists and analysts to accurately measure consumption patterns in the country. Besides, it leaves the data open to the charge that it does not fully capture the true and full picture of the Indian economy.[12]

Dr Pronab Sen, former chief statistician of India also admitted to Bloomberg: 'We have programmes for people below the poverty line, but we don't know the number of poor people.'[13] 'In 2023, the late Dr. Bibek Debroy, who was then Chairman of the prime minister's Economic Advisory Council, corroborated the logic of Sen's statement in an article in *The Hindu* that was co-authored with Aditya Sinha: 'Our ability to track inflation effectively has been severely undermined […] Our tools for understanding and managing our economic reality are grossly inadequate.'[14]

The Bloomberg article also stated[15]: 'It is an alarming problem for Prime Minister Narendra Modi, who is pitching India as the next big market for global investment and trade. Economists warn that the risk of policy errors will rise unless India moves quickly to update figures and remove barriers to accessing reliable data.'

The report provides an obvious example of the disconnect between reality and what the data captures: contrast the 24 per cent weight of the services sector in the CPI with the reality that the sector now accounts for about half the economy and a similar proportion of household spending, and you get an idea of the scale of the problem. Thus, in order to address the looming crisis in policymaking, and to improve the quality of data, the government in 2022 launched a new consumer expenditure survey to better capture consumption patterns in the Indian economy. However, the data collected by this survey was to be used for estimating GDP and CPI starting 2024–25. This lack of data tends to leave economists and analysts no choice but to depend on alternatives like fuel consumption and air traffic to gauge the health of the Indian economy.

Chief Statistician Samanta has vowed to 'create an ecosystem where data guides policymakers on the path of sustainable development'.[16] The government has been taking steps to correct the anomalies that have crept into the data collection exercise. It has made a list of 200 data sources, including GST collections, e-way bills for the interstate movement of goods and corporate filings, among others, to try and collect up-to-date and relevant data more efficiently. The government is also improving its data reporting systems so that individual ministries and departments report data on time, thereby reducing the time lag, so that policy formulations and decisions are in sync with realities on the ground.

POLITICIZATION OF DATA ERODES CREDIBILITY OF OFFICIAL STATISTICS

Another problem highlighted by some experts is the delay in making data available or altering it on account of a dispensation's political compulsions.

According to a report by the National University of Singapore's Institute of South Asian Studies, dated 18 March 2019, child malnutrition data collected in 2015–16 for the NFHS (round 4) was shared in October 2016 with the International Food Policy Research Institute (IFPRI).[17] While the data showed that, compared to 2004–05, there was a substantive reduction in child malnutrition, it was silent on the factors that drove this reduction, and on the performance of individual states.

Since no official explanation was provided, it led to speculation that the NDA government did not want to highlight data that showed the previous government (the UPA government, 2004–14) in a good light for the decrease in child malnutrition.

The same report mentions how several state governments inflated their data to declare themselves open defecation free under the Swachh Bharat Mission even as the CAG highlighted how, in several instances, this was not the case. What use would such data be in fashioning effective policy responses.

Further, the practice of revising data that has been collected adds to the frustration of analysts who are, therefore, unable to conclude with any degree of certainty about the direction and actual strength of the Indian economy. It gives rise to speculation about data tampering.

According to former RBI governor Shaktikanta Das, 'Monetary policymakers supplement official estimates with information on auxiliary variables to have a firmer assessment and minimize policy errors emanating from data revision.'[18]

This is a tacit admission that even officials do not rely entirely on the government's own figures. 'For instance, rather than use "bad data", economists at the RBI are likely using a combination of intuition and inflation numbers to set interest rates,' according to Sen. Moreover, there have also been allegations that India's impressive growth in recent years is partially due to data revisions.[19]

One of the major gaps in India's data collection process is the decision to defer the decadal population census, which was due in 2021. Although the government has claimed staff shortage to be the reason, many analysts speculated that governments are known to choose the timing of the release of census data to suit their electoral agenda.

Whatever be the reason, this does not augur well for the Indian economy. At a time when there is so much talk of reaping a demographic dividend by focusing on nurturing human capital, the lack of accurate data would be nothing less than disastrous. The fate of India's ambitious economic and social targets depends on it.

INDEPENDENT VERIFICATION OF THE AUTHENTICITY OF DATA

Although the Indian government has traditionally been the main collector and custodian of most important data points, the internet explosion in the last couple of decades has brought new data sources within the reach of both private corporations as well as private individuals. The Economic Survey of 2019 proposed that even the data collected by the government be democratized in the interest of social welfare, and thereby be considered a public good.

A NITI Aayog paper on 'Data Empowerment and Protection Architecture' (DEPA) stated that data is primarily an economic good. Moreover, that it is key to empowering individuals, who exert control over their personal data through a robust and dynamic regulatory, legislative and institutional framework, supported by technology design for secure data sharing.

However, it is important to note here that non-personal data—information that does not give away the identity of an individual from the available data—is critical to ensuring transparency and good governance, such as for welfare schemes.

The coming-of-age tools to collect and analyse big data in real time has provided both the government and the private sector with the capability to come out with technology-led solutions that result in efficient implementation. Big data is exactly that: sets of data that are growing in size and complexity. The process of analysing this data and extracting useful, actionable information to solve problems more efficiently across sectors is called data analytics.

The availability of big datasets as a public good, along with the development of applications to analyse them have given financial and technology businesses the wherewithal to mine mountains of diverse information, and thereby distil actionable insights that add value to society. But, as the same NITI Aayog paper pointed out, individuals and small businesses do not necessarily benefit from the democratization of data, even as companies and big businesses gain disproportionately from this.

In this context, the need to ensure adequate protections for individuals and communities is absolutely essential when using big datasets for good governance. Therefore, it is important to anonymize the data that is collected to protect the interests of individuals and communities. Sufficient safeguards in the realm of data sharing are necessary.

As the judicious use of data adds wealth and economic value, businesses are finding new ways to generate value from data.

According to the Intellectual Property (IP) Helpdesk of the European Commission, 'numerous facets of decision-making and business operations demonstrate the value of data. Data contributes to business in the following ways[20]:

- Offers market intelligence and projections to support companies' innovation and diversification.
- Assists in lowering business risk by guaranteeing prompt and precise decision-making.
- Identifies tasks requiring a lot of time and resources.
- Promotes efficient resource allocation by analysing gaps in various processes; these can be programmed to increase output.
- Enables companies to examine consumer behaviour and create customer retention plans.'

Simultaneously, there is a good deal of cutting-edge research under way to understand the uses of data for the betterment of society.

In recent times, another trend has become visible. Recognizing the growing importance of data and its criticality in creating value, there is a move in India, as in many other countries, to create a framework that clearly lists the obligations of both state and individuals with regard to non-personal and personal data as well.

WHY DATA PROTECTION IS IMPORTANT: THE AADHAAR CASE

In this context, it would be worth studying the Aadhaar case. In India, one of the main data collection points is Aadhaar, a unique 12-digit number that the government issues to each citizen. The Aadhaar stores every citizen's biometric data in a central database.

After Aadhaar was first sought to be introduced in 2010 by means of the National Identification Authority of India Bill, 2010, several PILs were filed in 2013 by prominent individuals and citizens groups, among them Justice K.S. Puttaswamy and Aruna Roy. Their argument was that Aadhaar violated an individual's fundamental right to privacy. The apprehension being that the data would give the state the means to profile citizens and track their movements—in short, engage in mass surveillance.

In 2018, a Supreme Court judgement gave its ruling in *Justice K.S. Puttaswamy* v. *Union of India*. By a 4:1 majority, the apex court upheld the Aadhaar Act enacted in 2016. It stated that the right to privacy could be restricted by the state if the 'restriction is proportional to a legitimate state aim. Reasoning that the efficient and transparent distribution of benefits and services to disadvantaged citizens is a legitimate aim, the Court concluded that the act did *not* violate the fundamental right to privacy. Further, it observed that there are enough safeguards in place to prevent Aadhaar from facilitating mass state surveillance.'[21]

However, the judgement did strike down as unconstitutional some individual provisions of the Act, such as for metadata collection and linking with bank accounts. It also established guidelines for protecting privacy in the context of Aadhaar, and emphasized the need for strong data protection mechanisms, strict safeguards against misuse, and transparency in the Aadhaar system. The court ruled that Aadhaar metadata could not be stored for more than six months.

Still, the issue of data privacy and protection continues to fester. Data, like all other information, can be lost, altered, corrupted or tampered with. It is a critical part of any data use regime to protect individuals from thefts of their confidential and personal data and being used for unauthorized or fraudulent purposes. In their endeavour to extract maximum benefits from data in the most efficient manner, companies and institutions must remember that their credibility rests on their ability to have a stringent data protection strategy in place to safeguard their information.

Since every organization and a vast number of individuals are generating, storing and sharing data at unprecedented rates, its protection is becoming increasingly important. Guaranteeing data privacy, shielding it from hacking, and ensuring that it can quickly be retrieved in case of tampering or loss is a critical part of any data protection strategy. The three key elements of data protection are[22]:

- **Confidentiality:** Ensuring that only authorized operators with relevant permissions can access any dataset.

- **Integrity:** Ensuring that all the information maintained by an organization is accurate and dependable.
- **Availability:** The information is kept secure but is easily accessible to authorized personnel at any given time.

These are particularly relevant as India ranked second globally in data breaches.[23]

THE DISTINCTION BETWEEN PERSONAL AND NON-PERSONAL DATA

As regards the rules of using non-personal or personal data, the distinction between the two seems easy enough. Personal data is any information that allows users to identify an individual from the data at hand. Non-personal data, on the other hand, is any information that does not allow for the identification of any individual from the data at hand. But, practically speaking, many a time it is not so easy to separate the personal from the non-personal data. For example, large databases of medical records do play a critical role in medical research and in the health insurance industry. Since such databases are essentially the aggregation of data collected from individual patients, maintaining anonymity and segregating the same is critical for ensuring that its use does not transgress an individual's privacy.

The main categories of non-personal data have been explained simply by PRS Legislative Research[24]:

- **Public non-personal data:** This refers to data that the government collects 'in the course of publicly funded works', such as 'anonymized data of land records or vehicle registration.'

- **Community non-personal data:** This pertains to 'raw or factual data (without any processing) which is sourced from a community of natural persons,' such as 'datasets collected by municipal corporations or public electric utilities'.
- **Private non-personal data:** This is 'data which is collected or generated by private entities through privately owned processes (derived insights, algorithms or proprietary knowledge)'.

Here, it is essential to keep in mind that personal data is usually a no-go area for companies and organizations, except with the express authorization of the individual concerned, and non-personal data, or originally personal data that has been anonymized by use of techniques, is the public good that is fuelling innovation and growth and generating pathbreaking insights and billions of dollars in value.

THE CHALLENGE POSED BY BIG DATA

While the limitless use that can be made of big data is a heady proposition, it has its issues as well. Big data needs large storage spaces, several complex and advanced technologies, and a large budget to store, manage and analyse within a secure environment and without infringing upon an individual's right to privacy.

Since the datasets expand manifold over time, these processes and their scalability present a significant challenge—the biggest of which being the threat of theft, or unauthorized use. Therefore, data security involves both strong technological and physical systems as also a robust legal system to be effective.

DATA PROTECTION IN INDIA

India amended its Information Technology Act, 2000, in 2008 to make it mandatory for companies to secure personal data within their custody, which is stored in their computer systems. The law mandated a fine for failing to do so; this marked India's first attempt to protect and secure data.[25]

In 2011, a rule was added, specifying the minimum requirements for the protection of personal data. Under this rule, businesses had to have a privacy policy, and had to get consent before collecting or transferring personal information; they had to also inform people about who this data was being shared with.[26] Over the next few years, several new rules and regulations were added to ensure data protection; but, these were done sporadically, resulting in several inconsistencies and loopholes. Many experts then began to call for a comprehensive data protection law.

In 2017, a nine-judge bench of the Supreme Court of India delivered a unanimous judgement in the case of *K.S. Puttaswamy* v. *Union of India*: 'Right to Privacy is an integral part of Right to Life and Personal Liberty guaranteed in Article 21 of the Constitution.'[27] Further, that the right to privacy was essential to the freedoms protected by all fundamental rights. Following this judgement, the Union government introduced the Personal Data Protection Bill before the Rajya Sabha. The bill was passed in August 2023 after a review by the Joint Committee of Parliament.[28]

The new law, the Digital Personal Data Protection Act (DPDP Act), 2023, on protecting personal data facilitates better targeting of service delivery, or formulation of evidence-based policies by the government, and allows the sharing of non-personal or anonymized data. Also, the National Strategy for Artificial Intelligence (NSAI) makes some types of government data available for 'public good' and requires businesses to share aggregated data.[29] The Ministry of Electronics and Information Technology established a committee of experts to suggest a data governance framework for the regulation of non-personal data. However, the country still does not have a law that specifically governs non-personal data.

In the realm of personal data, like the European Union's General Data Protection Regulation (GDPR)—which is hailed as the gold standard for the protection of consumer information—the DPDP Act emphasizes the need to obtain consent for data processing and has stringent measures for the breach of data privacy norms.

The law protects an individual's autonomy over their personal data. It also gives data principals, or individuals, a set of rights, which include the right to access, correct and erase personal data. Data fiduciaries, namely companies or institutions processing the data, have some obligations such as to ensure security, and inform principals about data breaches, among others.

KEY PROVISIONS OF THE DPDP ACT

Some of the key provisions of the Indian legislation are as follows:

Data fiduciaries and data processors: Data fiduciaries, namely companies or institutions processing the data, determine the purpose and means of processing personal data, while data processors process the data on behalf of the former. Both these classes of data intermediaries are required to protect the data they handle. They must take measures to ensure data protection, maintain transparency in data usage and, in case there's a breach, respond promptly.

Data principals: This term refers to the individuals whose data is being processed—that is, all of us, who generate data points every time we interact with a digital platform. The law gives data principals several rights, including access to their own data, the right to correct inaccurate information, and the right to erase personal data, or 'be forgotten' in the digital realm to ensure their digital autonomy under some conditions.

Data protection officer: Companies must appoint a data protection officer (DPO), who is responsible for ensuring compliance with the law. The DPO is the point of contact between the organization, the data principals and the authorities.

Grievance redressal: It is mandatory under the law for data fiduciaries to have mechanisms in place to address grievances and resolve complaints relating to data processing.

Data transfers: The law has stringent safeguards for transferring personal data outside India.

Exemptions: The law provides for situations where its data protection provisions will not be applicable. These include matters of national security and legal proceedings, among others.

The act attempts to foster a secure and accountable digital environment by balancing the rights of individuals with the requirements of institutions and businesses that handle data. In keeping with the law, the Indian government has established a data protection board to oversee and ensure its implementation.

Given the complex nature of the law and the problems in establishing such a vast framework, the government has adopted a phased approach under which some provisions are effective immediately while others have specific timelines to give businesses and entities time to adapt gradually.

Following the enactment of the law, many a business has had to modify its data practices to ensure compliance. Many have set up dedicated teams and resources for this. But companies with cross-border operations continue to face challenges in ensuring consistent data practices across regions, especially on cross-border data transfers.

The law gives individuals greater control and autonomy over their digital footprints. It has also led to an increase in data literacy in the sense that more individuals are now aware of the nuances of data privacy and their rights in the digital realm. Broadly, the DPDP Act seeks to shape a digital future that prioritizes individual rights, fosters innovation and ensures robust data security at the same time.

◆

It is essential that India internalize the commandments of data practice to meet its ambitious targets of social and economic development, and to forge ahead globally. The big data rush is only going to get bigger over time. Thus, governments need to ensure that accurate data is collected regularly and shared transparently for effective policy decisions, so that India can take its rightful place among the developed nations of the world.

12

INDIA: THE WAY FORWARD

The deep faith I developed in a newly independent India as a 16-year-old continues to burn bright within me as I cross 94. However, gifted as I am with the advantage of years, I am realistic enough to acknowledge that there are many hills to climb before India takes its rightful place on the global stage. The purpose of this book is to demonstrate that it is citizen-centric governance that ultimately determines whether a country is considered a 'viksit' nation or not.

If we take the examples of countries like the US, the UK, France, Germany, Canada, Australia and Japan or even countries like Singapore, Taiwan and South Korea, we find several common threads running through them—a relatively high level of economic activity and per capita income, almost 100 per cent literacy rates, respect for the rule of law, a focus on innovation, reliance on the market, acceptance of gender equality, and the availability of clean air and proper sanitation for its citizens, among others.

Besides, non-economic factors such as HDI, which quantifies a country's education levels, overall literacy and health into a single figure, are used to evaluate a nation's degree of development.

The most common economic metric used to determine whether a country is developed or developing is per capita GDP. However, there is no universally accepted GDP level to ascertain development. While some economists consider $12,000 to $15,000 per capita GDP to be sufficient for developed status, others do not consider a country developed unless its per capita GDP is above \$25,000 or \$30,000. According to the International Monetary Fund (IMF), the US per capita GDP in 2024 at current prices is about \$86,000.[1]

Countries that score well on the above parameters are considered well governed. Unfortunately, India ranks either poorly or at a mid-level in most of the global indices that rank countries on these parameters.

There are many global governance indices that evaluate where nations stand on the scale. Take, for instance, the World Bank's Worldwide Governance Indicators (WGI), which are described as 'a global compilation of data capturing household, business and citizen perceptions of the quality of governance in more than 200 economies'.[2]

WGI has six aspects of governance on which perceptions are sought. Four of these aspects have been covered to some extent in this book: the rule of law, the magnitude of corruption, the likelihood of political instability, and the quality of policy and its implementation. The last two aspects are regulatory quality, which focuses on the ease of doing business for the private sector, and voice and accountability, encompassing freedom of political participation, expression, association, and the media. The former has not been covered, and in the latter, only freedom of political participation is discussed. Regardless, India's ranking as of 2023 ranged from a low of 21.3 percentile in Political Stability and Absence of Violence/Terrorism, and a high of 67.9 percentile in Government Effectiveness.[3] The other four rankings are in the 40th and 50th percentiles. Not ideal for the world's fourth-largest economy.

Notwithstanding the undeniable progress India has made across spheres in nearly eight decades, it is important to view one snapshot of data points: India is the fourth largest economy in the world, but it is also a house divided. A March 2024 study by the World Inequality Lab showed that 'inequality skyrocketed since the early 2000s: the share of income held by the top 10 per cent has risen from 40 per cent in 2000 to 58 per cent in 2023, driven primarily by the top 1 per cent, whose share grew from 15 per cent to 23 per cent, while the middle 40 per cent saw a decline from 39 per cent to 27 per cent.' The share of the bottom 50 per cent in the total is 15 per cent, as can be seen in Figure 12.1.[4]

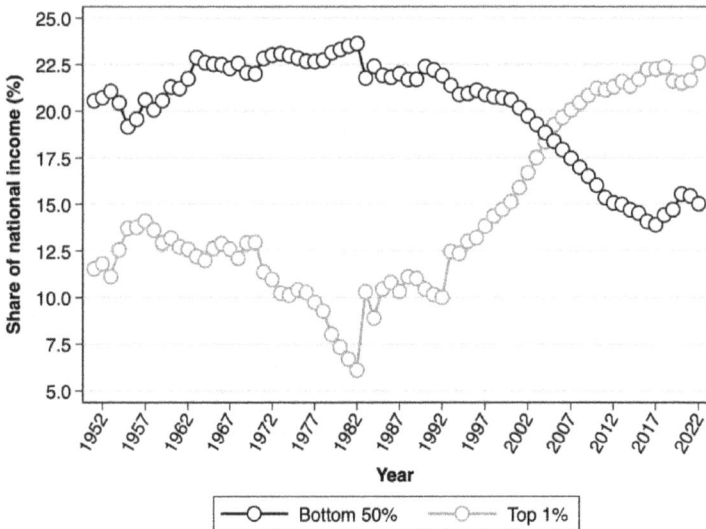

Figure 12.1: Bottom 50% vs top 1% national income shares, 1951–2022[5]

These data points reveal something important about the state of the nation:

- A large section of the population is excluded from the development process and lacks any kind of influence.
- The bottom 50 per cent who hold 15 per cent share of the income and are largely excluded from the

development process are precisely those who are
lagging behind in the spheres of health, education
and employment. Overall, they lack opportunities
for social mobility.

• These figures of disparities indicate the existence of
several fault lines in India: rural–urban, rich–poor,
gender and caste.

Considering that India is in a position to reap the benefits
of a demographic dividend, the above picture assumes
great importance. How will the country do so if half its
population is nowhere near acquiring quality health,
education and skills necessary for realizing the benefits
of the demographic dividend? These social determinants
create human capital and are drivers of development and
inclusive growth, yet our political class has not accorded
them the priority they deserve.

Experts say India has a window of three decades or so
to realize its demographic dividend. To create an efficient
workforce, skilling, upskilling and reskilling is needed, but
it is equally important to see that women, who comprise
half the population, also have a robust presence in the
workforce. For that, gender-based prejudices that operate
across areas, be it health or education, must be tackled.
Social schemes that do just that must be strengthened.

There is another significant point to consider. A large
section of the young workforce is located in the Hindi
heartland, which has lower indices of health, literacy,
education and training. If the rise in population figures is
centred in north India, some south Indian states show an
ageing population. All these aspects pose policy challenges.

But by far the greatest challenge India faces today
is that of addressing inequalities mirrored through
several dimensions. Reservation was one way that was

devised to set right the historical wrong done to certain communities who, on account of being from an SC or ST, could not access social, economic, political and cultural opportunities. The understanding being that formal equality—under Article 14 of the Constitution every person within India has the fundamental right to equality before the law and equal protection before the law— would not be able to address the entrenched inequalities of the communities so affected. Over time, reservation extended to backward castes and classes, and today socially better-off groups are also demanding reservation in education and public jobs. The reason for this is simple: all this is a reflection of the slow pace of job creation and the unemployable educated. Youth unemployment continues to be in double digits, which is unfortunate. Experts point out that a demographic dividend can as easily become a demographic 'bomb', for too many unemployed youth in a burgeoning workforce would only add to social unrest and chaos—not exactly ideal conditions for development and growth.

Such are the urgent issues facing India at this critical juncture. It is imperative for people who lead the nation and the institutions that guard our parliamentary democracy to rise to the occasion. For that matter, is the process by which citizens elect governments to power still strong enough to protect their interests?

Even now, the memories of India's first elections are fresh in my mind, when a largely illiterate society participated in the process with gusto, setting the tone for the next nearly eight decades, barring the aberration of Emergency. Even today, citizens exercise their right to vote, seeing it not only as a right but also a duty to send representatives to Parliament who will voice their needs, concerns and aspirations. They do so in the midst of brazen money power, and criminalization of politics casting a huge shadow on the electoral process.

By rights citizens expect their legislatures to debate issues of inequality, unemployment, discrimination, lack of healthcare and education. But, over the years, legislatures have had fewer sittings, fewer discussions on important legislations and policy matters, and less monitoring of the government. As for political executives such as the prime minister or chief ministers, a general concentration of power is seen, with political compulsions often dominating the task of governance. The bureaucracy, in study after study, has been associated with corruption. Implementation of policy and delivery of public services suffer.

World over, the trend is to have technocrats heading key ministries so as to be able to steer policy in key sectors in an increasingly complex world that is globally integrated at various levels. Similarly, domain experts have proved their worth in comparison to a generalized bureaucracy. That, plus a more meritorious, trained bureaucracy attuned to the needs of citizens, would make a difference.

As legislatures increasingly fail to keep the political executive accountable, citizens turn to the judiciary to redress their woes. Over the years, PILs have emerged as one of the most potent means of taking up issues that have a bearing on citizens' lives, and have to do with the violation of their constitutional and legal rights, and the apathy of those in power. However, the backlog of cases and the shortfall in the number of judges required slows down the process of justice, especially at the bottom most level, which is the first point of contact for citizens. That needs to be urgently addressed.

In a vast country like India, effective governance requires responding to diversity at the grassroots, and the distribution of legislative, executive and fiscal powers between the Union and states as laid down by the Constitution was meant to facilitate that. Although, over the years, centralizing tendencies have marred this arrangement.

We often tend to be deceived by appearances. Yes, the organs of the state as created by the Constitution for the working of India's parliamentary democracy are still there. But they need to work not just in letter but in spirit as well. When realpolitik overshadows the principles of governance, what you get is a flawed democracy.

Thus far, the issues of the bottom 50 per cent of the population were largely considered to be 'their' problems. A certain kind of economic growth was possible without them. Now, however, the circumstances have changed. For, the surge of growth that is capable of propelling India to superpower status is not possible if half the population is left behind—the half that constitutes a huge section of the workforce. Yes, the same workforce that is powering the dream of a demographic dividend in the decades to come.

This is the decisive moment, then—to have a yardstick of governance that thinks of even the last person in the line, in the spirit of 'leave no one behind'. In that yardstick lies the formula for inclusive growth, social cohesion, innovation and resilience, which will make the goal of superpower status achievable.

◆

I have faith in India. This is the faith not just of the 16-year-old who is still alive within me; it is the tempered conviction of a 94-year-old who recognizes the importance of a recalibration that puts a nation back in touch with first principles of governance so as to surge forward.

ACKNOWLEDGEMENTS

Writing *The Governance Gap* has been a multi-year journey of reflection, exploration and learning, and I owe a deep debt of gratitude to all those who supported me throughout.

First and foremost, I would like to thank my wife, Lalu, for her unwavering moral support and patience throughout this endeavour. Her encouragement sustained me during moments of doubt and long hours of work. My sons and daughters-in-law—Sudeep and Chandrika, Rajeev and Ritu—cheered me on throughout, always offering motivation when I needed it most. Rajeev took on the task of editing the book in the final stages, as my health prevented me from doing so, and I am deeply grateful to him. I must also thank my grandson, Aarya, who patiently located and delivered source after source for my research.

I am especially thankful to my secretary, Arun Sharma, who spent countless hours typing, revising and gathering materials, often working late into the night, to help me refine and organize my thoughts.

I would also like to extend my sincere thanks to my publisher, Rupa Publications. In particular, I am grateful to Kapish Mehra for believing in this manuscript and giving it a home, and to Dibakar Ghosh for his tireless support and problem-solving throughout the challenging publication process.

Research and content development are rarely solitary efforts; many helped me along the way. I thank Vikram Mukka and Aarnab Mitra for their assistance at various stages.

Over the years, my colleagues and teams across the various organizations I have worked with have played a crucial role in shaping my understanding of governance and leadership. Their experiences, perspectives and conversations have informed much of the thinking behind this book.

Finally, my heart goes out to all patriots and well-wishers of India. My observations stem from a deep love for my country and a firm belief that India is destined for greatness. I hope that this book, by sparking discussion on improving governance, will contribute, in some small way, to propelling India to claim its rightful place at the world's top table.

NOTES

1. DEMOCRACY IN ACTION

1   Quraishi, S.Y., *An Undocumented Wonder: The Making of the Great Indian Election*, Rupa Publications, New Delhi, 2014.

2   *Statistical Report on General Elections, 1951, to the First Lok Sabha, Volume 1*, Election Commission of India, New Delhi, 2003, 8, https://tinyurl.com/2s4h5x9m. Accessed on 20 February 2025.

3   Guha, Ramachandra, 'Democracy's Biggest Gamble: India's First Free Elections in 1952', *World Policy Journal*, Vol. 19, No. 1, 2002, 95–103, https://tinyurl.com/4nra4eab. Accessed on 6 June 2025.

4   Election Commission of India, *Report on the First General Elections in India 1951-52*, Government of India Press, New Delhi, 1955.

5   Misra, Salil, 'Under Nehru's Leadership, India's First Election Upheld Plurality, Rejected Communalism', *The Wire*, 24 February 2022, https://tinyurl.com/yhnwyypy. Accessed on 7 March 2024.

6   Shani, Ornit, *How India Became Democratic: Citizenship and Making of the Universal Adult Franchise*, Cambridge University Press, Cambridge, 2017.

7   Desai, Meghnad, *The Raisina Model: Indian Democracy at 70*, Penguin Books India, New Delhi, 2017.

8   Raisina Hill is an area of Lutyens' Delhi in the national capital and houses India's most important government buildings, including Rashtrapati Bhavan, the official residence of the President of India, and the Secretariat building, housing the Prime Minister's Office and several other important ministries.

9   'Chronology of Lok Sabha Elections (1952–1999)', *Hindustan Times*, 13 October 2003, https://tinyurl.com/52prt4yz. Accessed on 27 February 2025.

10 Furfur, 'Indian Election Results', *Wikimedia Commons*, 17 June 2024, https://tinyurl.com/2u7bvvxt. Accessed on 20 February 2025.

11 Desai, Meghnad, *The Raisina Model: Indian Democracy at 70*, Penguin Books India, New Delhi, 2017.

12 Vaishnav, Milan, and Danielle Smogard, 'A New Era in Indian Politics?' *Carnegie Endowment for International Peace*, 10 June 2014, https://tinyurl.com/bdefnaj7. Accessed on 7 March 2024.

13 FlyJet777, '2024 NDA Alliance Lok Sabha Seat Sharing of All Parties', *Wikimedia Commons*, 8 May 2024, https://tinyurl.com/2u2ynmxv. Accessed on 20 February 2025.

14 'First General Elections in India: All You Need to Know', *India Today*, 10 February 2016, https://tinyurl.com/4annphd2. Accessed on 7 March 2024.

15 Rai, Vinod, *Rethinking Good Governance: Holding to Account India's Institutions*, Rupa Publications, New Delhi, 2018.

16 Ibid.

17 Vaishnav, Milan, *When Crime Pays: Money and Muscle in Indian Politics*, HarperCollins, Gurgaon, 2017.

18 Ranjan, Mukesh, 'Record 46% of Newly-elected Lok Sabha MPs Facing Criminal Cases: Study', *The New Indian Express*, 6 June 2024, https://tinyurl.com/bp9u6zpe. Accessed on 27 February 2025.

19 Ibid.

20 Quraishi, S.Y., *An Undocumented Wonder: The Making of the Great Indian Election*, Rupa Publications, New Delhi, 2014.

21 Singh, Nandini, 'Lok Sabha Election 2024: How Much Does It Cost to Hold Elections in India?', *Business Standard*, 19 April 2024, https://tinyurl.com/bdfct9ys; 'Election Expenditure per Elector Up by Twenty Times in 2009 Compared to First General Elections', Press Information Bureau, Government of India, Election Commission, 11 March 2014, https://tinyurl.com/ycyr6nf5. Both accessed on 27 February 2025.

22 Garg, Subhash Chandra, *We Also Make Policy: An Insider's Account of How the Finance Ministry Functions*, HarperCollins India, New Delhi, 2023.

23 'BJP Got Lion's Share of Electoral Bonds till March 2023', *The Hindu*, 15 February 2024, https://tinyurl.com/573j5krs. Accessed on 7 March 2024.

24　Vermani, Elisha, 'Rs 570 Crore of Electoral Bonds Sold in January Alone, 94% Amount in Rs 1 Crore Denomination.' *The Wire*, 9 February 2024, https://tinyurl.com/pjr3prhd. Accessed on 7 March 2024.

25　'S Y Quraishi Writes: By Striking Down Electoral Bonds Scheme, Supreme Court has Lived Up to Its Role of Democracy's Guardian Angel', *The Indian Express*, 16 February 2024, https://tinyurl.com/mvxucnp5. Accessed on 7 March 2024.

26　Supreme Court of India, 'Civil Appeal No. 10044 of 2010 & Ors', *Central Information Commission*, 4 March 2020, https://tinyurl.com/2umffc37. Accessed on 7 March 2024.

27　'SC Leaves to Parliament to Cure Criminalisation of Politics', *The Week*, 4 April 2020, https://tinyurl.com/222bmnw3. Accessed on 7 March 2024.

2. HOUSE OF LAWMAKERS

1　Ray, Sanjana, and Debayan Dutta, 'Remembering Somnath Chatterjee: A Man Who Personified Democracy', 13 August 2019, https://tinyurl.com/5asyvxyt. Accessed on 27 February 2025.

2　Ibid.

3　Kashyap, Subhash C., *Blueprint of Political Reforms*, Shipra Publications, Delhi, 2020.

4　Ibid.

5　'70 Years of Parliament', *PRS Legislative Research*, 13 May 2022, https://tinyurl.com/9pea2pm4. Accessed on 27 February 2025.

6　Nair, Sobhana K, 'Parliament's Average Annual Sitting Days Down to 55 in the 17th Lok Sabha from 135 in the First', *The Hindu*, 12 February 2024, https://tinyurl.com/58k3hcna. Accessed on 27 February 2025.

7　Menon, Niranjana S., 'Vital Stats: Functioning of the 17th Lok Sabha', *PRS Legislative Research*, 10 February 2024, https://tinyurl.com/5ykt86kw. Accessed on 27 February 2025.

8　Gubbi, Manas, Niranjana S. Menon, and Siddharth Mandrekar Rao, 'Annual Review of State Laws 2022', *PRS Legislative Research*, 31 May 2023, https://tinyurl.com/3edmhcpu. Accessed on 27 February 2025.

9　Ibid.

10 Ibid.
11 Menon, Niranjana S., 'Vital Stats: Functioning of the 17th Lok Sabha', *PRS Legislative Research*, 10 February 2024, https://tinyurl.com/5ykt86kw. Accessed on 27 February 2025.
12 Ibid.
13 Jaiswal, Raunaq, and Nakul Patwardhan, 'Many MPs Are "Agriculturalists", but Why the Disconnect Between Parliament and Farmers?', *The Wire*, 28 January 2021, https://tinyurl.com/bdfexf4w. Accessed on 27 February 2025.
14 'Worst Message from Parliamentary Democracy Is Approval to Budget Without Discussion: Chidambaram', *The Hindu*, 24 March 2023, https://tinyurl.com/4ux7x5sz. Accessed on 6 June 2025.
15 Gubbi, Manas, Niranjana S. Menon, and Siddharth Mandrekar Rao, 'Annual Review of State Laws 2022', *PRS Legislative Research*, 31 May 2023, https://tinyurl.com/3edmhcpu. Accessed on 27 February 2025.
16 Question Hour usually lasts for an hour and is scheduled at the beginning of each parliamentary session. In the Lok Sabha, it occurs from approximately 11 a.m. to 12 noon, while in the Rajya Sabha, it is conducted at the same time on alternate days. However, the timing varies depending on the session's agenda or any other extraordinary circumstances.
17 Sen, Ronojoy, 'Has the Indian Parliament Stood the Test of Time?', *Observer Researcher Foundation*, 15 August 2022, https://tinyurl.com/j8n6sbpv. Accessed on 27 February 2025.
18 Sachdev, Vineet, 'MPs with Criminal Cases Increased in Last Decade: Report', *Hindustan Times*, 11 August 2021, https://tinyurl.com/4kvmmuun; Chatterjee, Mohua, '2014 vs 2019: A 26% Rise in MPs with Criminal History', *The Times of India*, 27 May 2019, https://tinyurl.com/mr3b2th4. Both accessed on 27 February 2025.
19 '251 of Newly Elected Lok Sabha MPs Face Criminal Cases, 27 Convicted: ADR', *Business Standard*, 6 June 2024, https://tinyurl.com/432wzerm. Accessed on 27 February 2025.
20 'Nearly Half of MLAs in India have Criminal Cases: ADR Analysis', *Frontline*, 20 July 2023, https://tinyurl.com/yvdsttdw. Accessed on 27 February 2025.

21 *Lily Thomas v. Union of India and Others* AIR (2013) 7 SCC 653.

22 Sen, Ronojoy, 'Has the Indian Parliament Stood the Test of Time?', *Observer Researcher Foundation*, 15 August 2022, https://tinyurl.com/j8n6sbpv. Accessed on 27 February 2025.

3. THE BUSINESS OF GOVERNANCE

1 Panandiker, V.A. Pai, *The Indian Cabinet: A Study in Governance*, Konark Publishers, Delhi, 1996.

2 Singh, N.K., *Portraits of Power: Half a Century of Being at Ringside*, Rupa Publications, New Delhi, 2020.

3 Mathai, M.O., *Reminiscences of the Nehru Age*, Vikas Publishing House, Noida, 1978.

4 Chowdhury, Neerja, *How Prime Ministers Decide*, Aleph Book Company, New Delhi, 2023.

5 Gandhi, Gopalkrishna, 'Review of Neerja Chowdhury's *How Prime Ministers Decide*: A Living Archive', *The Hindu*, 18 January 2024, https://tinyurl.com/mv6t26rt. Accessed on 7 March 2024.

6 'Centralisation of Power One of India's Main Problems: Raghuram Rajan', *NDTV*, 10 November 2018, https://tinyurl.com/43tu552h. Accessed on 7 March 2024.

7 Chaturvedi, B.K., 'Reform IAS, but Don't Throw the Baby Out With the Bathwater', *The Wire*, 1 March 2021, https://tinyurl.com/55ntn5pa. Accessed on 7 March 2024.

8 Ibid.

9 Saxena, Naresh Chandra, *What Ails the IAS and Why It Fails to Deliver*, Sage Publications, New Delhi, 2019.

10 'India Records Highest Rate of Bribery in Asia: Survey', *The Hindu*, 26 November 2020, https://tinyurl.com/4md74pww. Accessed on 10 June 2025.

11 'World Justice Project: Rule of Law Index® 2020', *World Justice Project*, 24 February 2020, 6, https://tinyurl.com/2j965bur. Accessed on 10 June 2025.

4. HOUSE OF JUSTICE AND JUSTICES

1 Kashyap, Subhash C., *Blueprint for Political Reforms*, Shipra Publications, Delhi, 2020.

2 'Pending Cases', *National Judicial Data Grid*, 24 February 2024, https://tinyurl.com/ytb4fmx5. Accessed on 24 February 2024.

3 Disposal refers to cases that go all the way to a judgement as well as cases that are dismissed. Deka, Kaushik, 'Why Law Minister Kiren Rijiju wants a Reboot of the Collegium System of Judges' Appointments', *India Today*, 20 September 2022, https://tinyurl.com/yc6393fz. Accessed on 28 February 2025.

4 Roy, Shubho, 'What's Choking the Indian Judiciary', *NDTV Profit*, 2023, 11 July 2023, https://tinyurl.com/yn9j4nhx. Accessed on 28 February 2025.

5 'State of the Judiciary: A Report on Infrastructure, Budgeting, Human Resources, and ICT', *Supreme Court of India*, 26 November 2023, https://tinyurl.com/54h6zhep. Accessed on 6 March 2025.

6 Ibid.

7 'Justice V.R. Krishna Iyer', Ministry of Law & Justice, Government of India, 8 September 2015, https://tinyurl.com/5n84ntfz. Accessed on 28 February 2025.

8 'Parliament and the Judiciary', *PRS Legislative Research*, 29 November 2016, https://tinyurl.com/yc5kya9w. Accessed on 10 June 2025.

9 Ibid.

10 Rajagopal, Krishnadas, 'SC Bench Strikes Down NJAC Act as "Unconstitutional and Void"', *The Hindu*, 4 December 2021, https://tinyurl.com/3p54byj2. Accessed on 10 June 2025.

11 'National Judicial Appointments Commission Act Notified', Ministry of Law & Justice, Government of India, 13 April 2015, https://tinyurl.com/3z8nbtnu. Accessed on 10 June 2025.

5. FEDERALISM: AN INTEGRAL PART OF THE GOVERNANCE STRUCTURE

1 Babar, Aniruddha, 'Dr B.R. Ambedkar's Contribution to Federalism Enshrined in the Constitution of India', *Fazl Ali College Journal*, Vol. 7, 2018, 43–55, https://tinyurl.com/yz5z5d3j. Accessed on 13 March 2024.

2 Moon, Vasant (ed.), *Dr. Babasaheb Ambedkar: Writings and Speeches, Vol. 13*, Dr. Ambedar Foundation, New Delhi, 2020, https://

tinyurl.com/45zjf34y. Accessed on 13 March 2024.

3   R. Mohan, *India's Federal Setup: A Journey Through Seven Decades*, Aakar Books, Delhi, 2023.

4   Bhattacharya, Shubhabrata, 'Congress Factionalism gave Life to Article 356', *The Sunday Guardian*, 9 April 2016, https://tinyurl.com/v2f6ajxy. Accessed on 11 June 2025.

5   'Sarkaria Commission', *Inter-State Council Secretariat*, 9 June 1983, https://tinyurl.com/mu38mbw6. Accessed on 13 March 2024.

6   Das, Anjishnu, '13 years in J&K, 10 Times in Manipur, UP: History of President's Rule', *The Indian Express*, 29 August 2023, https://tinyurl.com/2cw6fej9. Accessed on 13 March 2024.

7   'Maharashtra Drama Continues: Devendra Fadnavis is CM, Ajit Pawar His Deputy', *Hindustan Times*, 24 November 2019, https://tinyurl.com/am2nc66a. Accessed on 11 March 2025.

8   Ghanghas, Anil, 'Imposition of President's Rule in Indian States from Independence to 2020: An Analysis', *Studies in Indian Place Names*, Vol. 40, No. 70, 2020, 777, https://tinyurl.com/5aj64kpn. Accessed on 6 March 2025.

9   Rajagopalan, Shruti, Abishek Choutagunta, Christian Bjørnskov, and Stefan Voigt, 'How an SC Judgment Checked the Misuse of Article 356', *Hindustan Times*, 11 March 2024, https://tinyurl.com/5n7hu6tp. Accessed on 13 March 2024.

10 'Role of the Governor', *Interstate Council*, 19 May 2008, https://tinyurl.com/33fcetxu. Accessed on 13 March 2024.

11 'Seventh Schedule', Ministry of External Affairs, Government of India, https://tinyurl.com/ytrbpu7u. Accessed on 14 March 2024.

12 'Seventh Schedule: State, Union and Concurrent Lists Explained', *India Today*, 1 November 2021, https://tinyurl.com/2t7mvw9h. Accessed on 14 March 2024.

13 Chaturvedi, B.K., 'How the Union Govt Is Slowly but Surely Blurring India's Federal Structure', *The Wire*, 23 January 2024, https://tinyurl.com/mrxprs35. Accessed on 13 March 2024.

14 Roy, Chakshu, 'Governors as Chancellors: The Points of Conflict', *The Indian Express*, 28 August 2022, https://tinyurl.com/y4rdxw3v. Accessed on 13 March 2024.

15 Chowdhury, Subhankar, 'SC Seal on Chief Minister Mamata Banerjee's Authority in Selecting VCs: Bratya Basu', *The Telegraph*,

25 October 2024, https://tinyurl.com/2ptbnehs. Accessed on 11 March 2025.

16 'Bengal Governor Appoints Interim VC of Another State-run University Despite Mamata Banerjee's Threat to Block Funds', *The Indian Express*, 6 September 2023, https://tinyurl.com/mryfheut. Accessed on 11 March 2025.

17 Mallady, Shastry V., 'Governor's Interference Is Undermining the Autonomy of State Universities and Syndicate: MKU Faculty Association', *Lotus Times*, 9 July 2023, https://tinyurl.com/y37u7rhk. Accessed on 11 March 2025.

18 'West Bengal Assembly Passes Bill to Replace Governor with CM as Chancellor of State Universities', *The Times of India*, 4 August 2023, https://tinyurl.com/2627s9sv. Accessed on 11 March 2025.

6. RESERVATIONS: NOT A MAGIC BULLET TO RESOLVE BACKWARDNESS

1 'False Dichotomy: On Merit versus Reservation', *The Hindu*, 24 January 2022, https://tinyurl.com/4nutff4c. Accessed on 31 March 2024.

2 Saigal, Sonam, 'Ambedkar Would Be Pained to See That SC/ST Still Need Reservation', *The Hindu*, 7 December 2021, https://tinyurl.com/5e8wj5ea. Accessed on 31 March 2024.

3 Ranjan, Alok, 'Existing Reservation Quota Limit of the Indian States', *India Today*, 7 May 2021, https://tinyurl.com/5ymp5sab. Accessed on 28 February 2025.

4 'Reservation Guidelines', *Institute of Secretariat Training & Management, Government of India*, 24 January 2014, https://tinyurl.com/4fzdvada. Accessed on 6 March 2025.

5 Mihir R., 'Do Reservations Have to Be Below 50%? From Balaji [1962] to Indra Sawhney [1992]', *Supreme Court Observer*, 31 March 2021, https://tinyurl.com/mvdww973. Accessed on 31 March 2024.

6 Poddar, Umang, 'Does the EWS Judgment Remove the 50% Cap on Reservations?', *Scroll.in*, 20 November 2022, https://tinyurl.com/56bsmywj. Accessed on 31 March 2024.

7 'History of Reservation in India', *GoI Monitor*, 11 January 2019, https://tinyurl.com/ycxjs2ar; Venkatesh, Karthik, 'Ahead of the Curve: Revisiting Chhatrapati Shahu Maharaj's 1902 Decision to

Reserve Jobs for Backward Castes', *Firstpost*, 26 July 2021, https://tinyurl.com/2z5tpyf6. Both accessed on 31 March 2024.

8   'What Was Shahu Maharaj's Historic 1902 Reservation Order?', *The Satyashodak*, 26 July 2022, https://tinyurl.com/bde3amxm. Accessed on 31 March 2024.

9   Das, Bhagwan, 'Moments in a History of Reservations', *Economic & Political Weekly*, Vol. 35, No. 43–44, 2000, 3831–3834, https://tinyurl.com/y9spry7c. Accessed on 28 February 2025.

10   Saxena, Suvigya, 'Can Reservations and India Bloom Together', *Legal Service India*, https://tinyurl.com/4jd27smh. Accessed on 28 February 2025.

11   Das, Bhagwan, 'Moments in a History of Reservations', *Economic & Political Weekly*, Vol. 35, No. 43–44, 2000, 3831–3834, https://tinyurl.com/y9spry7c. Accessed on 28 February 2025.

12   Rajagopal, Krishnadas, 'Constitution Bench to Examine Validity of Extending Reservation of Seats for SCs/STs in LS, Assemblies', *The Hindu*, 20 September 2023, https://tinyurl.com/22tjt42a. Accessed on 31 March 2024.

13   Das, Bhagwan, 'Moments in a History of Reservations', *Economic & Political Weekly*, Vol. 35, No. 43–44, 2000, 3831–3834, https://tinyurl.com/y9spry7c. Accessed on 28 February 2025.

14   Ramakrishnan, Venkitesh, T.S. Subramanian, K. Venkateswaralu, Ravi Sharma, and Dionne Bunsha, 'Southern Record', *Frontline*, 5 May 2006, https://tinyurl.com/bdfudff6x. Accessed on 31 March 2024.

15   Nair, Sobhana K., 'Is there a Clear North-South Divide in Indian Politics?', *The Hindu*, 2 June 2023, https://tinyurl.com/63nt2tca. Accessed on 31 March 2024.

16   Vishwanath, Apurva, 'Reservation Criteria Shift from Caste to Income, Community to Individuals', *The Indian Express*, 8 November 2022, https://tinyurl.com/36rkrn7u. Accessed on 9 June 2025.

17   Pillalamarri, Akhilesh, 'The Future of Reservations in India', *The Diplomat*, 20 November 2022, https://tinyurl.com/3ru9kmam. Accessed on 31 March 2024.

18   Ibid.

19   Menon, Ramesh, 'The Dangers of Exploiting Reservation Issues

for Political Gain', *The Week*, 30 September 2017, https://tinyurl.com/5n83mr7m. Accessed on 31 March 2024.

20 Kumar, Sanjay, and Pranav Gupta, 'Are Marathas, Jats and Patels Economically Weak?', *Mint*, 20 September 2018, https://tinyurl.com/3drk65bp. Accessed on 31 March 2024.

21 Babu, D. Shyam, 'Wanna Be Weak? You Gotta Be Strong', *The Times of India*, 23 February 2024, https://tinyurl.com/yc292xjp. Accessed on 31 March 2024.

22 Kumar, Krishna, 'Jarange Patil Ends 17-day Fast After CM Eknath Shinde's Visit', *The Economic Times*, 14 September 2023, https://tinyurl.com/3eter4pz. Accessed on 11 June 2025.

23 'Ignited Hopes, No Jobs. Why Jats, Others Revolt', *IndiaSpend*, 23 February 2016, https://tinyurl.com/yrznvknh. Accessed on 31 March 2024.

24 Mehrotra, Santosh, 'Ten-year Record on Employment: Does the Reality Match the Promises or Claims?', *The Wire*. 7 January 2024, https://tinyurl.com/t9r5c66c. Accessed on 31 March 2024.

25 Nadkarni, M.V., 'Reservations can Help, and Hurt Too', *Deccan Herald*, 27 November 2023, https://tinyurl.com/mv8pjj6d. Accessed on 31 March 2024.

7. INDIAN AGRICULTURE: SPUTTERING ALONG

1 Frank, Andre Gunder, 'The Global Economy, AD 1400–1800: Comparisons and Relations', *Understanding Business: Markets*, Vivek Suneja (ed.), Routledge, London, 2000, 13.

2 Raju, Archishman, 'Nehru and the Spirit of Science', *The India Forum*, 30 September 2024, https://tinyurl.com/92cbcw5w. Accessed on 11 March 2025.

3 'Indian Agriculture under the Five Year Plans', *Insights IAS*, https://tinyurl.com/4pc4b9w2. Accessed on 11 March 2025.

4 Ibid.

5 'When the Big Dams Came Up', *The Hindu*, 20 March 2015, https://tinyurl.com/3rkzbjbt. Accessed on 9 June 2025.

6 'Indian Agriculture Under the Five Year Plans', *Insights IAS*, https://tinyurl.com/4pc4b9w2. Accessed on 11 March 2025.

7 'India Inflation Rate 1960–2025', *Macrotrends*, https://tinyurl.com/3au8cnwn. Accessed on 11 March 2025.

8   Aiyar, S.S.A., 'Drought Not a Big Calamity in India Anymore', *The Times of India*, 29 July 2012, https://tinyurl.com/46prf9m8. Accessed on 11 March 2025.

9   'India Wheat Imports by Year', *IndexMundi*, https://tinyurl.com/yhu5nms8. Accessed on 11 March 2025.

10   Malhotra, Inder, 'Swallowing the Humiliation', 12 July 2010, https://tinyurl.com/9e6jcbbx. Accessed on 11 March 2025.

11   G. Gopalkrishnan, *M.S. Swaminathan: One Man's Quest for a Hunger-free World*, Education Development Centre, Inc, Chennai, 2002, 47.

12   Chand, Ramesh, 'Agriculture in Post-Independent India: Looking Back and Looking Ahead', *ICAR Lecture Series #29*, 24 September 2021, https://tinyurl.com/6smbyrkj Accessed on 4 March 2025.

13   Ibid.

14   'Share of Agriculture in India's GDP Declined to 15% in FY23: Govt, *The Times of India*, 19 December 2023, https://tinyurl.com/mrhn3ws7. Accessed on 12 March 2025.

15   Richhariya, Jyotsna, 'Indian Agriculture Household Earns Just Rs. 10,218 in a Month: Govt', *Ground Report*, 8 August 2024, https://tinyurl.com/5b2mn2m9. Accessed on 11 March 2025.

16   'Agriculture and Allied Activities Sector Significantly Contributed to the Country's Overall Growth and Development by Ensuring Food Security: Latest Economic Survey', Ministry of Agriculture & Farmers Welfare, Government of India, 3 February 2023, https://tinyurl.com/28xt89km. Accessed on 11 March 2025.

17   'All India Report on Agriculture Census 2015–16', Ministry of Agriculture & Farmers Welfare, Government of India, 30 January 2020, https://tinyurl.com/4h89yrs6. Accessed on 11 March 2025.

18   In agriculture, monocropping is the practice of growing a single crop year after year on the same land, which allows for farmers to have consistent crops throughout their entire farm. Maize, soybeans and wheat are three common crops often monocropped. While this practice increases efficiency and yield, it can also lead to negative environmental impacts.

19   'Annual Review of Fertilizer Production and Consumption 2022–23: Highlights', *Indian Journal of Fertilisers*, Vol. 19, No. 9,

2024, 918–978, https://tinyurl.com/mryvsxfj. Accessed on 11 March 2025.

20 Das, Puja, 'Nearly 55% of Farm Land Getting Irrigation: NITI Aayog's Chand', *Mint*, 31 May 2023, https://tinyurl.com/3tn35yx9; 'Development of Irrigation in India—Water Resources, Irrigation Potential and Irrigation Systems of India and Tamil Nadu', *Tamil Nadu Agricultural University*, 28 March 2013, https://tinyurl.com/ymukpvc9. Both accessed on 11 March 2025.

21 'Saving the Harvest: Reducing the Food Loss and Waste', *National Academy of Agricultural Sciences*, 1 July 2019, https://tinyurl.com/3rynaxh8. Accessed on 11 March 2025.

22 Deepika M., '11 Major Problems Faced by Indian Farmers in Agriculture in 2024', *BigHaat*, 13 March 2023, https://tinyurl.com/3s6whj7m. Accessed on 11 March 2025.

23 'Union Budget 2023: Govt Raises Farm Credit Target by 11% to Rs 20 Lakh Crore for FY24', *The Times of India*, 1 February 2023, https://tinyurl.com/ydjjhtz5. Accessed on 11 March 2025.

24 Gulati, Ashok, and Ritika Juneja, 'Agricultural Credit System in India: Evolution, Effectiveness and Innovations', *ZEF Working Paper Series*, No. 184, 16 September 2019, https://tinyurl.com/353f3w6f. Accessed on 11 March 2025.

25 Ibid.

26 Dev, S. Mahendra, 'Union Budget 2024-25: Some Boost for Agriculture and Rural Economy', *Business Standard*, 24 July 2024, https://tinyurl.com/4r2y4d6b. Accessed on 11 June 2025.

27 'China's Growing Status in Innovation', *Federal Reserve Bank of St. Louis*, 30 April 2019, https://tinyurl.com/3xs53c6b. Accessed on 11 March 2025.

28 'India Can Learn Agri-Policy Lessons from China', *Financial Express*, 29 October 2019, https://tinyurl.com/z669bpvj. Accessed on 11 March 2025.

29 Gulati, Ashok, and Sakshi Gupta, 'Market Incentives, Direct Income Support for Farmers Are Far More Effective in Increasing Agricultural Productivity', *The Indian Express*, 31 October 2019, https://tinyurl.com/4afmntd8. Accessed on 11 March 2025.

30 Ibid.

31 'India Can Learn Agri-Policy Lessons from China', *Financial Express*, 29 October 2019, https://tinyurl.com/z669bpvj. Accessed on 11 March 2025.

32 Ibid.

33 Ibid.

34 'Composite Water Management Index', *NITI Aayog*, June 2018, https://tinyurl.com/4hpkxrpa. Accessed on 17 June 2025.

35 'Composite Water Management Index', *NITI Aayog*, August 2019, https://tinyurl.com/5xptnnv6. Accessed on 17 June 2025.

36 'Ensuring Optimum Utilization of Water in Agriculture Sector', Ministry of Jal Shakti, Government of India, 23 March 2023, https://tinyurl.com/7s5m8pt9. Accessed on 17 June 2025.

37 Mandel, Jonah, 'Israeli Desalination, Wastewater Treatment Becomes Global Model for Water Scarcity', *The Times of Israel*, 10 August 2023, https://tinyurl.com/3aynzk8x. Accessed on 17 June 2025.

38 Matto, Mahreen, Sumita Singhal, and Jyoti Parsad, 'Decentralised Wastewater Solutions the Need of the Hour for India', 14 October 2019, https://tinyurl.com/yc4e5abs. Accessed on 17 June 2025.

39 Gulati, Ashok, 'Farm Lessons from China and Israel', *Financial Express*, 15 February 2021, https://tinyurl.com/rzm7yer6. Accessed on 17 June 2025.

40 'The Indo-Israel Agricultural Cooperation Project', *MASHAV*, 4 June 2019, https://tinyurl.com/yc6xf5ex. Accessed on 17 June 2025.

41 Wilson, Anne, 'Smart Irrigation Technology Covers "More Crop Per Drop"', *MIT News*, 25 October 2023, https://tinyurl.com/j55j4scp. Accessed on 17 June 2025.

42 Nath, Prosenjit, 'Tackling India's Water Crisis: Learning from Israel's Success', *Organiser*, 27 January 2025, https://tinyurl.com/4ev6ka4v. Accessed on 17 June 2025.

43 Shetty, Kanishk, 'Strengthening Indo-Israel Agritech Cooperation', *Observer Research Foundation*, 26 July 2023, https://tinyurl.com/2rkm3t8a. Accessed on 17 June 2025.

44 Mishra, Piyush, 'India and Israel Sign Key Agriculture Deal to Boost Cooperation and Food Security', *India Today*, 9 April 2025,

https://tinyurl.com/3rtp4ej9. Accessed on 17 June 2025.

45 Ibid.

46 Ibid.

47 'Agriculture', Statistical Year Book India 2014, Ministry of Statistics and Program Implementation, Government of India, 31 December 2014, https://tinyurl.com/2wewwkuw. Accessed on 11 March 2025.

48 Ibid.

49 'Digital Agriculture Mission: Tech for Transforming Farmers' Lives', Ministry of Agriculture & Farmers Welfare, Government of India, 4 September 2024, https://tinyurl.com/kkmhek5c. Accessed on 11 March 2025.

50 Saini, Shweta, Siraj Hussain, and Pulkit Khatri, 'Farm Loan Waivers in India: Assessing Impact and Looking Ahead', *NABARD* and *Bharat Krishak Samaj*, 6 December 2021, https://tinyurl.com/2seefar4. Accessed on 12 March 2025.

51 'Credit Culture Destroyed? Only 50% Gain from Farm Loan Waivers, Says Study', *The Times of India*, 26 July 2022, https://tinyurl.com/4ftdpzmx. Accessed on 5 March 2025.

52 Ibid.

53 Textor, C., 'Public Expenditure on Agriculture, Forestry and Water Resource Projects in China from 2014 to 2024', *Statista*, 29 January 2025, https://tinyurl.com/27nmwvft. Accessed on 12 March 2025.

54 'Summary of the Union Budget 2024–2025', Ministry of Finance, Government of India, 23 July 2024, https://tinyurl.com/5hfbsh27; 'Union Budget 2024–25: Spotlight', *india.gov.in*, https://tinyurl.com/msncm2xz. Both accessed on 12 March 2025.

8. A DEEPLY UNJUST EDUCATION SYSTEM

1 Singhvi, Abhishek, 'India's Basic Constitutional Values Need Eternal Vigilance', *Hindustan Times*, 29 November 2024, https://tinyurl.com/2rjy2bew. Accessed on 12 March 2025.

2 'Women & Men in India-2017', Ministry of Statistics & Programme Implementation, Government of India, 15 January 2019, https://tinyurl.com/37f23mvy. Accessed on 5 March 2025.

3   'Literacy Is Rising, But We Can Do Better', *Deccan Herald*, 23 June 2025, https://tinyurl.com/mry9apnv. Accessed on 8 July 2025.

4   Nanda, Prashant K., 'India has the highest population of illiterate adults: UNESCO', *Mint*, 29 January 2014, https://tinyurl.com/3buvtffs. Accessed on 12 March 2025.

5   'Women & Men in India-2017', Ministry of Statistics & Programme Implementation, Government of India, 15 January 2019, https://tinyurl.com/37f23mvy. Accessed on 5 March 2025.

6   Ibid.

7   Stanfield, James Ronald, and Jacqueline Bloom Stanfield, *Interviews with John Kenneth Galbraith*, University Press of Mississippi, Jackson, MS, 2004, 156.

8   'Performance Grading Index of All States and UTs on School Education 2017–18, Ministry of Human Resource Development, Government of India, 12 March 2019, https://tinyurl.com/2ua76h9u. Accessed on 12 March 2025.

9   'What is PISA Test? India is Taking Part First Time Since 2009; Check Questions, Rankings, Scores, Subjects', *Financial Express*, 11 September 2018, https://tinyurl.com/yyw5exff. Accessed on 11 June 2025.

10   Rajagopalan, Sridhar, 'Unpacking the PISA Test: Why Do Indians Struggle with Certain Types of Tests?', *Hindustan Times*, 10 July 2019, https://tinyurl.com/bdzbc6ms; Vishnoi, Anubhuti, 'Poor PISA Score: Govt Blames "Disconnect" with India', *The Indian Express*, 3 September 2012, https://tinyurl.com/3bhr7f76. Both accessed on 10 June 2025.

11   Bhattacharyya, Ranajit, 'Annual Status of Education Report (ASER 2023: Beyond Basics) Was Released in New Delhi', *ASER Centre*, 17 January 2024, https://tinyurl.com/59f5xphh. Accessed on 1 July 2025.

12   Bhattacharya, Saptarshi, 'India has Not Taken Education Seriously Since Independence: Prof. Krishna Kumar', *The Hindu Centre for Politics and Public Policy*, 20 January 2023, https://tinyurl.com/yc3c8srw. Accessed on 10 June 2025.

13   Ibid.

14   Tilak, Jandhyala B.G., 'Five Decades of Underinvestment in Education', Vol. 32, No. 36, 1997, 2239–2241, https://tinyurl.com/rka9r49r. Accessed on 12 March 2025.

15 Stiglitz, Joseph E., 'Some Lessons from the East Asian Miracle', *The World Bank Research Observer*, Vol. 11, No. 2, 1996, 151–177, https://tinyurl.com/2797fxyp. Accessed on 12 March 2025.

16 Balaji, B. Preedip, Vinay M.S., J.S. Mohan Raju, 'A Policy Review of Public Libraries in India', *Indian Institute for Human Settlements*, Working Paper, 2018, https://tinyurl.com/u4ncu78u. Accessed on 12 March 2025.

17 '250 Million Children Out-of-School: What You Need to Know About UNESCO's Latest Education Data', *UNESCO*, 21 September 2023, https://tinyurl.com/eumu73d2. Accessed on 12 March 2025.

18 'Status of Learning Achievements in India: A Review of Empirical Research', *Azim Premji Foundation*, 2 March 2005, https://tinyurl.com/3xh7kbes. Accessed on 12 March 2025.

19 Ibid.

20 Ibid.

21 Sarangapani, Padma M., Bindu Thirumalai, Anusha Ramanathan, Ruchi Kumar, and Mythili Ramchand, 'No Teacher, No Class: State of the Education Report for India, 2021', *UNESCO*, https://tinyurl.com/2xb4j7ep. Accessed on 12 March 2025.

22 'Status of Learning Achievements in India: A Review of Empirical Research', *Azim Premji Foundation*, 2 March 2005, https://tinyurl.com/3xh7kbes. Accessed on 12 March 2025.

23 'Nehru's Approach to Primary Education Lamentable: Amartya', *The Economic Times*, 4 July 2011, https://tinyurl.com/4f2zz3nb. Accessed on 12 March 2025.

24 Sharma, Sanjay, Interim Union Budget 2024–25: The Need for 6% of GDP in the Indian Education Sector, Major Roadblocks and More', *The Times of India*, 29 January 2024, https://tinyurl.com/7p948ed2. Accessed on 12 March 2025.

25 Jhingran, Dhir, 'ASER 2024 Delivered Good News. But There is Still a Mountain to Climb', *The Indian Express*, 6 February 2025, https://tinyurl.com/3mvnt87t. Accessed on 12 March 2025.

26 'Nehru's Approach to Primary Education Lamentable: Amartya', *The Economic Times*, 4 July 2011, https://tinyurl.com/4f2zz3nb. Accessed on 12 March 2025.

9. PUBLIC HEALTH: IN NEED OF REVITALIZATION

1   'WHO Remains Firmly Committed to the Principles Set Out in the Preamble to the Constitution', *World Health Organization*, https://tinyurl.com/2srnpbnm. Accessed on 12 March 2025.

2   Rao, K. Sujatha, *Do We Care? India's Health System*, Oxford University Press, New Delhi, 2017, 12.

3   *Public Health For All*, K. Srinath Reddy (ed.), India International Centre Quarterly, New Delhi, Vol. 49, Nos. 3 and 4, 2022–2023, 2.

4   Arora, Simran, '7 Decades of Wellness: How Life Expectancy Increased in India the Last 75 Years', *Times Now*, 11 August 2022, https://tinyurl.com/mww7uxkk; Chakrabarti, Angana, 'Women in India Live Longer than Men But Don't Have Healthier Lives, Finds New Report', *The Print*, 11 July 2021, https://tinyurl.com/4aczssfb. Both accessed on 12 March 2025.

5   *Public Health For All*, K. Srinath Reddy (ed.), India International Centre Quarterly, New Delhi, Vol. 49, Nos. 3 and 4, 2022–2023, 2.

6   'Prime Minister Shri Narendra Modi Led Government Has Made Indian Healthcare Future-Ready: Dr. Subhas Sarkar', Ministry of Education, Government of India, 23 December 2022, https://tinyurl.com/3cy43fft; 'World Health Statistics 2015', *World Health Organization*, https://tinyurl.com/575jabtj; Chauhan, L.S., Public Health in India: Issues and Challenges, *Indian Journal of Public Health*, Vol. 55, No. 2, 2011, 88–91. https://tinyurl.com/3wuuzrk9. All accessed on 12 March 2025.

7   *Public Health For All*, K. Srinath Reddy (ed.), India International Centre Quarterly, New Delhi, Vol. 49, Nos. 3 and 4, 2022–2023, 1.

8   Rao, K. Sujatha, *Do We Care? India's Health System*, Oxford University Press, New Delhi, 2017, 13.

9   Ibid. 298–299

10 Ibid.

11 'About Pradhan Mantri Jan Arogya Yojana (PM-JAY)', *National Health Authority, Government of India*, https://tinyurl.com/2s3w2tc4. Accessed on 12 March 2025.

12 'Committed to Advancing the Agenda of Universal Health Coverage through Affordable and Accessible Healthcare for All', Ministry of Health and Family Welfare, Government of India, 18 December 2017, https://tinyurl.com/y6tzfcjw. Accessed on 12 March 2025.

13 'Share of Government Health Expenditure in Total Health Expenditure Increases from 28.6 Per Cent in FY14 to 40.6 Per Cent in FY19', Ministry of Finance, Government of India, 31 January 2023, https://tinyurl.com/23cahn2a. Accessed on 12 March 2025.

14 Zhang, Wenyi, 'Health Expenditure in China as a Proportion of Gross Domestic Product (GDP) from 2013 to 2023', *Statista*, 19 November 2024, https://tinyurl.com/muunvtk9; 'Sri Lanka Healthcare Spending 2000–2025', *Macrotrends*, https://tinyurl.com/2ye9mnrh. Both accessed on 12 March 2025.

15 Kaul, Rhythma, 'India Accounts for 28% of 10.6 Million TB Cases in 2021: WHO Report', *Hindustan Times*, 28 October 2022, https://tinyurl.com/bdfrk4hu. Accessed on 11 June 2025.

16 'New HIV Cases Down in India by 44% Since 2010: Anupriya Patel', *The Hindu*, 25 September 2024, https://tinyurl.com/mw95prnx. Accessed on 12 March 2025.

17 Kumar, Ashwani, Neena Valecha, Tanu Jain, and Aditya P. Dash, 'Burden of Malaria in India: Retrospective and Prospective View', *American Journal of Tropical Medicine and Hygiene*, Vol. 77, No. 6, 2007, https://tinyurl.com/3x7ydbmw. Accessed on 12 March 2025.

18 Agrawal, V.K., and V.K. Sashindran, 'Lymphatic Filariasis in India: Problems, Challenges and New Initiatives', *Medical Journal Armed Forces India*, Vol. 62, No. 4, 2011, 359–362, https://tinyurl.com/dd93e7hf. Accessed on 12 March 2025.

19 Porecha, Maitri, 'India Accounts for 52% of World's New Leprosy Patients, Says Health Minister', *The Hindu*, 17 February 2023, https://tinyurl.com/y75bwp8t. Accessed on 12 March 2025.

20 Prasad, Seema, 'India Had Over 11% of Global Hepatitis Burden in 2022, with 35.3 Million Cases', *Down to Earth*, 10 April 2024, https://tinyurl.com/285fw746. Accessed on 12 March 2025.

21 Lakshminarayanan, Subitha, and Ramakrishnan Jayalakshmy, 'Diarrheal Diseases Among Children in India: Current Scenario and Future Perspectives', *Journal of Natural Science, Biology and Medicine*, Vol. 6, No. 1, 2015, 24–28, https://tinyurl.com/ye23t96u. Accessed on 12 March 2025.

22 Chauhan, L.S., Public Health in India: Issues and Challenges, *Indian Journal of Public Health*, Vol. 55, No. 2, 2011, 88–91. https://tinyurl.com/3wuuzrk9. Accessed on 12 March 2025.

23 Buttan, Sandeep, 'At 8 Million, India Has the World's Largest Blind Population. Nearly Half of It Was Preventable', *Firstpost*, 7 April 2022, https://tinyurl.com/mr3m2etd; Krishnan Sathishkumar, Meesha Chaturvedi, Priyanka Das, S. Stephen, and Prashant Mathur, 'Cancer Incidence Estimates for 2022 & Projection for 2025: Result from National Cancer Registry Programme, India', *Indian Journal of Medical Research*, Vol. 156, No. 4–5, 2023, 598–607, https://tinyurl.com/yc6tf6d7. Accessed on 12 March 2025.

24 Sharma, Deepak, 'The State of India's Health Security: GHS Index 2021 Rankings and Trends', *The Times of India*, 23 July 2023, https://tinyurl.com/mrxrzxda. Accessed on 12 March 2025.

25 Ibid.

26 Ibid.

27 Ibid.

28 Ibid.

29 Ibid.

30 Bell, Jessica A., and Jennifer B. Nuzzo, 'Global Health Security Index: Advancing Collective Action and Accountability Amid Global Crisis, 2021', *Johns Hopkins*, 29 November 2021, https://tinyurl.com/28zya8su. Accessed on 5 March 2025.

31 'Zero Case: India's Polio Eradication Saga', Ministry of Health and Family Welfare, Government of India, 19 November 2024, https://tinyurl.com/43mce495. Accessed on 12 March 2025.

32 'WHO Acknowledges India's Success in Declining TB Incidence by 16% and TB Mortality Reduction by 18% Since 2015', Ministry of Health and Family Welfare, Government of India, 8 November 2023, https://tinyurl.com/3hu5z8n3. Accessed on 12 March 2025.

33 Sengar, Namit Singh, 'India Needs to Add 2 Billion Sq Ft in Healthcare Real Estate to Meet Population Needs: Report', *News18*, 25 November 2023, https://tinyurl.com/3j4546fb. Accessed on 12 March 2025.

34 'India Facing Deficit of 2 Billion Sq Ft of Healthcare Space to Cater to Current Population Need: Study', *Biospectrum*, 23 November 2023, https://tinyurl.com/2wfu6y5x. Accessed on 5 March 2025.

35 Singh, Angesh, 'How Many Doctors Are Produced in India Every Year?', *Knya*, 2 July 2024, https://tinyurl.com/3w2j3bbs. Accessed on 12 March 2025.

36 'Why Medical Education in India Needs Urgent Reforms', *India Today*, 8 January 2022, https://tinyurl.com/56zcusrb. Accessed on 12 March 2025.

37 'Update on Ratio of Patients and Doctors/Nurses', Ministry of Health and Family Welfare, Government of India, 12 December 2023, https://tinyurl.com/2sj2yu9b. Accessed on 12 March 2025.

38 Ibid.

39 'Urban Population (% of Total Population)–India', *United Nations Population Division*, https://tinyurl.com/5n6hzrx6. Accessed on 12 March 2025.

40 'National Health Account (NHA) Estimates 2020–21 and 2021–22', *Ministry of Health and Family Welfare, Government of India*, https://tinyurl.com/3fkmrbej. Accessed on 12 March 2025.

41 'PayNearby: Bharat Health Index (BHI) 2023', *Estrade*, 11 August 2023, https://tinyurl.com/ybfdhr27. Accessed on 12 March 2025.

42 'Only 25% of Semi-rural, Rural Population Has Health Facilities within Reach', *Business Standard*, 11 August 2023, https://tinyurl.com/5em67paw. Accessed on 12 March 2025.

43 Player, Jacob, 'Healthcare Access in Rural Communities in India', *Ballard Brief*, 2019, https://tinyurl.com/6f7u23s2. Accessed on 12 March 2025.

44 Sharma, Dinesh C., 'India Still Struggles with Rural Doctor Shortages', *The Lancet*, Vol. 386, No. 10011, 2015, 2381–2382, https://tinyurl.com/ykkftfu2. Accessed on 12 March 2025.

45 Ibid.

46 Player, Jacob, 'Healthcare Access in Rural Communities in India', *Ballard Brief*, 2019, https://tinyurl.com/6f7u23s2. Accessed on 12 March 2025.

47 Ibid.

48 'Over 7.3M Tourists Likely to Visit India for Medical Purposes in 2024, *Medical Buyer*, 15 July 2024, https://tinyurl.com/2hm4esyu. Accessed on 12 March 2025.

49 Mabiyan, Rashmi, 'Is India Doing Enough to Carve a Niche in

Medical Tourism?', *ETHealthWorld*, 20 November 2019, https://tinyurl.com/erbz4e64. Accessed on 12 March 2025.

50　Katz, Alexandra, 'India Emerges as New Destination for Russian Medical Tourists', *Russia Beyond*, 16 April 2015, https://tinyurl.com/yxtsdyfc. Accessed on 12 March 2025.

51　Agrawal, Sanjana, Gopal Chauhan, Abhiruchi Galhotra, and Sonu Goel, 'Five Years of National Health Policy in India: Critical Analysis of the Public Health Expenditure from 2017 to 2022 and Way Forward', *Indian Journal of Community Medicine*, Vol. 49, No. 6, 2024, 883–885, https://tinyurl.com/4zvtu34t. Accessed on 3 July 2025.

52　*Public Health For All*, K. Srinath Reddy (ed.), India International Centre Quarterly, New Delhi, Vol. 49, Nos. 3 and 4, 2022–2023, 10.

53　Ibid. 8

54　Rao, K. Sujatha, *Do We Care? India's Health System*, Oxford University Press, New Delhi, 2017, 298–299.

55　'Social Groups Press for Immediate Rollout of Right to Health Act'22, *The Times if India*, 23 January 2025, https://tinyurl.com/3x8zwtdc. Accessed on 12 March 2025.

56　'India: Human Capital Index 2020', *World Bank*, 1 January 2020, https://tinyurl.com/ytesktpk. Accessed on 12 March 2025.

10. HUMAN CAPITAL: THE STORY OF INDIA'S WORKFORCE POTENTIAL

1　'Achieving the Demographic Dividend: An Operational Tool for Country-Specific Investment Decision-Making in Pre-Dividend Countries', *World Bank*, 22 February 2019, https://tinyurl.com/4mu75w26. Accessed on 12 March 2025.

2　'Telling Numbers: Over Half of India's Population is Still Under Age 30, Slight Dip in Last 5 Years', *The Indian Express*, 11 May 2022, https://tinyurl.com/2uj6tuha. Accessed on 12 March 2025.

3　'Reaping the Demographic Dividend', *EY India*, 11 April 2023, https://tinyurl.com/4rny4y2x. Accessed on 12 March 2025.

4　'Human Capital and Educational Policies', *OECD*, https://tinyurl.com/ywtmv5xk. Accessed on 12 March 2025.

5　'The Human Capital Project: Frequently Asked Questions', *World Bank*, 19 March 2019, https://tinyurl.com/mr77zcun. Accessed on 12 March 2025.

6   'Achieving the Demographic Dividend: An Operational Tool for
    Country-Specific Investment Decision-Making in Pre-Dividend
    Countries', *World Bank*, 22 February 2019, https://tinyurl.
    com/3n2bz8bk. Accessed on 12 March 2025.

7   'Human Capital: Gaining from Differential Demographic
    Dividend', *Financial Express*, 16 October 2020, https://tinyurl.
    com/483j4j3w. Accessed on 12 March 2025.

8   'India Ranks 116 in World Bank's Human Capital Index', *The
    Hindu*, 17 September 2020, https://tinyurl.com/uxr3nmhx.
    Accessed on 12 March 2025.

9   'The Human Capital Project: Frequently Asked Questions', *World
    Bank*, 19 March 2019, https://tinyurl.com/mr77zcun. Accessed
    on 12 March 2025.

10 'Only 50% Class 5 Students Can Read Class 2 Text, Learning Gap
    by Class 3: Report', *India Today*, 31 January 2025, https://tinyurl.
    com/2xx5s56c. Accessed on 12 March 2025.

11 Khurana, Kriti, 'S&P Global Market Intelligence Finds India's
    Influential Growth Potential Rests on Its Labor Force, Exports
    and Startups', *S&P Global*, 17 August 2023, https://tinyurl.com/
    yjz9m5xr. Accessed on 12 March 2025.

12 'Reaping the Demographic Dividend', *EY India*, 11 April 2023,
    https://tinyurl.com/4rny4y2x. Accessed on 12 March 2025.

13 Ibid.

14 Ibid.

15 Malin, Sophie, and Ashima Tyagi, 'India's Demographic
    Dividend: The Key to Unlocking Its Global Ambitions', *S&P
    Global*, 3 August 2023, https://tinyurl.com/bzr6e9bz. Accessed
    on 12 March 2025.

16 Kaushik, Mansvini, '43% Indian Women Are STEM Grads But
    Only 14% Are Employed as Scientists, Engineers', *Forbes India*,
    23 July 2021, https://tinyurl.com/4rreux95. Accessed on
    12 March 2025.

17 Jha, Anuja, '100 Crore Indians Have No Extra Money to Spend:
    Report', *India Today*, 26 February 2025 https://tinyurl.com/
    mpv4utxc. Accessed on 11 June 2025.

18 'Analysis of Sharp Increase in Youth Unemployment', Ministry of
    Labour and Employment, Government of India, 9 August 2023,

https://tinyurl.com/249newzb. Accessed on 12 March 2025.

19 Sharma, Milan, 'Youth Unemployment in India at 10.2%, Says Union Labour Minister', *India Today*, 28 November 2024, https://tinyurl.com/yyk7rdxr. Accessed on 12 March 2025.

20 'Female Labour Force Participation Rate (LFPR) Rose to 37 Per Cent in 2022–2023 from 23.3 Per Cent in 2017–2018', Ministry of Finance, Government of India, 22 July 2024, https://tinyurl.com/yffn6dyd. Accessed on 12 March 2025.

21 Ortiz-Ospina, Esteban, Sandra Tzvetkova, and Max Roser, 'Women's Employment', *Our World in Data*, March 2018, https://tinyurl.com/yfm9k9s4. Accessed on 12 March 2025.

22 'Female Labor Force Participation', *World Bank*, 10 January 2022, https://tinyurl.com/2djzb72h. Accessed on 12 March 2025.

23 Malin, Sophie, and Ashima Tyagi, 'India's Demographic Dividend: The Key to Unlocking Its Global Ambitions', *S&P Global*, 3 August 2023, https://tinyurl.com/bzr6e9bz. Accessed on 12 March 2025.

24 'Employment Statistics in Focus-April 2023: Female Labour Utilization in India', *Directorate General of Employment*, 1 May 2023, 14, https://tinyurl.com/45d6yr6c. Accessed on 12 March 2025.

25 'Labour Market Indicators Show Substantial Improvement in Last Few Years: Economic Survey 2024–25', Ministry of Labour & Employment, Government of India, 31 January 2025, https://tinyurl.com/y4hx2nwz. Accessed on 12 March 2025.

26 Salve, Prachi, 'DataViz: Govt's Skill Development Scheme Placed Only 18% Candidates', *IndiaSpend*, 19 September 2023, https://tinyurl.com/2sebkuze. Accessed on 12 March 2025.

27 Mehrotra, Santosh, and Harshil Sharma, 'Govt's Push Towards Skilling: Big Funding, Poor Outcomes', *The Wire*, 7 February 2025, https://tinyurl.com/y5bm4332. Accessed on 11 June 2025.

28 'Daily Update: August 8, 2023', *S&P Global*, https://tinyurl.com/eddezvk9. Accessed on 12 March 2025.

29 'Q2 2023 *ManpowerGroup* Employment Outlook Survey', ManpowerGroup, 21 June 2023, https://tinyurl.com/59x6xrt6. Accessed on 12 March 2025.

30 'Look Forward: India's Moment, Vol. 3', *S&P Global Market Intelligence*, 2 August 2023, https://tinyurl.com/ub8tcetp. Accessed on 5 March 2025.

31 'Labour Market Indicators Show Substantial Improvement in Last Few Years: Economic Survey 2024–25', Ministry of Labour & Employment, Government of India, 31 January 2025, https://tinyurl.com/y4hx2nwz. Accessed on 12 March 2025.

32 'Is AI a Threat to Your Job? Economic Survey Flags Sectors, Income-levels at Risk', *India Today*, 1 February 2025, https://tinyurl.com/23d9638m. Accessed on 12 March 2025.

33 'By Leveraging Its Young, Dynamic, and Tech-Savvy Population, India Has the Potential to Create a Workforce That Can Utilise AI to Augment Their Work and Productivity—Economic Survey 2024–25, Ministry of Labour and Employment, Government of India, 31 January 2025, https://tinyurl.com/3acm87zf. Accessed on 12 March 2025.

34 Roy, Tapas, and Sudas Roy, 'Engineering Education in India', *Economic & Political Weekly*, Vol. 58, No. 1, 2023, https://tinyurl.com/mu4fmjdv. Accessed on 12 March 2025.

11. CRITICALITY OF DATA IN DECISION-MAKING

1 'History of Census in India', Ministry of Home Affairs, Government of India, https://tinyurl.com/5jnb7f4r. Accessed on 12 March 2025.

2 Ibid.

3 Ibid.

4 '"Only 15 Paise Reaches the Needy": SC Quotes Rajiv Gandhi in Its Aadhaar Verdict', *Hindustan Times*, 11 June 2017, https://tinyurl.com/y73nh6vp. Accessed on 12 March 2025.

5 'Pradhan Mantri Jan Dhan Yojana (PMJDY)—National Mission for Financial Inclusion, Completes Nine Years of Successful Implementation', Ministry of Finance, Government of India, 28 August 2023, https://tinyurl.com/n5wnky9v. Accessed on 5 March 2025.

6 Ibid.

7 'India's Data Problem Is Real, Fixing Quality a Pressing Priority', *The New Indian Express*, 10 July 2023, https://tinyurl.com/5azzpju4. Accessed on 12 March 2025.

8 Sheriff M., Kaunain, '2 Billion Jabs: India Crosses Global Covid Milestone', *The Indian Express*, 18 July 2022, https://tinyurl.

com/3rsdce8m. Accessed on 12 March 2025.

9 Beniwal, Vrishti, 'Spotty Economic Data in India Jeopardizes a Fast-Growing Market', *Bloomberg*, 14 July 2023, https://tinyurl. com/3yu4p89k. Accessed on 12 March 2025.

10 Ibid.

11 Ibid.

12 Ibid.

13 Ibid.

14 Debroy, Bibek, and Aditya Sinha, 'How the CPI Basket Conceals the Inflation Picture', *The Hindu*, 13 July 2023, https://tinyurl. com/3wjysjm6. Accessed on 12 March 2025.

15 Beniwal, Vrishti, 'Spotty Economic Data in India Jeopardizes a Fast-Growing Market', *Bloomberg*, 14 July 2023, https://tinyurl. com/3yu4p89k. Accessed on 12 March 2025.

16 Ibid.

17 Maiorano, Diego, 'Politicization of Data Under the Modi Regime', *ISAS Insights*, 18 March 2019, https://tinyurl. com/4xw9mbd6. Accessed on 12 March 2025.

18 Beniwal, Vrishti, 'Spotty Economic Data in India Jeopardizes a Fast-Growing Market', *Bloomberg*, 14 July 2023, https://tinyurl. com/3yu4p89k. Accessed on 12 March 2025.

19 Ibid.

20 'Data Protection—The Regime in India (Part-I)', *European Commission*, 4 January 2024, https://tinyurl.com/64kbh6kz. Accessed on 12 March 2025.

21 'Aadhaar Review: Beghar Foundation v Justice K.S. Puttuswamy (Retd)', *Supreme Court Observer*, https://tinyurl.com/2k2c6ev6. Accessed on 12 March 2025.

22 'Why is Data Protection Important?', *PECB*, 10 November 2021, https://tinyurl.com/mr2z82rk. Accessed on 12 March 2025.

23 'India Suffered Second-Highest Data Breaches in 2022 with 450 Million Records Exposed: Report', *CNBC TV18*, 3 March 2023, https://tinyurl.com/3f7jyn37. Accessed on 12 March 2025.

24 'Non-Personal Data Governance Framework', *PRS Legislative Research*, 28 July 2020, https://tinyurl.com/yc3j43pe. Accessed on 11 June 2025.

25 'Section 43A: Compensation for Failure to Protect Data', *India*

Code, 27 October 2009, https://tinyurl.com/4kdet9yn. Accessed on 12 March 2025.

26 'The Information Technology (Reasonable Security Practices and Procedures and Sensitive Personal Data or Information) Rules, 2011', *Indian Kanoon*, 11 April 2011, https://tinyurl. com/5n6uht5e. Accessed on 12 March 2025.

27 Mahapatra, Dhananjay, and Amit Anand Choudhary, 'Right to Privacy Is a Fundamental Right, It Is Intrinsic to Right to Life, Supreme Court', *The Times of India*, 24 August 2017, https:// tinyurl.com/jj2fws9m. Accessed on 12 March 2025.

28 'The Digital Personal Data Protection Act, 2023 (Act 22 of 2023)', *Indian Kanoon*, 11 August 2023, https://tinyurl.com/ yvd6de7f. Accessed on 12 March 2025.

29 'National Strategy for Artificial Intelligence', *NITI Aayog*, June 2018, https://tinyurl.com/2smc685x. Accessed on 12 March 2025.

12. INDIA: THE WAY FORWARD

1 Biswas, Soutik, 'India: Is the Fastest-Growing Big Economy Losing Steam?', *BBC*, 11 December 2024, https://tinyurl.com/ mr3rvf9m. Accessed on 20 May 2025.

2 'Worldwide Governance Indicators', *World Bank Group*, 30 October 2024, https://tinyurl.com/3hz5jxeh. Accessed on 10 June 2025.

3 Ibid.

4 'Inequality in 2024, A Closer at Six Regions', *World Inequality Database*, 19 November 2024, https://tinyurl.com/yeytz52w. Accessed on 12 March 2025.

5 Bharti, Nitin Kumar, Lucas Chancel, Thomas Piketty, and Anmol Somanchi, 'Income and Wealth Inequality in India 1922–2023: The Rise of the Billionaire Raj', Working Paper No. 2024/09, *The World Inequality Lab*, 2024, https://tinyurl.com/mudh7khz. Accessed on 5 March 2025.

www.ingramcontent.com/pod-product-compliance
Lightning Source LLC
Chambersburg PA
CBHW031538260326
41914CB00039B/1995/J